RED
BLANKET

JOHN HARCH, M.D.

ISBN 979-8-6423-6745-2

REDBLANKETBOOK.COM

PREFACE

———

THIS STORY HAS BEEN CARRIED BY ME, or perhaps has followed me, since 1987. I always thought I might get it down on paper, but the constraints of job, family, and life caused me to make only halting progress.

About 18 years ago, I wrote my first chapter, the one about Doruk, which in retrospect, was a necessary catharsis rather than the start of a book. I could finally set aside some of the haunting emotion and guilt surrounding that event and move on. Over the next ten years, I wrote a few more chapters, but had made little headway until late in 2015, when a former college fraternity brother shamed me into getting serious about writing the whole thing instead of just talking about it. At that point, the stories came pouring out, as if they wanted to be told. Thanks, Rob.

You may wonder how I can describe these incidents in such detail when they happened so long ago. I kept a journal,

1

starting early in my internship, documenting anything I saw or did that seemed noteworthy. Intermittently, I would pull out the journal, and reading it would curl my toes. It still does. And there remain tales in it which are not described in this book.

Every encounter you will read here is true, to the best of my knowledge, no matter how outrageous it may sound. The accounts were taken from my direct experience, or were related to me by a medical professional who had experienced the event firsthand.

To produce a narrative that would flow smoothly and be easy to read, I took some literary license regarding chronology. Some cases were moved in time to be grouped with others. I tried to reproduce the patient histories and conversations as they occurred, but the accuracy is only as good as my memory, and my journal.

The names of patients, nurses, doctors, and others have been changed to maintain confidentiality. Do not conclude that any character in this story refers to any real person; the characters themselves must be considered fictional, even though the story itself is factually accurate.

The documentation of mistakes, complications, and less-than-ideal care was done to give the reader a realistic look at life in a big, public hospital, not to denigrate the institution or the personnel. Large teaching hospitals, especially in the inner city (including LA County-USC Medical Center), provide overall excellent service to a huge population, and they welcome the indigent. These hospitals are staffed by

To my loving mother, who tirelessly modeled hard work, truth, and compassion—and to my wife, whose intelligence and generosity have brought me immeasurable joy.

CONTENTS

many dedicated, skillful people who function at a high level despite the challenging conditions. Most of us who trained in general surgery would ask to be taken to a public trauma center if severely injured.

The descriptions of individual cases often include a reference to the patient's race or ethnicity. While this may seem unnecessary or pejorative, it sometimes provided useful medical information, and it represents the method used at the time (and still used in many places). I decided to retain this feature for some of the cases, although it may seem politically incorrect today.

This is the true story of my initiation, my training, my coming of age in the profession we call surgery.

CHAPTER ONE

OUTSIDER

A **BONE WAS STICKING THROUGH A** hole in his blue jeans, and he didn't know it.

"Get your hands off me, assholes!" he yelled.

"Intoxicated 27-year-old crashed his motorcycle into a guardrail," said a paramedic. "Blood pressure's a little low."

"Goddammit, let me go!" he screamed, thrashing around. His head lay in a pool of blood on the gurney, blonde hair bathed in the dark, crimson-blue liquid. A huge chunk of scalp was peeled back, exposing a large, white expanse of skull. I couldn't take my eyes off the splintered end of his femur, still hanging out of his jeans at mid-thigh.

"John," said Dr. Eva Brandt, my senior general surgery resident, "get a towel, shove that scalp back in place, and apply some pressure. And I need IV access!"

I pressed the flap of scalp back onto his head, trying to slow the bleeding.

"Fuck you!" he bellowed, turning his head in my direction. He tried to bite me, and I pulled my hands back just in time to save my fingers. When he started spitting, I felt some saliva hit my face. One glob landed on my shirt, another on a nurse's pants.

Some police arrived and helped control him. We put both arms and his good leg in leather restraints. We covered his face with a surgical mask so he couldn't spit on us any longer.

"Get that leg in some traction," ordered Eva.

"You bastards!" yelled the patient.

Everyone was annoyed and pissed at this guy. The yelling, the cursing, the biting, the spitting; and we were supposed to save his ass. I started thinking about some of the times I got drunk at Northwestern University as an undergrad. One night, a bunch of us had driven from campus (just north of Chicago) up to a little rural bar in Wisconsin. It was about 90 minutes away, but we made the drive because we liked the bar owner, and he'd serve anyone, even the youngest guys. We got pretty plowed over the course of several hours, and then had to drive home.

We gathered in the parking lot to choose drivers from our group of stumbling, laughing idiots. When nearly everyone had been packed off, I got behind the wheel, with three other very drunk guys in the car with me. Did I drive slowly and carefully? No, I wanted to beat everyone back to campus despite leaving last. It made no sense, but that's what you do when you've had ten beers. I drove 90 miles per hour down the twisting country roads. At one point, a cat ran across the road in front of me. By the time I saw it, it was too late. I heard a *ba-bump* and felt a little thud under the wheels. I never had time to react, so I just kept the accelerator floored. We made it back about the same time as everyone else.

All I could think of now, looking at this belligerent drunk, was, "This could have been me." I could have killed or injured myself and everyone in my car. Or people in other cars. Or pedestrians (just like the cat). My life would have been dramatically different.

"Hey, man, calm down or we're gonna have to paralyze you," said Eva. She looked at me and added, "There's no way to know if this guy's just a mean drunk or has a bad head injury. We're gonna need a head CT."

Then I thought, "If I had crashed my car that night five years ago and sustained a head injury, I might have acted this way. And everyone would have thought I was a complete jackass. Would the doctors and nurses have been sympathetic and professional enough to give me good medical care?"

"Hey, buddy," said Eva. "Stop thrashing around. We're trying to help you."

"Fuck…you…bitch," he said from behind the mask. Gradually, his breathing had become more labored and fast.

7

Eva was now able to get close enough to check his chest and listen to his lung sounds.

"John," said Eva, "feel his rib cage here."

I put my hand on his ribs. They weren't firm like ribs should be; instead they were crunchy and able to be pushed inward with just a little pressure. He had multiple broken ribs, for sure.

Eva put her stethoscope on his chest wall. "Diminished breath sounds," she declared. "Get me a chest tube tray and a 36 French chest tube."

Now the patient was gasping for air. His eyes were bulging and he started to turn blue. He wasn't screaming obscenities at us anymore. In fact, he stopped fighting us altogether.

Eva ripped open the chest tube tray. Without injecting any anesthesia, she made a small slash over a rib. She placed a big clamp into the incision and between the ribs, plunging it into the chest cavity. A whoosh of air rushed out of the hole she'd created in the chest wall. The patient started to breathe again and let out a moan. Eva rammed a large, clear, plastic tube into the hole and sutured it to his skin. Blood shot out of the tube in spurts each time the patient coughed, painting the floor with big, red splotches. The whole process had taken about a minute. Eva's efficiency at preventing a respiratory arrest and death was stunning. I hoped I could be that good someday, and that confident.

Right now, however, I was less than a month into my surgical internship. It had started with less excitement but more anxiety three weeks previously.

The year was 1982. July 1 was the start of a week thought by many to be the most dangerous time of year for a patient to enter a teaching hospital. The recent fifth-year residents have been replaced by fourth-year residents, fourth- by third-, etc. But the most significant peril is that the seasoned interns, the infantry of the hospital, are suddenly relieved of their menial and exhausting duties by the new recruits (fresh out of medical school), who are expected to scramble through the minefield of hands-on patient care. Unfortunately, the downside risk of a misstep is borne by the patient. This danger is clearly understood by the faculty and all the other residents who are senior to the new interns.

And so, on this day, I found myself standing outside a meeting room on a quiet upper floor of a cavernous, 2,000-bed hospital—Los Angeles County-University of Southern California (USC) Medical Center—as my fellow interns began to assemble. It was 6:50 a.m. I noticed a bathroom around the back of a vacant nursing station. I stopped in to double check everything: my hair, my face, my clothes. The room was tiny and the fixtures ancient. Faded paint was peeling off the walls and ceiling. I looked down. There was no toilet seat. In fact, there was no hardware to even attach a seat. If you needed to sit, it had to be right on top of the damn bowl.

We'd been told to show up in shirt, tie, and white coat. Everyone complied, except the single, petite woman among us, who appeared in skirt, blouse, and white coat. I had a foreboding that I didn't fit in very well, that I might be out of my league. This, because of my middle-class upbringing.

The interns filed into the small classroom and were directed to sit in the first two rows. Some of the chief residents occupied the last row, one in bloody, rumpled greens, a few snoozing. They had an unflappable, stoic look about them. A half-dozen senior faculty were scattered around the room. A distinguished-looking doctor in a clean, white coat addressed us from a podium at the front of the room.

"Good morning. My name is Pat O'Donnelly. I'm the chief of surgery and the director of this residency program. I'd like to welcome the new general surgery intern class of 1982 to LA County-USC."

He scanned the group of nervous interns and continued, "You will rotate through the trauma services and all the subspecialties. Each trauma service is identified by the day of the week; so, for instance, when assigned to the Saturday Service, you will cover all trauma and general surgery cases from 7 am on Saturday until 7 am on Sunday. You are responsible for the admission and care of patients on your service, and should know the details of each and every case. You are expected to arrive promptly for work each day, and for the educational conferences held each week. A record of your attendance will be maintained." He paused, possibly for emphasis on this last point.

"While you are working in this hospital, remember that you are representing the Department of Surgery, and your appearance and behavior, even in stressful situations, should be appropriate. As you are already aware, this program is pyramidal. At the end of four months, evaluations will be completed, and we will select six of you to proceed to the second year."

I looked to my right, my left, and behind me. There were ten of us altogether. I didn't know it when I made my list for the residency match, but four of the ten of us would be "cut." Only six would continue in general surgery. The other four would have to seek another direction, possibly in one of the medical specialties. For those of us who sought a surgical career, being cast into the nonsurgical specialties would be the ultimate humiliation. Furthermore, these rejects were required to finish the remaining eight months of internship like lame ducks, painfully slogging through the long days and longer nights with the shame of having been "deselected," usually for unclear and perhaps arbitrary reasons. This pyramidal structure therefore created a cutthroat environment that influenced our thoughts, our actions, even our alliances. One might say it was our version of the TV show *Survivor*, circa 1982. Because of the negative aspects of this traditional pyramidal arrangement, and the angst it caused everyone over the years, our faculty abandoned it the very next year.

I tried to size up my competitors, and I saw them scrutinizing me as well. The other nine appeared qualified and confident. As we introduced ourselves, the anxiety level in the room began to rise.

"I'm B. Rutherford Wilkinson III, from the University of Michigan School of Medicine."

"No shit," I thought. "Gives his first name as a single letter." He was a thin, pale, smug-looking guy, whose face was now turned up just a bit as though he were sniffing the air.

"Kathryn Telina, from the University of North Carolina at Chapel Hill." She spoke softly, but assertively.

Dr. O'Donnelly then motioned to two young doctors near the front who seemed to know each other and had been intermittently whispering and grinning. "Gentlemen? Care to introduce yourselves?"

"Well, I'm James Cline, and…I…uh…oh, yeah, I remember. I went to USC Medical School!" This cut the tension, and everyone laughed or at least smiled. James, sporting a slightly balding pate and a pointed nose, was a little older than the rest of us and didn't appear very concerned about the upcoming year. His fellow USC grad calmly introduced himself as Mike Miller and said nothing more. Dr. O'Donnelly smiled at the pair paternally, then nodded to the next intern.

"Billy Goodwin. Howard University College of Medicine." This guy stood out. He was the only black physician among us. He was lean and had a very tight haircut. The muscles of his face were taut and defined. He was confident. I liked him immediately.

Dr. O'Donnelly gestured to me.

"John Harch, UCLA." University of California, Los Angeles, was the crosstown rival to USC in more than just medical academics. I scanned the room. Polite nods and smiles, mostly. How did I look to them? How did I look to the senior people, the important ones?

The remaining interns introduced themselves. This was definitely no group of slouches. I wondered how many of them had inside connections with the chief of surgery that might trump the hard work and raw intellectual ability of the others. And were there a few who might be flat-out brilliant?

As I ruminated on the "cut," I was mentally biting my nails. I had serious doubts about my chances here, which were intensified by my sense of being a socioeconomic outsider to this insular, privileged world of the physician.

I glanced to the far left. I recognized Dr. Rollins, third in command of this surgery department, slouched in a chair. He was short; at most maybe 5 feet, 8 inches. He had a head of short, curly hair. His arms were folded as he scanned the group of interns. When my eyes met his, he stared back at me with cold detachment. He had interviewed me months ago, and the interview had gone very poorly. So poorly, in fact, that I had thrown my interview materials in the trash can outside his office in frustration afterward. "I'll never get in here," I thought. Nonetheless, I had been accepted. I couldn't understand this paradox. Now, however, a sickening feeling crept over me. What if their plan was to get a year of hard labor out of me, and it was predetermined that I was one of the four to be cut? It now seemed so clear.

"These handouts will outline your assignments and hospital policies," concluded Dr. O'Donnelly. "Welcome and good luck."

I felt profoundly alone. As we stood and moved toward the front of the room, the intern on my left elbowed me and said, "Well that was enough bullshit to get your panties in a wad, wasn't it?" As I turned and smiled, he stuck out his hand. "Skip Cline. Nice to meet you." Apparently, James Cline, the joker, went as "Skip."

"John Harch. My pleasure."

His handshake was sincere, and he had a sardonic grin that made me think I had stumbled on a true comrade.

"I spent four years here as a medical student," Skip said. "Don't let them get under your skin with all this pompous crap."

As we picked up our assignments, Skip looked at the schedule and said, "Sweet! You got ENT first. No problem." Then he groaned. "Oh, crushed testicles! I've got burns first."

We met several of the other interns. As we were exiting the room, B. Rutherford Wilkinson III introduced himself with a dead fish handshake, noting that he was the third generation in his family to embark on a general surgery career. And, by the way, his father was currently the chief of surgery at the University Michigan.

Skip and I raised our eyebrows obligingly, looked at each other, and struggled to maintain straight faces. Still, in the back of my mind, there was apprehension that one of the six spots was probably already gone. In fact, if Skip and his cohort had been here for four years, I guessed that three spots were gone, and I knew virtually nothing about the rest of the interns.

Feeling jangled and preoccupied by the discussion in the new intern meeting, I took the stairs down to the fourth floor, location of the ENT (ear, nose, and throat) ward. My team hadn't arrived yet, so I decided to kill some time by visiting the staff cafeteria on the first floor. This huge room was occupied by about 100 nurses and doctors, who sat in small groups discussing the previous night's adventures.

"Shit! We delivered 37 babies in the last 24 hours. We had four crash C-sections, a bad shoulder dystocia, and a couple pairs of twins. It was crazy. And there wasn't much attending help…"

"Look, man. I'm not getting stuck with all those people Kelly was too goddamn lazy to work up last night. They're all going back to him later this morning, once I get 'em sorted out…"

Even though the food was free, I wasn't hungry. I sat by myself, anxious, brooding, sipping a glass of orange juice. Up to this point, I had my life under control, but now I had a very uncertain future.

My thoughts drifted to my girlfriend, Lori, and our relationship. A mutual friend had given me her phone number 18 months ago, and she had reluctantly agreed to meet me for a drink.

Neither of us was very smitten on that first date. We were serious people; she with an English degree, working as a magazine editor; me with a biology degree, clawing my way through medical school. We casually probed to see what kind of mind the other had, what values, what hopes.

"I don't believe in marriage," she said at one point.

"Really?" I responded. "Why not?"

"Well, I just don't think I could commit to loving one person for the rest of my life. I think it's an irrational expectation."

"I'm a long way from that kind of commitment too," I said. With over a year of med school remaining and at least five years of surgery residency, I wanted no part of a long-term relationship. On this point, at least, we were a great match. It didn't take long to realize that we had a lot more in common than a desire to remain single. We had similar beliefs on politics. We were both ex-Catholics. We believed in maintaining our physical fitness.

I looked at my watch. Fifteen minutes had passed while I daydreamed. I got up and wandered back upstairs. A tall, thin, bearded doctor strode onto the ward.

"I'm Dan Johnson, fourth-year ENT. Nice to meet you."

Two interns soon appeared. The first was tall, with curly hair, a bounce in his step, and an impish look about him. The other one was short, chubby, and seemed more reserved.

"Hey, I'm Mark Lane," said the tall one.

"Hi, I'm Bob Allen," said the short one. "We're both ENT interns."

"Good to meet you guys," I said, shaking their hands. "I'm a general surgery intern—at least until the end of this year."

"What do you mean?" asked Mark.

"Well, they're gonna give four out of the ten of us the boot at the end of this year," I explained. "We just don't know who that'll be."

"What?!" exclaimed Bob. "That's crazy. I'm glad they don't do that to us."

"Yeah, I'm pretty worried about it," I admitted.

"You're gonna make it," said Mark. "I can tell."

I smiled. "We'll see," I replied. He was being polite—he knew nothing about the cut or me or my competition. Still, I appreciated the sentiment.

Dan announced we'd start with rounds, so we could get a feel for the service. We walked to the first patient room. There was no door, just a six-foot-wide entryway leading to a communal, 30-foot-by-30-foot room with six beds positioned around the perimeter. There were curtains that could be pulled around each bed for privacy, but most of them were retracted, with each patient able to see all the others. I soon discovered that all the wards were arranged this way. There were only a few private rooms for special circumstances, such as infection isolation. We stopped at the first bed.

"This is Jorge Pena," said Dan. "He's a 55-year-old man from El Salvador, now in the U.S. for about a year. He's developed this fungating mass on his nose over the past three months, and we're trying to figure out what it is."

I looked closely at Jorge. He appeared older than 55. He looked back at me passively. Coming out of both nostrils and hanging off the end of his nose was a fleshy mass. It was pink, moist, large—about the size of a golf ball—and looked like something you might see in a low-budget, science-fiction movie.

"We've done biopsies, cultures, an array of lab tests, but no one knows exactly what this is. It doesn't look like cancer under the microscope. We'll probably just have to resect it, but we don't want to remove his nose, because it'll leave him pretty disfigured. And bleeding could be a big problem if we operate."

I nodded to Jorge, who nodded back. He made no comment, asked no questions, and his face reflected helplessness and resignation that I would see again and again in this hospital. As we left the bedside, Mark whispered to me, "Gnarliest fuckin' thing I've seen in a long time, man."

In the second bed was Edward, a 23-year-old man who had swallowed a mixture of Drano and furniture polish in an ill-conceived suicide gesture. Dan explained that Edward had burned his mouth, but they were unsure how much of the caustic liquid made it into his esophagus. His lips and tongue were very swollen, and he looked miserable. He attempted to speak, but it was unintelligible, and so painful that he abandoned the effort.

"Dr. Harch," said Dan, in a mock-authoritative tone, "why is this patient on the ENT ward?"

I was uncertain what he was getting at. "Well, I guess because of the burns to his mouth," I said.

"Yes, but what about his esophagus? What will happen if it gets all scarred and he can't swallow?"

I was thinking. "You could…put in…a feeding gastrostomy?" I ventured, referring to a rubber tube placed through the abdominal wall and directly into his stomach.

"Yes, but are you going to make the poor guy eat that way the rest of his life?"

"Uh…" I didn't know. I was embarrassed, but I'd never heard the problem discussed before.

"That's where your boys, the general surgeons, would come in," he said. "Edward would need his esophagus resected. Then they'd transfer a segment of colon up into his chest, connect it up, and, voila, a new esophagus. It's a big damn surgery, and we're hoping he doesn't need it. Right, Edward?" he asked, patting him on the leg. The patient nodded.

The exchange between Dan and me was known as pimping: asking a student, intern, or resident a series of questions to see what they knew about a subject. It could be good-natured and informative, as with Dan or, if handled maliciously, intimidating and humiliating.

We went from bed to bed, hearing sad and sometimes ridiculous stories, all three interns taking notes. We stopped in the hallway before entering the next room.

In a low voice, Dan said, "Next, we'll see Terri. She's 30 years old, and last week made her third suicide attempt by putting a .38 under her chin and firing it. The bullet split her mandible, went through her tongue, alveolar bone, and nose, and lodged in the subcutaneous tissues in her upper forehead. She suffered no significant damage to any critical structure. We were able to repair and clean up some of the damage, but she'll need more surgery later, when the swelling and inflammation are down."

We entered the room. Terri was morbidly obese—about 400 pounds. She looked up, smiled a little, and mumbled, with difficulty, "Hi, Doter Josen." She had sutured incisions over her chin and forehead, and the middle of her face was grossly swollen and suffused with a deep violet discoloration. She squinted at us through two little slits between puffy eyelids.

"Hi, Terri. These are my new interns, Drs. Lane, Allen, and Harch. Were you able to drink or eat anything this morning?" asked Dan.

"Yeth. I finithed thum of the thof thiet they gabe me," she replied.

"Great," said Dan. "We'll probably keep you on a soft diet for a few more days. Then you can go home, once the psych people finish your evaluation. Sound OK?"

"I geth tho," whispered Terri.

We walked back into the hallway. As before, Dan moved toward us and lowered his voice.

"This next case is at least as pathetic as the last one. Mrs. Parsons was a heavy smoker, and she turned up with throat cancer. We resected it, but it recurred. We irradiated her neck and had to place a tracheostomy. Unfortunately, she's had further recurrence of her cancer."

We walked into the cramped, single-bed room. A woman in her late fifties sat cross-legged in bed. She looked thin but reasonably healthy, except for her neck, from which protruded a plastic tracheostomy tube. Around and above the tube, the skin was reddish brown, irregular, and thick. Her entire neck looked rigid, and she had to turn her shoulders to look left or right. I also noticed that with each heartbeat, the tracheostomy tube rocked up and down.

"How's your pain today, Mrs. Parsons?" asked Dan.

She covered her tracheostomy with one finger, and whispered hoarsely, "About the same."

Dan added, "Well, we're going to adjust your pain meds today and have a conference about your treatment plan."

"More radiation?" she asked, finger again on the trach tube.

"No, I don't think so," Dan responded. "Maybe some chemotherapy."

"Will it help?" she inquired.

"I don't know," Dan said, "but I certainly hope so."

We left the room, and Dan stopped us when we were out of Mrs. Parsons' earshot. "We really don't have much left to offer her. Our main goals are to control her pain, try to keep some nutrition going in, and maintain an airway. But there's one worrisome problem. Did you see that trach tube bobbing up and down?"

I nodded my head emphatically, not sure of the significance of what I'd seen.

"Well," said Dan, "when a trach tube is in place for a long time, especially with locally recurrent cancer and radiation, it can end up rubbing against the innominate artery, which is closely adjacent. After a few million heartbeats, the tube can erode into the artery, and then all hell breaks loose."

There was a long silence.

"What can you do if that happens?" asked Mark.

"Kiss your ass good-bye," said Dan. "That artery is about a half-inch in diameter. You can try to insert your finger alongside the trach to compress the artery, but it's usually all over by the time you arrive."

This series of heartbreaking stories, described so objectively by Dan, was beginning to depress the three of us, but no one dared show anything more than cool, scientific consideration. Showing emotion would emphasize our neophyte status.

We finished rounds, and Dan assigned us our "scut work." This was the name given to the daily list of tedious tasks required to keep the services running: replacing IVs, drawing blood, retrieving X-Rays, finding lab results, etc. In many large, private hospitals most of this work would be done by hospital-employed technicians, phlebotomists, nurses, and clerks. But in a county hospital such as this one, interns were like slaves. They worked long hours, mostly, it seemed, occupied with endless scut work. The arrangement saved millions of dollars in wages. The real education and training of the interns, therefore, occurred on rounds, in conferences, and in brief hallway discussions with an upper-level resident.

Mark and Bob, who'd been medical students at USC, dragged me around the hospital, showing me where to get supplies, drop off blood samples, and schedule tests.

"If you're gonna work here and survive, you need to understand something," said Mark. "This is a county hospital. It's just like the VA. No matter how fucking bad an employee is, they can't be fired."

"Yeah," agreed Bob. "They can sit on their asses, refuse to do things, even kill people. Their union will protect them."

"Not all of 'em are that way," added Mark. "Some will actually help you, especially the nurses. But others will obstruct and frustrate the shit out of you every chance they get. They hate us. They think we're spoiled, privileged brats... which, of course, some of us are." He smiled.

"What's the key to success?" I asked.

"Find all the good ones," said Bob.

"Yeah," said Mark. "Look for the ones who're willing to help. We'll point some of 'em out while you're on ENT with us. The other bastards have to be begged or bribed or threatened."

"But it has to be done carefully," warned Bob. "They know they're protected. Remember that you're just a doctor. You're temporary. When you're gone, they'll still be here obstructing someone else's progress. You're just a snot nose to them."

About this time, we got a call from Dan to come up to the admitting area on the fourth floor. When we arrived, he had his back to us, and was hunched over a gurney in a corner of the room. Lying supine (face up) in front of him was a young woman with all four extremities held down in hard leather restraints. When Dan turned toward us, he had a disgusted look on his face.

Jamie was 18 years old and had a history of severe psychiatric disease. A week ago, she had begun to bite her right lower lip. Despite her parents' efforts to stop her, she managed to chew away part of her lip. Over the past few days, she continued the self-mutilation, and now had a large chunk of lower lip and skin missing below the right side of her mouth. It was possible to see about five of her teeth and the gums below them even when her mouth was closed. As we observed, she tried to catch more of the tissue between her teeth, and Dan stopped her by inserting a wooden tongue blade. She scowled at us without speaking.

With the help of a psychiatric resident and Jamie's mother, a plan was made to wire Jamie's jaw shut while an appropriate regimen of sedatives and antipsychotics could be prepared. Jamie had tried to escape from this medical evaluation, and thus, the need for the restraints.

To draw Jamie's blood, Mark held her shoulders, I put all my weight on her arm, and Bob (the best phlebotomist among us) sat on her legs while he stuck her vein. Shortly thereafter, Dan took her to the OR and wired her jaw shut. We spent the afternoon with Dan in the clinic, then it was time to start my first night on general surgery call.

When I arrived on the emergency admitting ward, called 9200, all 10 beds were full, and there was one new patient waiting in the hallway. The senior resident in charge, Phil

Conway, welcomed me and asked me to get started on the new patient. He then disappeared upstairs to begin an operation on a gunshot victim.

I walked over to the first patient I would evaluate on my own as a new intern. He was a young, Hispanic guy. The white sheet pulled up to his neck had a little blood stain at the level of his abdomen. I asked him, "*Habla ingles?*" He shook his head no. Having been told that there were always interpreters available, I asked the clerk to call for a Spanish translator. She smiled oddly, started to say something, then picked up the phone and made the call. I waited.

In about five minutes the elevator doors opened. I was chagrined to find that the elevator disgorged not an interpreter, but my next patient, a 40-year-old lady who I was told had a sick gallbladder. She, too, spoke no English. Stubbornly, I waited a few minutes longer, only to be greeted by another gurney holding a 35-year-old man who'd gotten drunk and jumped off a balcony. He had a broken leg, lacerations, a concussion, and unknown abdominal injuries. It was glaringly clear to me that I had to jump in immediately and use my broken Spanish with unconjugated verbs. I shot a quick glance at the clerk, who had a little grin on her face. She looked quickly down at the papers on her desk and said nothing.

I completed my rudimentary history and physical on Jose Garcia, who had a single stab wound to the abdomen. I was in a hurry to get to my next two patients, so I stopped a passing nurse, and asked her to place a nasogastric tube in Jose (a requirement for nearly all our trauma patients).

She paused, looked at my name badge, and said, "Look here, intern boy. I don't know you. And I have no way of knowing whether you know what the hell you're doing. So, until I figure out how good you are, you can place your own damn NG tubes." She stared at me, waiting for a response. I was dumbfounded, and stared back at her for a second, probably with my mouth partway open. Then, without another word, she stomped off in the direction she had been heading when I so rudely interrupted her.

I had to decide how to respond to what might easily be considered "impertinence" in the minds of many physicians. After all, the hierarchical structure of medicine—at least in those days—required that nurses follow doctors' orders without question and, typically, without comment. Although brand new, I was a doctor. But LAC-USC was its own world and, apparently, was governed by its own set of rules. Mark and Bob had warned me.

I quickly decided that confronting this nurse would mark me as a pompous rookie. Besides, I'd be wasting valuable time. I grabbed an NG tube, explained my intentions as best I could to Jose, and then ran the tube down one of his nostrils and into his stomach. He coughed, gagged, and choked, eyes bulging in disbelief. I taped the tube to his nose and moved on to my next charge.

We admitted 10 or 12 patients that night. While we interns drew blood, ordered and chased down X-Rays, and dictated notes, the residents appeared intermittently to reassess our collection of the sick and injured. Some would be taken to the OR; others would be "cleared" of immediate need for surgery and sent to a nonemergency ward.

At one point, Phil Conway returned from the OR and wanted to make rounds. We stopped at the bedside of an older lady with possible acute diverticulitis. I recited the details of her history, exam, and labs. As I was summing up, he asked, "What IV fluid are you using?"

"Ringer's lactate," I said.

"Why?" he asked. The pimping was under way.

"Well…uh…isn't that what we use on everyone?"

"I hope that's not the answer you give on staff rounds, because they'll eat you alive," he said. "You need to think about what you're hanging in these IVs. We use Ringer's lactate or normal saline on the young trauma patients because they need volume, and it doesn't really matter what you pick. But an older, hypertensive patient? Maybe something else, perhaps with less salt. How much sodium chloride in Ringer's?"

"I don't know," I said.

"How much sodium chloride in normal saline?"

"Not sure."

"How much potassium in each?" he asked.

I just shook my head.

"Well, I suggest you find out. It's written right on the side of the IV bag. You'll have the right solution for your patient, and it might save you from dismemberment on formal rounds."

Around 2 a.m., there was a brief lull in the action on 9200. I decided to return to the ENT ward to check on the sorry group of patients I'd met the previous morning. As I entered the darkened ward hallway, I could hear breathing and muffled snoring. I peered into Jorge's and Edward's room; everyone was asleep. Over to Terri's room and all was quiet. I peeked into Mrs. Parson's room. The coarse sound of air flowing in and out of her tracheostomy was audible, then it stopped. She whispered, "Who's there?"

"It's just me, Dr. Harch, your intern. Everything OK?"

A moment of silence.

"I'm in a lot of pain. Can you ask my nurse for some pain medicine?"

"Sure. I'll speak to her right now."

I found a nurse and communicated the request, then remembered Jamie. Dan told me that after he wired her jaw shut, she started bending over to her restrained hands and using the new wires on her teeth to tear the skin off her fingers. This prompted him to secure her wrists in hard restraints way out to the side of the bed, and apply a posey (shirt-like restraint) to keep her from reaching her hands. They also wrapped her hands in gauze and tape. How was she doing now? Was she still hurting herself? The nurse directed me to the three-bed room at the front of the ward.

I walked to the room and pushed the door open slowly and silently. The long, narrow room was dark except for a low-wattage, bare bulb high on the wall to my left. The three beds lay to the right. I stopped at the first bed, which held a young woman recovering from surgery to repair injuries from stab wounds to her face. In the faint glow, I could barely make out the vital signs recorded at the foot of the bed. The temperature, blood pressure, and pulse all looked OK, and the patient was asleep.

I moved to the foot of the next bed and picked up the vital signs sheet. My eyes had begun to adjust to the darkness. The vitals looked alright, but I had an eerie feeling. I slowly raised my gaze from the clipboard to the head of the bed. There was Jamie. The upper half of her body was raised up at 45 degrees, held back by the posey, her arms pinned down by the hard restraints. The dim light in the room now reflected ominously off the pearly edges of her possessed eyes. Her upper lip was pulled up in a muscular, twitching contraction, like a silent, snarling dog, exposing the gleaming metal wires which now caged her teeth. Her hair was wild and tangled, and her neck muscles were rigid. A drop of saliva appeared from between two teeth, ran out the corner of her mutilated mouth and down her chin, falling on her gown. She was motionless, but her face was screaming, "If I could get out of these restraints and remove these wires, I would chew off some pieces of you!"

By now, all the hairs on my arms and the back of my neck were standing on end. I felt as though I were the next victim in a horror movie. It seemed that my mere presence was taunting her, and her restraints were a poor guarantee of my safety. Without looking away from her, I set the clipboard down and slowly backed out of the room. A bit shaken, I made my way back to 9200.

No one on the Tuesday Service got a wink of sleep that night. When 7:00 approached on Wednesday morning, I heard talk of "pass-on rounds." This ritual occurred each morning as a fresh surgical team showed up to assume care of those souls remaining from the prior 24 hours. For the team finishing its day of call, the important decision to be made was, do any of these patients need emergent or urgent surgery? If not, they should be transferred to the ward for recovery and discharge. Otherwise, they remained on 9200 for further observation. The incoming team would either operate on these people and keep them on its service or complete their workup and return them to the team that originally admitted them.

It was therefore important to keep tabs on the progress and effectiveness of each patient's workup as the day or night advanced. It was a matter of pride to "clean up" the admitting ward from 4 a.m. to 7 a.m., thereby passing on as few patients as possible. Finally, someone had to present these leftover patients to the new team in detail, no small task if you had raced around all night pursuing menial duties without synthesizing the history, lab work, X-Rays, and exams on numerous patients.

At 6:45 a.m., we still had nine patients lying on gurneys. Both residents and all three medical students were upstairs operating. The other intern had gone downstairs to schedule some X-Ray studies. I suddenly realized that I, on my second day here, might be the default verbal "presenter" of a thousand bits of information currently unknown to me. Further, this data would have to be digested by me in the next 15 minutes and then succinctly summarized. It was an impossible assignment, and I was panic-stricken.

I began to dart around gathering the charts. Which of these guys is Raul Gomez, the suspected acute appendicitis who arrived 30 minutes ago? What was the latest blood count on the stab wound to the back? Did we get the X-Rays on the guy who fell out the second story window? Oh, God!

Just then, Phil strode onto the ward, tired and bloody, and saved me from certain humiliation. He flashed me a quick grin, then casually reviewed each case, intermittently asking me for a critical blood test or X-Ray, which I could sometimes provide. When pass-ons ended, I had a huge new list of scut work to complete. I walked into the ICU to get started and ran into Skip.

"Harch," he exclaimed, "you survived your first call night in this dungeon! How'd they treat you?"

"Not too bad. It was busy, and we got no sleep, but…"

Just then, a beautiful ICU nurse walked past us, and we both gawked.

"Who is that?" I asked.

"Oh," laughed Skip, "that's Darla, also known as Low Gomco."

"Low Gomco?"

"Yeah. She has a gorgeous friend who works in here, too, named Tiffany, or High Gomco. They have a reputation for getting busy with the residents...thus, their nicknames."

I just shook my head. The origin of the names must have derived from our suction machines in the hospital, made by the Gomco Company. When writing orders for suction, one would write either low or high Gomco, depending on how much suction was desired.

"Of course," said Skip, "while I was a medical student here, they never gave me the time of day. But one look at either of them, and I pop a chubby."

CHAPTER TWO

SHARKS

BEHIND THE HOSPITAL, UP A STEEP SET of concrete stairs and across an asphalt plaza, was the interns' and residents' dormitory. Many of us, particularly interns, decided to live there because of the convenience. We didn't have to look for an apartment in Los Angeles. We didn't have to sit in freeway traffic when we had an emergency call to the hospital. It was simple and inexpensive, but it was depressing. The old four-story building was as dingy as the old hospital. The rooms were small, featuring a twin bed, a bedside table, a phone, a built-in set of drawers, a tiny closet, and a bathroom. That was it. By good fortune, my window looked down on the plaza, which contained a basketball court.

One evening during my first week at LAC-USC, I made it back to the dorm room around 7 p.m. At about 7:15, I looked out the window and saw three guys shooting baskets. It was summer, so there was still enough light to get a game. I hadn't slept much the prior three days, but I really needed some exercise. I threw on my shorts and shoes and hurried down.

When I walked onto the court, I realized that one of the three guys was Billy, the black intern who'd impressed me on our first day. We reintroduced ourselves, and arranged the teams so we could play together. We were a good fit: we played team defense, I could hit a few outside shots, he could hit from anywhere and drive the basket. He had competitive intensity and was in great condition. We smoked the other team in four consecutive games.

When the other two guys walked off, Billy said, "Hey, that was great. I like teammates who play defense. Don't typically see mucha that in pickup games." Thus started a long friendship based on our mutual love of basketball and medicine.

Two days later, I found myself on call for ENT night clinic. The nurse asked me if I was available to see a man who had had his tongue bitten off by his girlfriend. I told her I was, and sat down to await his arrival.

While sitting there, I could hear a woman, perhaps 30 years old, grunting and straining, nearly crying, as if she were struggling repeatedly to accomplish something like a bowel movement. She sounded so distressed that I got up and approached the exam booth, carefully pulling back the curtain a few inches, saying, "Can I help you with anything?"

The image presented to me just didn't compute. Kneeling on a gurney, half-naked, was a "woman," earrings and breasts dangling, hunched over a plastic urine bottle, into which she had placed "her" penis. She was trying to urinate, without success. I was surprised but tried not to show it. She sobbed, "I just…can't…pee," tears rolling down her cheeks.

I said, "I'll try to get you some help," and I closed the curtain.

I found Dan a few exam rooms away. Describing the scene I'd just witnessed, I asked what was going on and what could be done, since the patient seemed so miserable.

He said, "Oh, that's Kim, who's partway through her transsexual change from man to woman. She has leukemia and a blood clotting disorder. She's here for recurrent nose-bleeds. Maybe she bled into her bladder and formed just enough clot to obstruct her urethra. We'll have to place a Foley if she can't pee."

Just then, the nurse touched my arm and said, "Dr. Harch, the guy with the bitten-off tongue is here." She guided me to another exam room and pulled the curtain aside.

Carlos was sitting on the edge of a gurney, with dried blood on his chin, neck, shirt, and pants. He occasionally spat a little fresh blood into a kidney basin. He looked angry.

I introduced myself and asked him what had happened.

"I wush kishing my girrfren an she bi off my chung."

35

"Why did she do that?" I asked.

"I have nyo fucking igea," he said. "That cun."

I asked him to open his mouth. Sure enough, about three-quarters of an inch of his tongue was missing; the remaining part was ragged and oozing slightly. It looked like the edge of a partially eaten hamburger. I brought Dan over for a look; he said there was nothing we could do but let it heal. After Dan left, Carlos looked me straight in the eye and, in a hushed voice, said, "Whe I geh ou a here, I'm guh-a kirr a bish. I mea i…wai and shee. I wirr kirr her." It took me a few moments to realize he was saying that when he gets out of the hospital, he would kill his girlfriend…wait and see. His tone and his eyes were very convincing, and there was little doubt in my mind that he was serious.

I finished checking out Carlos, admitted him, and put him on antibiotics. I also notified security about Carlos's threat, hoping the police would follow up. My suspicion was that Carlos may have been doing more than kissing an unwilling woman, who now had more to fear than sexual assault.

During the first week, the interns were reminded to attend Morbidity and Mortality (M and M) Conference at 8:30 a.m. on Saturday. To be late or absent would require a very good excuse, and illness didn't qualify. The concept of M and M is to collect all the problems and complications from the previous week and discuss them as a group. The goal is to examine thought processes, surgical technique, and hospital systems to avoid similar mistakes in the future.

The physician in charge of each problem case is required to stand and explain and/or defend the actions which brought on the misadventure.

At 8:20 on Saturday morning, after an early start to finish ward rounds, I entered the small conference room and intentionally sat in the back row.

Dr. O'Donnelly began, "Thank you for coming to the Morbidity and Mortality Conference for the General Surgical Services. Dr. Shipman, would you present the misdiagnosis of appendicitis?"

Dr. Shipman, a third-year resident, stepped to the podium and described the case of a young woman who was taken to surgery for appendicitis but was instead found to have infection in her tubes and ovaries (a fairly common mistake, as I was to find out later).

One of the attending physicians said, "Tell us again what the preoperative pelvic exam showed."

"Right-sided tenderness without a mass," replied Dr. Shipman.

Another attending asked, "Are you sure there was no left-sided tenderness or cervical motion tenderness?"

"Yes, sir," said Dr. Shipman. "I'm sure."

Yet another attending asked, "Did you actually do a pelvic exam?"

"Yes, sir," said Dr. Shipman, defensively. He looked like a cornered dog.

The attendings were trying to sort out whether adequate consideration had been given to the actual diagnosis, pelvic inflammatory disease (PID), which is common in the young female population and is the result of sexual activity. Although PID can be very difficult to distinguish from appendicitis, it is treated with antibiotics, not surgery.

The grilling went on and on. Suggestions were made that the history taking could have been better. Other diagnostic tests could have been done, or they could have observed the patient longer. The unspoken implication was that the young doctor had hurried to the operating room just to get another case under his belt. Truthfully, nearly all the residents were eager to accrue a large file of surgical cases. Some were a little too eager, a few much too eager. The senior staff believed it was their sworn duty to discourage this behavior, even though they likely had done the same thing years before. Finally, there were no more questions for Dr. Shipman, and he retreated quickly to his seat.

Next up was Dr. Alvarez. He was presenting and defending the case of a young man stabbed in the abdomen.

It is important to point out that LA County-USC Medical Center was one of the few hospitals in America at the time that used "expectant observation" to manage stab-wound patients. In nearly every other hospital, it was gospel to take all abdominal stab-wound patients to the OR. But at our institution, we simply had too many stab wounds and too few surgeons, anesthesiologists, and operating rooms to explore them all. So we watched the stable ones for six to eight hours. If they developed signs of bleeding or intestinal perforation, off to the OR they would go. If not, they'd get transferred to the ward and discharged when they were out of danger. With this approach, perhaps 30 to 40 percent of these patients avoided an operation. Dr. Alvarez's patient had been one of those managed nonoperatively, but had later gotten into trouble and had to be taken to surgery. In our parlance, this is a missed injury, and our attending staff hated to see it happen.

The hyenas jumped all over Dr. Alvarez, ripping at his hindquarters. How many times was the temperature checked? Was the red cell count followed closely? Did the white blood cell count rise? Was a bad or early decision made to move the patient just to clear out the admitting ward? The resident was trying to fend off the onslaught, but he wasn't very successful. After about ten minutes of aggressive questioning and seemingly inadequate responses, Dr. Alvarez ended up slinking to his seat, reeking of guilt and embarrassment.

This continued for an hour and a half. A few of the senior residents stood their ground and came out unscathed, but most of the others, especially the younger ones, got chewed up. When the conference ended, the interns exited very quietly, dreading the day we'd be placed on this sacrificial altar.

In the hallway, Phil Conway pulled me aside. He had been the chief resident on call with me for my first night of general surgery call, had advised me to learn about IV fluids, and had saved me from having to do pass-on rounds. We had developed a good working relationship that night, and now he could see that some of the interns, including me, were unnerved by the M and M Conference. He had some papers in his hand.

"Hey, John," he said, "I have something I want you to read tonight." Then he gave me a little document I have kept to this day. He didn't give it to any of the other interns that day, at least not while I was watching. So why me? It is reproduced below, exactly as it appeared that morning.

HOW TO SWIM WITH SHARKS: A PRIMER
Voltaire Cousteau

Actually, <u>nobody</u> wants to swim with sharks. It is not an acknowledged sport, and it is neither enjoyable nor exhilarating. These instructions are written primarily for the benefit of those who, by virtue of their occupation, find they <u>must</u> swim and find that the water is infested with sharks.

It is of obvious importance to learn that the waters are shark infested before commencing to swim. It is safe to assume that this initial determination has already been made. If the waters were clearly not shark infested, this would be of little interest or value. If the waters were shark infested, the naïve swimmer is by now probably beyond help; at the very least he has doubtless lost any interest in learning how to swim with sharks.

Finally, swimming with sharks is like any other skill; it cannot be learned from books alone; the novice must practice in order to develop the skill. The follow-

ing rules simply set forth the fundamental principles which, if followed, will make it possible to survive while becoming expert through the practice.

Rules:

1. <u>*Assume unidentified fish are sharks.*</u> *Not all sharks look like sharks, and some fish which are not sharks sometimes act like sharks. Unless you have witnessed docile behavior in the presence of shed blood on more than one occasion, it is best to assume an unknown species is a shark. Inexperienced swimmers have been mangled by assuming that docile behavior in the absence of blood indicates that the fish is not a shark.*

2. <u>*Do not bleed.*</u> *It is a cardinal principle that if you are injured either by accident or by intent, you must not bleed. Experience shows that bleeding prompts an even more aggressive attack and will often provoke the participation of sharks which are uninvolved or, as noted above, are usually docile.*

   Admittedly, it is difficult not to bleed when injured. Indeed, at first this may seem impossible. Diligent practice, however, will permit the experienced swimmer to sustain a serious laceration without bleeding and without even exhibiting any loss of composure. This hemostatic reflex can in part be conditioned, but there may be constitutional aspects as well. Those who cannot learn to control their bleeding should not attempt to swim with sharks, for the peril is too great.

The control of bleeding has a positive protective element for the swimmer. The shark will be confused as to whether or not his attack has injured you, and confusion is to the swimmer's advantage. On the other hand, the shark may know he has injured you and be puzzled as to why you do not bleed or show distress. This also has a profound effect on sharks. They begin questioning their own potency or, alternatively, believe the swimmer has supernatural powers.

3. *Counter any aggression promptly. Sharks rarely attack a swimmer without warning. Usually there is some tentative, exploratory aggressive action. It is important that the swimmer recognize that this behavior is a prelude to an attack and takes prompt and vigorous remedial action. The appropriate countermove is a sharp blow to the nose. Almost invariably—this will prevent a full-scale attack, for it makes it clear that you understand the shark's intentions and are prepared to use whatever force is necessary to repel his aggressive actions. Some swimmers mistakenly believe that an ingratiating attitude will dispel an attack under these circum-*

stances. This is not correct; such a response provokes a shark attack. Those who hold this erroneous view can usually be identified by their missing limb.

4. <u>Get out if someone is bleeding.</u> If a swimmer (or shark) has been injured and is bleeding, get out of the water promptly. The presence of blood and the thrashing of water will elicit aggressive behavior even in the most docile of sharks. This latter group, poorly skilled in attacking, often behaves irrationally and may attack uninvolved swimmers or sharks. Some are so inept that in the confusion they injure themselves.

    No useful purpose is served in attempting to rescue the injured swimmer. He either will or will not survive the attack, and your intervention cannot protect him once blood has been shed. Those who survive such an attack rarely venture to swim with sharks again, an attitude which is readily understandable.

    The lack of effective countermeasures to a fully developed shark attack emphasizes the importance of the earlier rules.

5. <u>Use anticipatory retaliation.</u> A constant danger to the skilled swimmer is that the sharks will forget that he is skilled and may attack in error. Some sharks

have notoriously poor memories in this regard. This memory loss can be prevented by a program of anticipatory retaliation. The skilled swimmer should engage in these activities periodically, and the periods should be less than the memory span of the shark. Thus, it is not possible to state fixed intervals. The procedure may need to be repeated frequently with forgetful sharks and need be done only once for sharks with total recall.

The procedure is essentially the same as described under rule 3—a sharp blow to the nose. Here, however, the blow is unexpected and serves to remind the shark that you are both alert and unafraid. Swimmers should take care not to injure the shark and draw blood during this exercise for two reasons: First, sharks often bleed profusely, and this leads to the chaotic situation described under rule 4. Second, if swimmers act in this fashion it may not be possible to distinguish swimmers from sharks. Indeed, renegade swimmers are far worse than sharks, for none of the rules or measures described here is effective in controlling their aggressive behavior.

6. *Disorganize an organized attack. Usually, sharks are sufficiently self-centered that they do not act in concert against a swimmer. This lack of organiza-*

tion greatly reduces the risk of swimming among sharks. However, upon occasion, the sharks may launch a coordinated attack upon a swimmer or even upon one of their numbers. While the latter event is of no particular concern to a swimmer, it is essential that one knows how to handle an organized shark attack directed against a swimmer.

The proper strategy is diversion. Sharks can be diverted from their organized attack in one of two ways. First, sharks as a group are especially prone to internal dissension. An experienced swimmer can divert an organized attack by introducing something, often minor or trivial, which sets the sharks to fighting among themselves. Usually by the time the internal conflict is settled, the sharks cannot even recall what they were getting about to do, much less get organized to do it.

A second mechanism of diversion is to introduce something which so enrages the members of the group that they begin to lash out in all directions, even attacking inanimate objects in their fury.

What should be introduced? Unfortunately, different things prompt internal dissension or blind fury in different groups of sharks. Here one must be experienced in dealing with a given group of sharks, for what enrages one group will pass unnoticed by another.

It is scarcely necessary to state that it is unethical for a swimmer under attack by a group of sharks to counter the attack by diverting them to another swimmer. It is, however, common to see this done by novice swimmers and by sharks when they fall under a concerted attack.[1]

This essay has appeared in many medical journals and undoubtedly has been passed around in other professions, especially business. I had never seen it before. It did, however, strike me as extremely apropos of my current situation, and would become more so if I were selected to stay in this residency program.

But how do you avoid swimming with sharks? From my observation of the M and M Conference, it appeared that swimming was mandatory. How to not bleed if attacked? How to deliver the preemptive blow without overstepping your lowly position in the hierarchy? As it turns out, these are very difficult questions to answer.

---

[1] Little is known about the author, who died in Paris in 1912. He may have been a descendant of Francois Voltaire and an ancestor of Jacques Cousteau. Apparently, this essay was written for sponge divers. Because it may have broader applications, it was translated from the French by Richard J. Johns, an obscure French scholar and Massey Professor, and Director of the Department of Biomedical Engineering. The Johns Hopkins University and Hospital, 720 Rutland Avenue, Baltimore, Maryland, 21205. Perspectives in Biology and Medicine—Summer, 1973.

Late one night toward the end of my stint on ENT, I got an emergency beep from the ENT ward. I called the desk, and the clerk said, "Dr. Harch, you need to come right now! Please! Right now!" I hoped the problem was anything other than the lady with the bobbing tracheostomy. I was close by, just three floors down, so I sprinted up the stairs and flew into the hallway.

There were two terrified nurses standing outside Mrs. Parsons' room, one of them with blood spattered all over her white uniform. They were yelling and pointing into the room. I couldn't understand much more than, "Hurry, hurry!"

I dashed into the room. A short Filipina nurse stood at the bedside with a towel pressed to Mrs. Parsons' neck. The nurse was covered in blood. There was blood on the wall behind her, running down in rivulets. She said, "Doctor, I tried to stop the bleeding, but…"

Mrs. Parsons was white and motionless, and I knew she had emptied most of her blood volume onto that luckless nurse and the wall. The nurse was crying now, and I took her hand off the towel and checked Mrs. Parsons for a pulse. There was none. I told the nurse she did everything she could have done, and that we expected this. I suggested she go wash up, and then stood for a while with Mrs. Parsons, trying to process what had transpired. This was the first time someone had died while in my care. Eventually, I would spend less and less time at the bedside reflecting like this. Now, however, it seemed like a terribly sudden transition from a speaking, thinking human to the shell of a person devoid of any vital force.

CHAPTER THREE

DRUGS
AND ALCOHOL

NIGHT CALL COULD BRING TERROR FOR
new interns at LA County-USC, a terror not understood by outsiders. We had clawed our way
into this internship, but now we had to solve problems we
hadn't faced before on our own. Suddenly, we were making
decisions that affected whether people lived or died. Deep
inside, we were petrified that we might miss a clue or a diagnosis, or reach a faulty conclusion and injure or kill someone.

Many of my rotations in medical school had been at
institutions like UCLA or Cedars-Sinai, where students,

and even interns, were very closely supervised. But at the county hospital the intern was the first one called, and the intern was expected to get the job done. You could call your resident for help, but if you called too frequently, it was poor form. It showed lack of confidence. We sought help from one another, but because of the workload, we were often left to our own limited knowledge and experience, typically late at night.

Sometimes we filled the role of physician on call (POC). We carried a beeper, which went off continuously, it seemed, since we were responsible for more than a hundred patients distributed on different floors. The most common calls were for fever workups (time-consuming), low blood pressure (frightening at 3 a.m.—to both patients and interns— when residents weren't easily accessible), falls from bed, confusion, the violent patient, critical lab results, bleeding, and wound problems.

The POC was sometimes assigned to cover the surgical intensive care units. Here were located the sickest of the sick. Most were on ventilators that required frequent adjustment. Blood was taken every few hours, and IV lines had to be maintained. X-Rays were ordered and interpreted by the intern.

While serving as POC, you might also be called to the admitting ward when the admitting team was overwhelmed. You could get called to the OR to assist on emergency operations, which could mean holding retractors for hours.

One evening, I was assigned to be POC for the ICU. I arrived at 5 p.m. to take report on each critically ill patient. The second-year resident, Craig Kelly, was already there, getting ready to leave the hospital. As usual, he was in a hurry, and his top priority wasn't patient care.

"It's about time, Harch," said Craig, standing next to an unconscious patient. "I need to get out of here. Let me tell you about this lady, and I use that term very loosely. This is Tammy, and she's 35. She's been smoking since she was two, I think. She's got terrible peripheral vascular disease, and the vascular service has been operating on her for several years. You know, fem-pop, fem-stop, fem-chop. She's had bilateral AKAs. She's also a drugee and a boozer, and has organic brain syndrome."

"OK," I said, scribbling notes furiously. What he meant was that because of clogged arteries (from smoking), they had tried to bring blood flow down to the small arteries in Tammy's legs. These operations (femoral artery-to-popliteal artery bypasses, or fem-pop bypasses) had failed, or clotted (stopped). The ultimate result was amputation, or fem-chop. Bilateral meant both sides, and AKA referred to above-knee amputation. The shorthand slang for this series of failures in vascular surgery was fem-pop, fem-stop, fem-chop.

"Anyway, she recently developed gangrene on her stumps, along with infection, and we admitted her for antibiotics. Meanwhile, her boyfriend, who's also a lowlife, decides he wants to marry her, which they do right on the fuckin' ward. But she gets septic and has to be moved in here. She's sick as shit and trying to die. Do what you have to do to keep her alive and not bug me; I got a big date tonight."

I looked at Tammy. She had tubes and hoses coming out of every orifice. Her face was swollen. You might say she was on her last legs, but…

"One more thing: the new husband, Buddy, stands next to the bed all day long…at least as long as the nurses will let him. I kicked him outta here before you came in. He'll ask you about 10 times tonight when he can take her home. He's probably fried his brain just like Tammy and doesn't realize the only place she's going is to the eternal care unit. OK, I'm outta here."

He turned to go, then stopped, looked at me and added, "By the way, has anyone here told you that no one from UCLA has ever made it through the pyramid and been kept in this surgery program?"

I was stunned by this comment, so casual yet so brutal. I was silent for a moment, then replied, "I didn't know that."

"Well, it's just a fact. Thought you should know." Then he walked away in a rush to make his date.

I immediately started stewing over this exchange. What kind of prick would say that? Or was he the only one straightforward enough to tell me the truth? Was it confirmation of my suspicions regarding Dr. Rollins?

This train of thought forced me to consider how I ended up here in such a precarious situation. Midway through my fourth year of medical school, I applied to numerous general surgery programs, mostly in the western United States. After traveling around for a series of nerve-wracking interviews, I (along with every other graduating medical student) made a list of my preferred programs, first to last. Meanwhile, the residency program directors also made a list of their preferred students, first to last. All that information was thrown into a computer for the "residency match," whereupon each student was summarily "matched" to an institution. There was no way to predict or change the result. Therefore, on the whim of a computer program, thousands of brand-new doctors suddenly committed the next three to seven years of their lives to a training program and were spread around the country like dandelion seeds on the wind.

On match day, Lori and I drove to UCLA to receive the news (those were the days before personal computers and smartphones; the only way to reliably get such news was in person).

Lori and I had been dating for about 15 months. I hadn't discussed with her how I ranked my choices for the match. In fact, I listed as number one the well-known and well-respected Parkland program in Dallas, Texas, the place President Kennedy was taken when shot. I believed it was the best of the programs I had considered, and figured getting in was a long shot. If I was accepted, however, the opportunity would be phenomenal, and I just couldn't pass it up. Lori and I would have to figure out what to do with our relationship.

I gathered with 143 fellow UCLA medical students in one large room to discover our destinies. When handed my letter, I turned to Lori and said, "I want you to open it. But

I have to make a confession. I listed Parkland first...because I think it would be such a fantastic place to train. But my chances are so close to zero....I think I'll be at Irvine, still close enough for us to be together."

She looked at me with obvious disappointment, realizing that I had left her out of a decision that might separate us geographically and end our relationship. I felt like a rat. She opened the letter and was silent. She looked quizzically at me and handed me the letter, saying, "I'm not sure what you got." I took the letter and looked at it. I was expecting to read UC Irvine Medical Center, where I'd had a great interview. I thought my chances of getting in were very good, and I'd placed it second on my list of choices. It was located about 40 minutes away from Lori's apartment.

Instead, the letter read LAC-USC MC. For about 60 seconds, Lori and I couldn't decipher my fate.

"John," Lori said, "it's USC. You got into USC."

Then I realized that the program was Los Angeles County-USC Medical Center, which had been the third choice on my list. Lori knew I would be conflicted about this result. It was known as a strong training program, but was notorious for its punishing work schedule over the course of five years.

This outcome, unanticipated by both of us, meant that I'd be located just a few miles from Lori. She lived in Hollywood, on a little street behind the Hollywood Bowl. She was the managing editor of *Motorcyclist Magazine* at the time. In fact, on our first date, she told me that Honda had given her a motorcycle. She was riding it back and forth to work on the busy city streets. I was shocked because she didn't look at all like a motorcycle mama. I told her, "You're way too pretty to end up mangled underneath a car. You know, at the hospital, we call them 'donor cycles.'" She thought the comment was condescending, but gave up motorcycle riding not long after. Whether our conversation led to this decision was unclear to me, but I was happy that she was back in her car.

When the result of the match had settled in, we smiled and hugged, because we knew we'd be able to stay together without uprooting her or having a long-distance relationship. But I worried about the lasting damage I might have done with my unilateral decision to select a program as far away as Texas for my first choice. Was she permanently offended because I hadn't even discussed it with her? Hurt because I ranked her below my selfish professional goals? If so, she didn't share it with me.

I was saved from my inner torment by Skip, who arrived to give me report on his ICU patient. "Shit," he said, "some guy on the ward is crashing and we have to take him back to the OR. I just have a minute."

"Go," I said.

"Uh…my guy is Esteban," Skip said, dragging me to an adjacent bed. "Poor bastard is 26, and he got trapped between a loading dock and a truck that backed up. He was stuck there for over six minutes because he couldn't yell or move, and no one knew he was in trouble. They brought him to the ER, where he had no blood pressure. He had an ER thoracotomy and was taken to the OR, where they removed a ruptured spleen. Because of the downtime, his squash is probably shot, and they may harvest his organs for transplant. He's circling the drain. Just try to keep him alive for the transplant team. If he needs blood pressure support, call somebody smarter than me...which means anybody. I gotta run. Good luck, amigo."

I moved closer to Esteban for a better look. He had signs of the horrible mishap he'd suffered. All the skin from his waist to his forehead was a splotchy, reddish-purple color; it's what we call traumatic asphyxia (the pressure of being crushed forces blood out of the small capillaries and into the skin, where it remains for days). I raised one of Esteban's eyelids; even the "whites" of his eyes were red. Skip's comment about his "squash" referred to his brain, which was presumed irreversibly damaged from the prolonged low blood pressure and lack of breathing. This doomed man, simply doing his job a few hours ago, was almost exactly my age.

The next patient belonged to the Saturday Service. The junior resident was Marc Feinberg, and rumor had it he was the meanest resident in the program, at least to interns. I hadn't crossed paths with him much before this.

"Dr. Feinberg's across the hall in the residents' library," said Darla. "You can get report from him there."

"Thanks, Darla," I said. As she turned to resume care of her patient, I watched her longer than I needed to. Ever since Skip told me about Darla and Tiffany, I couldn't walk into the ICU without getting distracted by their presence. Spending most of my days and many of my nights in the hospital didn't help matters much. As I walked toward the door, I felt guilty about my thoughts; not because of what Darla or Tiffany might think, but because I had a girlfriend—a kind, smart, good-looking girlfriend who cared about me. Still…Darla, Tiffany…High and Low Gomco…

The residents' library was a room set aside for the residents as a sort of refuge. It wasn't a sleep room, but rather a place to hide, to prepare for a presentation, or just recover after being on call. As a matter of tradition, interns were strictly forbidden from entering this room. We were not yet accepted into the fraternity. I knocked on the door, and a resident opened it about six inches.

"Yeah?" said the resident.

"Is Dr. Feinberg here?" I asked. "I'm the POC and I need to do ICU checkout." I looked over his shoulder. The room was a shambles. There was a broken-down couch on the left and a long table in the middle of the room covered with big surgical textbooks and cafeteria trays. In one corner a resident in bloody greens snoozed in a big, soft, easy chair, his head back and mouth open. There were partially eaten donuts on the floor, along with paper plates, trash, and surgical journals. It looked like an archaeological excavation site for a strange, not-so-long-lost culture.

Feinberg walked to the door but didn't invite me in. "I'll meet you in the ICU in a couple minutes." He shut the door in my face.

"Thanks for the nice welcome, asshole," I thought. It was driven home that I wasn't one of them; not yet, possibly not ever. I went back to the ICU.

In a few minutes, Feinberg showed up. "This is Shayna," he said, "a 30-year-old lady who told her husband that she was depressed and wanted to kill herself. He got his gun out and loaded it. He handed it to her and said, 'Here, shoot yourself.' And she did; in the abdomen. She sustained stomach, colon, and liver injuries, which were repaired, but she lost a lot of blood. She's reasonably stable, but she just spiked a fever and needs a fever workup. And I'd like to recheck her coagulation status tonight."

"I got it," I said.

"And don't do anything heroic with my patients. You're not ready for that yet. Call me if you have any doubt about what to do."

"Sure thing," I promised.

The final patient in the ICU was Linda, a 46-year-old woman who had been a heavy drinker for many years. She had developed cirrhosis of the liver, resulting in repeated upper gastrointestinal bleeding episodes and many hospital admissions. She belonged to my favorite resident, Nick Givens, who'd given me a brief rundown on her earlier in the day.

Nick was three years ahead of me in the residency. He was married and had four kids. He was straitlaced; never a cussword or negative comment about another person out of him. He was deeply religious. Despite his wholesomeness, we got along well. In my brief time at LA County, he'd already provided me with several articles pertaining to a sick or complicated patient we'd shared. He was an unending font of information and was respected for his technical abilities in the OR.

Nick walked into the ICU and greeted the nurses. "Hello, ladies. Everything OK in here?"

"So far, so good," said Darla. "Even Linda's holding her own."

Looking to me, Nick said, "You already know a little about Linda. She bled really hard on this admission. Right now, her bleeding seems to have stopped. She's still on Pitressin. We're checking her hematocrits and coags frequently. I want you to keep a close eye on her tonight because she has a significant risk of dying."

"I will," I said, trying to focus on Linda and not Darla. Nick said goodbye and hurried off to his other duties.

Cirrhosis of the liver is a particularly foul and complex medical problem. There are numerous causes for it, including chronic hepatitis, but most of the people we treated at LA County had earned their disease through a love affair with alcohol. These patients develop bleeding from the esophagus (typically manifested by vomiting of blood or clots), yellow jaundice, and muscle wasting. As a result, we refer to them as bleeding, yellow canaries.

Linda was my yellow canary. And Nick's. I respected him more than anyone in the program. So I tried to focus on her that night, realizing that I had other ICU patients and possibly new work with the admitting team to juggle as well.

They were getting slammed on 9200. I got called for backup around 1 a.m. All the residents were operating. All the interns were occupied. A 30-year-old pregnant woman had been hit by a car while walking. When she arrived in the ER, the nurses discovered her fetus on the stretcher between her legs, still attached to the umbilical cord. They had cut the cord and removed the dead fetus before I was asked to start her trauma workup.

This young woman also had a broken femur and a fractured pelvis. It was my job to begin assessing whether she had a significant intra-abdominal injury (or, for that matter, an injury anywhere else). Unfortunately, her poor English, my poor Spanish, and the wild urgency of the night prevented me from having any sensitive discussion of her calamity. I could only say I was sorry, and get on with the task of seeing that she didn't die too. I started piecing together the details of the accident and her medical history. She was despondent, scared, and alone. If we could confidently exclude other injuries, she'd have to be transferred to the ortho ward to fix her fractured femur. If she didn't pass the placenta, she'd need a D and C (dilatation and curettage) by the OB-GYN residents. Her tragic day was evolving into a grueling hospital stay.

Just then I got a beep from ICU. Linda's blood pressure was low and her IVs weren't working. That was another charming feature about cirrhotic patients: their veins were usually all used up. I headed directly to the ICU.

As I entered the room, Buddy (the guy who'd married Tammy in the hospital) grabbed my arm and asked, "Hey, Doc, can you tell me how she's doin' tonight? I want to take her home tomorrow."

"I'll have to talk to you later," I said, and I hustled over to Linda's bed. Her blood pressure was 65, heart rate 118. She needed fluid, but both IVs had stopped working, so I had no way to help her at this moment. Dark, bloody fluid poured out of her stomach drainage tube.

I put tourniquets on both arms. Darla and I started working feverishly to get an IV going. In this crisis, I was able to suppress my obsession with Darla, temporarily. In a few minutes Darla established a decent line. We gave blood when it arrived. I poked holes all over Linda's arms, legs, and feet, but managed to establish an IV that flowed only very slowly.

"Dr. Harch," said Darla, "I had to stop Linda's Pitressin when the IVs quit working. Now we're running blood and platelets. We can't run Pitressin without another reliable line."

"What's her blood pressure now?" I asked.

"About 95 systolic."

"Let's hold the Pitressin. Let me know if she drops her pressure or cuts loose bleeding."

Pitressin is a medication that slows bleeding in cirrhotics. What Linda really needed was a central venous line, which is a long IV tube placed in the neck or just below the collar bone and into a large vein. Multiple medications and blood products can be given quickly through a line like this. But I hadn't been trained to place central lines, and it was a little dangerous to attempt. I could have called Nick at that moment, 3 a.m., but he was recovering from nearly 48 hours of nonstop work and surgery. He was only now getting a few hours of sleep. Let him sleep, I thought, and I'll cross my fingers for Linda.

I got lucky, and so did Linda. She struggled along with marginal vital signs for the next few hours, but didn't bleed hard. Meanwhile, Tammy's blood pressure was dwindling a little. I walked over and ordered some IV fluids. Buddy was asleep in a chair and he woke up.

"Doc, how's she doin'? Is she gettin' better?"

"Well, Buddy, she's really, really sick," I explained. "She's got a bad infection, and her blood pressure is low."

"Am I gonna get to take her home?" he asked, eyes welling up.

"I don't know," I said, lying. "We're doing everything we can, but she's in pretty bad shape."

Tears rolled down his face. "You guys gotta save her."

I turned to see Darla watching this exchange. She reached up to adjust some IV lines and her fitted white dress hiked way up on her perfectly smooth thigh. Despite Buddy's desperate pleading and all the critical responsibilities around me, I found myself lusting after her again. Why was I so distracted by every attractive woman I encountered in the hospital? My thoughts flashed to Lori. She might understand; after all, she wasn't exactly a girl scout in her past. I recalled a conversation we had a few months after we met.

"What was your longest relationship before we got together?" I asked.

"I dated a guy named Ryan for about two years."

"What was he like?"

"Well, we met at the restaurant where I was a waitress and he was a bartender. We were both students at UCI. He was a biology major."

"Just like me," I said.

"No…not just like you," she said, laughing. "Ryan didn't want to play by anyone else's rules. Among other things, he liked to experiment with recreational drugs."

"Did you participate?"

"Uh…yeah. He really believed the drugs enhanced one's intellectual and emotional consciousness…or awareness. That fascinated me. He was also a very sensuous person, which tied into the drugs."

"So, what kind of drugs did you guys do?"

"Well, before I met Ryan, the only thing I used was pot, infrequently. But he introduced me to amyl nitrate, which we inhaled, and cocaine, Quaaludes, psilocybin mushrooms, and LSD. It made good sex even better."

"Jesus Christ! My little English major magazine editor was a wild thing!"

"Well, don't jump to conclusions. It wasn't quite as crazy as it sounds."

"What did you think of all the drugs?"

"It was exciting, and different, and…mind-expanding."

"Didn't using those drugs scare you?"

"Not really, because he was very familiar with them… and he knew exactly what to take, how much, what to expect, and what environment to be in while you were taking them."

"How often did you do this?"

"Just a few times for each drug. I just wanted to know what it was like. But it was stupid. Messed up my academic performance at the time. And the last time I took LSD, it scared me. It was too intense, so I didn't do it again."

"LSD…wow. I've never taken LSD. Too scared I'd do something insane."

"That wasn't the only unorthodox thing about him," she said, waiting for me to meet her gaze.

"What else?" I asked.

"He was bisexual."

"Really."

"Yes…that was part of his appeal for me. I figured there wouldn't be any pressure from him for a committed relationship, like marriage."

"What about you? Are you bisexual?"

"No. Sometimes I wish I were sexually attracted to women because I think women, in general, are much nicer than men. But it's just not my thing."

"Well, that's good to hear," I smiled. "So, I guess you guys had an open relationship?"

"Our understanding was that either one of us could have sex with others. As it turns out, I didn't ever do it, but

Ryan had a relationship with an older guy he'd see about once a month."

"And how many guys was that guy having sex with?"

"Lots. He was very active in the gay community."

"Lori, do you know what's been going on at UCLA the past year or so?"

"No."

"Someone noticed a cluster of gay men in LA developing rare infections and cancers. It's thought to be lifestyle related, and it's killing them. They're trying to sort out the cause right now. You're lucky you didn't get sick."

"You know, there was whispering about some of his friends from Laguna Beach getting sick."

"How long since you last saw him?"

"I don't know. About nine months."

This revelation left a pit in my stomach. Although researchers didn't understand much about the disease that would later be called HIV/AIDS, they knew it could be deadly. "We better both cross our fingers," I said.

Nick arrived at about 6:30 a.m. and I gave him a full report. He was upset that the Pitressin had been stopped. Didn't I know that the Pitressin was an essential component of her care? That she might have bled to death without it? I should have called him to put the central line in.

I apologized and tried to explain, but he wasn't satisfied. He said his sleep wasn't as important as Linda's life. It made me uneasy that he didn't seem angry; instead, he was disappointed. I gave reports on the rest of the ICU patients as each team arrived. Then I left to start my duties for the new day. But a cloud of shame hung over me. I was sure that my actions had likely cost me any slim chance I had to make the intern cut, which was only six weeks away.

CHAPTER FOUR

REALLY, RUSS?

THE ALARM JOLTED ME FROM A DEEP sleep at 6 a.m. I showered, downed a stale donut, and got dressed. I tossed my stethoscope in a pocket of my white coat, then dashed across the plaza in the rising light of dawn for the first day of Friday Service.

I arrived on the ward at 6:20. My chief resident, Pete Miller, was already there. Within minutes, the junior resident, Tim Dantz, and three med students showed up. We introduced ourselves. At 6:29, the other intern walked in. It was B. Rutherford Wilkinson III, my fellow general surgery intern with the dead-fish handshake. He greeted Pete and Tim, introducing himself as "Russ," and stated he was pleased to be on their service. He gave a token nod to the rest of us.

"Let's get going," said Pete. "We've got a big service." Stopping at the first bed, he said, "This is Hector Ramirez. He's three days status-post surgery for perforated appendicitis. What are his temps doing?"

Russ grabbed the vitals sheet and said, "T max 101.4 last night, sir."

"OK," said Pete. "Let's get a look at that wound." I started forward, but Russ stepped in front of me and pulled the bedsheet and blanket aside. He removed the top dressing, then roughly pulled out the gauze packing from the wound. The patient winced.

"Hmmm, looks kinda soupy," said Pete. "Let's irrigate that wound with betadine and saline. Get him up and coughing. Get a CBC and chem 7. And check his intraoperative cultures. Dr. Harch, what bacteria would you expect to find in those cultures?"

This was my first general surgery rotation. I knew some bacteriology from my medical student rotations, but hadn't studied appendicitis in any depth. "E. coli..." I said, trying to pull up the other names.

"That's one," said Pete.

"B. fragilis, Klebsiella, and Serratia," blurted out Russ.

"Very good, Russ," said Pete. Russ was beaming.

We moved to the next bed. Russ tried for the vitals sheet, but I already had it.

"This is Enrique Garcia," Pete stated, nodding to the patient. "He sustained gunshot wounds to the left lower quadrant and left lower extremity last Friday. We resected 18 inches of damaged small bowel, a chunk of shredded colon, and hung up a colostomy. How are his temps?"

"No fever the last 24 hours," I responded. "Vitals OK."

Pete checked the patient's abdomen. "Soft, wound looks OK. Lookin' pretty good. Come back here and change this dressing. Make sure his labs are up to date. Get him walking. Get his Foley catheter out."

We moved across the hall to the women's room and stopped at the bed of a 40-year-old obese woman.

"Mrs. Hererra is five days status-post cholecystectomy," said Pete. "She's doing fine but won't get up and move. Her wound looks good, but she was a little warm yesterday afternoon. What did her temps do last night?"

Russ had the vitals. "Low-grade fevers of 100.6, 100.2, and 100.5, sir."

"You don't need to call me sir," said Pete. "Let's get a UA, culture if needed, CBC, and a chest X-Ray. I'll bet she's brewing a pneumonia. Get her out of bed, walk her, and snake her. If you can get a sputum specimen, send it off for culture."

Mrs. Hererra was in for a bad morning. She didn't want to move because she had a big incision across her right upper quadrant, through all the muscles, making it very painful to get up. The extra weight she carried made it even tougher. We'd return later to inflict on her all the actions just ordered by Pete. The worst of it would be the snaking, which we also called snogging. It was the brutal LA County method to make people cough and clear their lungs. I'd learned about it from my intern buddies on ENT. We would take a thin, red, rubber tube and slide it down one nostril. That was unpleasant enough, but then we shoved the tube down farther, going through the vocal cords and into the trachea. The patient would cough like hell. Sometimes patients would reach up and try to rip the tube out, and we'd restrain their arms. Other times they'd grab their incisions and hold on while they coughed. It was cruel, but it worked. It was just another dirty job the intern had to do.

There were about 19 patients on the service. At each bedside, Russ and I and the students took notes: name, age, birthdate, medical record number, history, surgery done, labs, and X-Rays. Later (usually at night), we would transcribe all this data onto one 3x5 card for each patient, in very tiny print. The little stack of cards would be carried in our shirt pockets at all times. That way, we could pull the card out to refresh our memories before or during rounds. With so many patients, it was an absolute necessity.

When we finished rounds, Russ and I split up the patients so we could start on the giant pile of scut work so effortlessly created by Pete. Russ was rather insistent on which patients he did and didn't want. I was insistent only about not wanting an argument on the first day, so I agreed to his preferences. I ended up with Mrs. Hererra, of course, and 10 of the 19 patients.

Russ took two medical students and disappeared to do his work. The remaining student and I started at the top of our work list. By midmorning, we got to Mrs. Hererra. She was still lying in bed like a big slug. We needed blood for the labs. Because of her weight, her veins were very hard to find, and it took three sticks with needle and syringe to get her blood.

Next, the snogging. I said, "*Necesito poner un tubito en su nariz para ayudar usted a toser. Es necesario para prevenir pneumonia,*" which translates loosely to "I need to place a small tube in your nose to help you to cough. It's necessary to prevent pneumonia." Too simple an explanation for the horrible thing I was about to do. She nodded, but the look on her face told me she didn't really understand.

I produced the rubber tube, lubricated it, and passed it into one of her nostrils. She leaned her head back away from me a little, eyes bulging, but I pushed the tube forward. She gagged, and I pushed it in another two inches and down into her trachea. Immediately, she coughed violently and clutched her abdomen, letting out a little scream. I wiggled the tube in and out, stimulating more coughs, followed by the crackling sound of sputum being loosened and brought up. Her eyes welled up and tears rolled down her face. The student was appalled. I felt like a medieval torturer, but it worked. She brought up some globs of green sputum, which we collected in a specimen cup for culture. She continued to hold her incision with both hands, weeping silently.

When I finished, Mrs. Hererra gave me a look that seemed to say, "You may be my doctor, and you say you're helping me, but you really hurt me, you mean son of a bitch."

I repeated my earlier statement. *"Lo siento, pero es necesario para prevenir pneumonia."* We weren't done, however. After another brief and grammatically incorrect explanation, and with great difficulty, the student and I dragged her out of bed and forced her to walk, painfully, to the bathroom. There we obtained a urine specimen to check for infection. We moved her to a wheelchair, and the student whisked her down to the third floor for a chest X-Ray. When she returned, her IV had infiltrated and I had to stick her two more times to establish a new, working one. The two of us had spent well over an hour on essential post-op care that would go mostly unnoticed by the rest of the team.

The intimacy of these bedside activities is inescapable. We assault people with sharp objects. We shove tubes in their noses and other orifices, and sometimes cut holes in them to place other tubes. We probe their vaginas and rectums with our fingers. We put our hands in their wounds and, during surgery, inside their bodies. We pull and push them out of bed half-naked, our arms wrapped around their sweaty bodies, and force them to walk. Typically, they haven't bathed properly in days, so they stink, and they know it. Their hair is a matted mess and their modesty has been surrendered. They are vulnerable and scared, and they're in pain. Doing what is right for these patients each day (not what is easy) demands knowledge and skill, but also fortitude. Communicating that you know you're about to hurt someone, then being as gentle as possible, makes the pain of disease and illness more tolerable. The physical connection then becomes an emotional connection—the essence of compassionate medicine.

We worked until about 4:30 p.m., when it was time for afternoon rounds. We again walked bed to bed, now reviewing all labs and X-Rays, with Pete making sure all the work had been completed. Mrs. Hererra's chest X-Ray showed early pneumonia, and we started her on antibiotics. Pete found some new chores for us to do.

Around 6 p.m., I was nearly finished. When I passed one of the patient rooms, I saw Russ's med students hovering over a patient. They were struggling to start an IV. The patient was obviously unhappy, realizing that an uncomfortable procedure had become painful when left to inexperienced members of the team.

"Where's Russ?" I asked.

"He, uh…went home a little while ago. Asked us to do a few things and restart this IV," explained one of the students.

"Went home?" I almost shouted.

"Yeah, he said he had reading to do."

"You guys should be at home, reading," I growled. "What else needs to be done?"

"Mr. Ramirez still needs his wound cleaned out and re-dressed," the other student said.

Now I was really pissed off. It was shameful to make students deal with difficult IV starts and an open post-op wound. Those tasks were hard enough for new interns.

"Just go home, you guys," I said. I finished Russ's work, seething the whole time. By now, it was a little after 7 p.m. I made a phone call. "Hi, Lori, how are you?"

"Fine. Are you still at the hospital?"

"Yeah. It's been a long day. Can I come over tonight? I gotta get outta here."

"Of course. I'd love to see you. Have you eaten?"

"Uh…no. Haven't had time."

"Come on over. I'll have some food ready."

"Thanks. See you in about 30 minutes."

I hurried out of the hospital—no, I ran out. I decided not to waste time going to the dorm to change clothes. It was starting to get dark as I approached the parking garage. The area around LA County Hospital was seedy; drunks stumbled around, drug addicts wandered the campus looking for things to steal, crazy people stood or sat talking to themselves, and there was gang activity in the nearby park.

I scanned the walkways, bushes, and doorways. I was parked on the second floor. As I opened the door to the stairwell, I looked in without entering, as I usually did. No one there. I sprinted up the stairs and out the door. All clear. As I drove out of the garage, my anxiety level started to drop; not only because I'd avoided a hostile encounter, but because I was getting a little break from internship. And I didn't have to return to my stark dorm room alone.

I contemplated my circumstances as I drove west toward Hollywood. I had worked so long and hard for this surgical internship. Now I felt no one gave a shit whether I succeeded or not, except Lori, Billy (my basketball buddy), and maybe Skip. And none of them could have any impact on my chances at the residency. It was discouraging, especially since I was putting in 110 hours a week.

I knocked on Lori's apartment door. She opened it, smiled, and said, "You actually made it!"

I planted a big kiss on her lips and hugged her.

"How was your day?" she asked. The smell of real, home-made food filled the apartment.

I summarized the events of my first day on the Friday Service, including my torture of Mrs. Herrera and my inter-actions with Russ.

"Honey, don't let him take advantage of you or get under your skin," she said.

"Well, it's not that easy to walk the line. Everyone is watching everything we do. I don't want to be too aggressive with him...but I don't want to get rolled over, either."

"But don't you think all these people will see him for what he is?"

"I don't know. Remember that his dad is the chief of surgery somewhere. It probably doesn't matter if he's a suck-up or a lazy bastard. He knows he has an advantage. His dad probably talks to Dr. O'Donnelly regularly."

"Look," said Lori. "You're smart, you work really hard, and you give a damn. They'll see it. I think your chances are as good as anybody's."

These were the words of a supportive girlfriend; things she had to say. They didn't comfort me much because she didn't know this surgery training system from the inside.

"I hope you're right. But remember, everybody's smart. And most everyone is working his ass off right now. I need to start thinking about what I'm gonna do if I don't make the cut."

"You'll make it. And if they're too stupid to keep you, you're better off somewhere else."

She might have said, "We're better off somewhere else." But she didn't, given our tacit agreement to avoid discussing long-term plans. It left all options open for both of us.

"How was your day?" I asked.

"Oh, about the same. Derrick acted like an idiot, as usual, but most of the guys behaved themselves, and they're meeting their deadlines." She enjoyed her editorial job at *Motorcyclist Magazine*, but there was a certain amount of stress each month just before the magazine went to the printer.

"Will you have to work late next week when you ship?"

"Just late enough that I'll get to take you out to dinner and bill it to the company."

We ate dinner and talked. I got a few beeps but handled everything by phone. It got to be about 10:30 and the sleeplessness was catching up with me. I tilted my head toward the bedroom and she smiled, saying, "Let's go."

We pulled each other's clothes off and fell into each other's arms. She was long and lean and smooth and sensuous. This was true escape from internship.

Two mornings later, the Friday Service team started earlier than usual because of staff rounds. This instructional process occurred once each week, on each service, when surgeons from the local community would come in to make rounds with the teams. All these surgeons were graduates of our surgical residency. By participating, they got to see interesting cases, and we benefitted from their advice. Occasionally they assisted on elective cases or even took call with us to help with emergency cases.

Staff rounds were at 8 a.m. Pete asked us to come in around 6 to inspect wounds and change dressings, draw blood, and check labs. The students had to retrieve all pertinent X-Rays. Everything had to be clean and tidy on the service by 8.

Three staff surgeons arrived just before 8 and were introduced. We set out for the patient rooms. It was the interns' job to present the patients to the staff. Russ and I had memorized the information on each 3x5 card as best we could. We rattled off the details for each case. Sometimes the staff asked for minutia we couldn't provide, facts about surgeries we hadn't witnessed. It was nerve wracking.

When I finished presenting Mr. Garcia, one surgeon asked me why he received a colostomy.

"Because of his colon injury and the contamination," I said confidently. This is what I'd been told.

"Yes, but why not just remove the injured colon, wash the belly out, start antibiotics, and reconnect the ends of the bowel?" he persisted.

I didn't have enough knowledge about colon trauma to give a good answer. I stood there thinking, embarrassed.

"Because of the experience in World War II and the Korean War," piped in Russ. "They learned that the risk of anastomotic breakdown and infection was too high."

"That's right," nodded the staff guy. "Very good."

I was humiliated, and angry. Now I understood why Russ was leaving his work to the students and dumping the time-consuming patients on me: so he could be reading this information in the evening. He was behaving like a privileged punk who had grown up with music lessons, summer camps, tennis courts, and the expectation that he'd naturally wind up being a successful surgeon. Why should he shoulder his share of the workload now? The gulf between him and me seemed wide and deep.

I was raised in a family that was barely middle class. My father was the son of immigrant, working-class Czechoslovakian parents. He attended college briefly, got distracted by golf and beer drinking, and eventually became a machinist. His income was modest, especially considering he supported a wife and four children.

At age 41, my father began to experience fatigue and poor appetite. He ignored his worsening symptoms because it was unacceptable for a male in his cultural circle to complain or seek a doctor's care. In fact, he had never visited a doctor in his entire life. He deteriorated, developed jaundice, and exploratory surgery revealed extensive, inoperable stomach cancer.

We went to the hospital to see him after his surgery. Young children were not allowed to visit seriously ill family members in the hospital in those days, so the five of us stood a short distance from his hospital room window and waved. I remember the moment vividly, looking across an expanse of thick, tangled ivy toward that window, as he waved back, forced a little smile, and put on a good front for us. I can't imagine how distressing it must have been for him to look at his wife and four small kids (the youngest, my sister, being four), knowing that he would soon be dead, leaving us to survive on our own. This thought has haunted me for years, and continues to haunt me to this day. It was the last time I saw him. He died nine days later. It was the day before my eighth birthday.

My mother was one of nine children born to Italian immigrant parents. As the only family of "dagos" in a small town in upstate New York, they were treated with considerable hostility. They were tough, however, and survived on my grandfather's meager salary as the production manager at a small but growing Italian cheese factory. My mom attended college and became a nurse, eventually caring for our injured soldiers on the island of Okinawa during WWII, then working as a surgical nurse after the war. She quit nursing after getting married, but had to return to work after my dad died. Although we never lacked food, shelter, or basic necessities, there were few luxury items. Vacations were simple and short. As kids, we learned to earn the money for things we wanted but didn't need.

The ENT residents had spread the word that they were receiving so many drunks with cut up faces at night that they were looking for interns to help sew them up. It's not that we didn't have enough to do each day, but we were dying to do some actual surgery, even if it was suturing skin.

One night, Billy and I showed up at the clinic. There were three or four people with facial lacerations waiting to be treated. They were holding bloody bandages against their wounds. Some were so drunk that they were half-asleep—or completely asleep—on gurneys. We each took a patient and started to collect supplies.

We didn't sedate these drunks—they were already self-medicated. The real challenge was keeping them still so we could work. My guy was really drunk and had fallen onto something, sustaining several lacerations on the left side of his face. Now he was mumbling and rolling around on a gurney in an unpredictable way. I placed some sterile drapes and started injecting some numbing lidocaine, which stings. The guy opened his mouth and let out an "arrrhhh-hhhhh" that sounded like what I imagined a pirate would say, followed by a blast of rank, alcohol-infused breath that nearly knocked me over.

The struggle began. I would irrigate dirt out of the wounds, and he would turn away. I would inject lidocaine; he would shout and roll around. He would belch; I would ignore the stench and place sutures. When he wasn't writhing around, he'd fall asleep. I fumbled a lot because my suturing skills were limited. Keeping the field sterile was impossible.

Two beds over, Billy was working. His patient was a little more awake (translation: not so drunk), but initially wasn't saying much. She was a young Hispanic woman who'd been slashed on the face. When Billy started to inject, she said, loudly, "What the fuck are you doing?"

"I'm getting you numbed up so I can fix this cut on your face," he said, and he continued to work.

She looked at him closely, peering from under the green cloth drape. "Hey," she said, "get this nigger off me."

Billy calmly responded, "Well, that rolled off your tongue pretty easily. I bet you've used that word before." He shot me a quick glance.

"Well…maybe I have…and maybe I haven't," she said.

There was a pause. The patient seemed about to nod off.

"Do you want me to continue?" he asked. "I'm trying to stitch you up."

"Yeah…go ahead," she said.

I finally finished my suture job. It didn't look bad but didn't look great, given that my marginal abilities had been tested in the middle of a skirmish. The patient let out another big "arrrhhhhhhh" and stuck his head over the side of the gurney. Then he vomited all over the floor, splashing some on my shoes and pants. I was grateful this hadn't happened 10 minutes earlier.

I walked over to see how Billy was doing. He was finishing. The repair was very nice. He'd done the very best he could. "We're all done," he said to the patient. "We'll get you a prescription for pain medicine and an appointment to come back to remove the sutures."

"Thanks," said his patient. "And... sorry, Doc."

"No problem," he said. "Let's forget it."

Billy and I left the clinic. As we walked down the hall, I asked, "How often does shit like that happen to you?"

"Oh, here and there."

"Don't you get mad as hell? I mean, how do you remain so calm?"

"The chief of surgery at my medical school is a very influential man in my life—second only to my own father. At times like this I always recall a phrase he repeatedly stressed, 'Equanimity under duress,' as the hallmark of surgical discipline. He emphasized that ours is the noblest profession, and even when patients are abusive, we should maintain a higher standard."

"That's a great lesson…but hard to put into action at the moment you're insulted. I admire how cool you stayed. It would piss me off."

"Oh, yeah, it pisses me off, but I don't want to get down on their level. It doesn't solve anything."

"I guess you're right. Better to take the high road."

"My parents also taught me to practice forgiveness. And I try. But I keep that little guiding principle about equanimity written on an index card and taped to the wall above the desk in my dorm room."

Side by side, we trudged off to the dorm to get some sleep.

Friday rolled around. Our team would be responsible for every trauma and general surgery problem for the ensuing 24 hours. I was asked to admit a sick alcoholic to the ICU, so I pushed her bed down the hall myself. The receiving nurse was Tiffany, High Gomco. Uh-oh. I was in danger of losing my ability to function coherently.

"Hi, Dr. Harch," she said. "Is this your admit?" She blinked her gorgeous green eyes.

"Uh…yeah," I said. I searched her eyes for anything unspoken.

"Do you have orders?" She raised her eyebrows a little, as if to say, "It's all business, Buster."

"I'm about to write them," I said, as I recovered a tiny amount of brainpower and resumed patient care.

The team was fortunate to make it to the cafeteria for dinner that evening. This didn't always happen. When we came back up to 9200, we had a new patient. A 38-year-old drunk guy had jumped or fallen out the back of a pickup truck and broken his femur. We had to check him out for other injuries, but we knew he needed the fracture fixed, so we called an orthopedic consult. A short time later, the elevator opened and out walked Pete and a guy I didn't know. He was the ortho resident on call, and Pete introduced him to me. His name was Bret. I went to the bedside with them. While they were talking and examining the patient, I noticed that Bret had several big scars on his face, more on his neck, and one visible on his chest in the V of skin above his scrub shirt. He also had multiple scars on his arms, some of which were six or eight inches long. Bret made a plan to take the patient for surgery after we cleared him of any other injuries.

When Bret walked off the ward, Pete came over to me and said, "Do you know who that is?"

"No," I said.

"Bret was a medical student here a few years ago. On a slow call night, he went into that sleep room right there," Pete gestured to the room just behind the clerk's desk, "to take a quick nap. Some crazy guy who had been beaten up got out of bed in room one over there and had a knife on him. He went into the sleep room and stabbed Bret about 25 times. They stopped the guy, but Bret had to be taken straight to the OR by his own admitting team. He nearly died. He lost his spleen and needed hours of surgery to fix all the other injuries. It took him more than a year to recover. He ended up going into Ortho."

"Holy shit," I said. "Poor guy. How many times has something like that happened around here?"

"Never before, never since, to my knowledge. But it just reminds you how many crazy people there are sitting on this admitting ward."

As we approached midnight, things quieted down a little. Because we had most of our work done, Russ decided to get some sleep. Given what I'd heard earlier, I didn't want any part of that sleep room, so I found a quiet spot to do some reading.

Around 1 a.m., the phone at the desk rang. It was the ER. They had a young guy with a gunshot to the chest and a very low blood pressure. Unbeknownst to us, this was the start of a very bad night. Pete and Tim ran to the elevator. I asked if I could go with them since I was caught up on my work. They said, "Hell, yeah." Russ was asleep, and I didn't wake him.

The emergency room occupied a huge space, with exam rooms positioned around the perimeter. In the center of this bustling gateway to the hospital was C-booth, a dedicated trauma treatment area with three beds side by side, where the severely injured were brought for assessment. When we arrived, there was a big commotion, with people shouting and rushing around. Our patient was on the middle gurney in C-booth. Pete and Tim strode to the bedside, where they observed a single entry wound on the patient's right chest. He was barely conscious and had a blood pressure of about 60. Tim placed a chest tube in about 90 seconds, and blood poured out the tube and into the collection chamber.

Pete shouted, "Hey, Harch, call the OR and tell them we have a red blanket. We're coming straight up." He looked at Tim and said, "I hope we can get him up there. I'd rather not crack his chest here."

Red blanket was a designation given to an extreme emergency which required immediate surgery. It could be declared only by a general surgery resident or attending staff member. The surgical staff had to drop everything and prepare for the patient's arrival. It was universally understood that this privilege was never to be abused with a less-than-emergent case.

I called upstairs. A nurse answered and I said, "Dr. Miller has a red blanket in C-booth. Gunshot to the right chest with big chest tube output. They're coming up now." We quickly moved the patient to the fifteenth floor.

"Let's scrub," said Pete. "Harch, c'mon."

I was thrilled! Interns didn't get to the OR very often at LA County, especially on a weekend call night when we were meant to be the menial scut puppies. We scrubbed in, and Pete made a big, curved incision on the right chest. He carried it down between the ribs and entered the chest cavity. He handed me the rib spreader. I inserted it and cranked it open. Blood poured out, flowing onto the table, then cascading to the floor. We peered in. There was a big hole in the lower part of the lung, which was still bleeding profusely. Pete clamped the lung and the bleeding slowed. With some further dissection, the bleeding vessels were found, tied off, and a chunk of lung was removed. Pete let Tim do some of the repair work and closure of the chest incision.

"Do you know why we like you to participate in these cases, if circumstances allow?" asked Tim.

"So I can help...and learn?" I responded.

"Yes," said Tim. "See one, do one, teach one. That's the LA County way."

I scrubbed out and wrote orders for the ICU.

Just then, the phone rang. Tim and I were wanted on 9200 for consults and new patients. We headed down. My first patient was a guy who got a claw hammer to the neck. While I was working, two more patients appeared from the elevator in close succession. I looked around. Where was

Russ? I walked over to the sleep room. He was asleep with his head in a book.

"Hey, Russ," I snarled, "get up. We've got workups to do."

"Oh, um…yeah, OK…" he mumbled.

I started on the next patient. After about ten minutes, I hadn't seen Russ. I returned to the sleep room. He had fallen asleep again. "Hey, Russ," I said, raising my voice, "Get your ass outta bed. There's work to do." He slowly rolled out of bed, looking annoyed.

Over the next three hours, we got slammed, receiving eight new patients. Tim and Pete disappeared into the OR with the students. Suddenly I realized it was 6:40 a.m. It appeared that Russ and I would have to present everyone for pass-ons, and a sense of panic started to rise in me.

I went to get all the charts. Where was Russ? I asked the clerk, who said he might be gathering labs. He'd better return by 7, I thought. I poured over the charts so I could at least make an effort to present the patients. My head was spinning.

At 7 a.m., a gaggle of residents, interns, and med students sauntered in, looking clean and fresh. Billy was in the group. I was holding all the charts and looking desperately at the elevator, but no reinforcements appeared to save me. I felt like the Lone Ranger, but without a mask.

I started with a guy stabbed in the groin; they asked if he had a bruit (swishing sound suggesting a connection between artery and vein). I hadn't checked. It was a very small detail, now magnified by the sea of faces looking at me for answers.

We moved to the bed of a guy with a possible bowel obstruction that Russ had worked up. I was superficially aware of the details, but there was no formal note from Russ to guide me. I stumbled through the presentation. They asked to see his abdominal X-Rays, and I couldn't produce them. In better circumstances, the students would have fetched them, but they were all upstairs in surgery.

We went from bed to bed. I did an OK job on a few of my patients but was missing details on multiple others, including one who I didn't know at all because she'd arrived at 6:55. At nearly every bedside, someone from the Saturday Service would ask for a piece of history or lab work that wasn't done or wasn't available. It was excruciating to be responsible for such a disorganized mess. Every now and then I'd shoot a look at Billy, who was suffering with me. He appeared to be on the verge of saying something to defend me or deflect the criticism, but I would give him a return look that was meant to say, "No useful purpose is served in attempting to rescue the injured swimmer. He either will or will not survive the attack, and your intervention cannot protect him once blood has been shed." I was doing my best not to bleed.

Eventually, in response to each inadequate presentation, the chief resident started saying, "Well, OK. Let's just move on to the next patient," in a disgusted tone. Pass-on rounds like this meant that the incoming team needed a huge effort to sort out the disarray, and it's a painful way to start the day.

Near the end of rounds, I noticed Russ at the back of the crowd of doctors, watching. He didn't offer any help. I walked out to the desk feeling depressed about my performance. I also knew that I had a lot more work to do: any patients that arrived before 7 still had to be worked up by our team, and we were expected to finish all the mundane tasks we'd dropped in the chaos of the last few hours.

I found Russ in the hallway. "Where the hell did you go just before 7?" I asked.

"To get labs and stuff...for rounds," he replied.

"Well, it didn't do me any fuckin' good," I said. "You might have chimed in with some of those labs when I was struggling. Or produced an X-Ray or two when I needed them. Or you might have presented the patients you worked up and know better than I do."

"You were doing fine," he said. Then it dawned on me that he'd simply decided to stay out of the water. He turned around and walked away.

Billy was still on the ward getting instructions from his residents on how to begin cleaning up the disaster we had left them. He was shaking his head.

"Man, you got hung out to dry. That was totally unfair," he said. "Where was Russ, that little shit? He should have presented his patients, at least."

"Says he was gathering labs," I answered. "I swear I have to watch the guy all the time. He's lazy, and he loves it when I look bad."

"Yeah, I've heard similar stuff from other interns. But the residents...they know you aren't responsible for pass-ons. They could've given you a break."

"I don't know," I said. "I guess that's the way it goes here. My chances of making the cut seem to shrink every day."

"No way, man. You're good. You're good. Don't worry."

But I worried. And I vowed that on future call nights, I'd start acting like a junior resident: I'd keep better track of every patient on our ward all night long so I wouldn't get caught off guard again and look like a moron.

CHAPTER FIVE

SEE ONE, DO ONE, TEACH ONE

I WAS SWEATING INSIDE MY GOWN AND gloves while we prepared to insert a central venous line in a comatose trauma patient. Nick Givens was the chief resident on the Saturday Service, and he agreed to teach me the technique for placing these specialized IV lines. Neither of us wanted a replay of the night I couldn't get a line in and had to forego giving critical drugs.

Nick identified the exact location just below the patient's collar bone. I picked up the introducing trocar, a thick, hollow needle, four intimidating inches in length. I loaded it onto a syringe, like attaching an ice pick on the end of a stick. It looked like a weapon (and in the wrong hands, is very much one). I placed the tip of this huge needle against the patient's skin and took a deep breath. The skin puckered inward at the point of the needle. I pushed forward through the skin and toward the vein. After an inch, no blood.

"Further?" I asked.

"Yes," Nick said calmly.

I was scared to pass the trocar further, but I did, drawing back on the syringe plunger as the entire syringe and trocar moved forward. Suddenly, venous blood rushed into the syringe. Success! I inserted the thin, plastic line and sutured it in place.

"Nice job," said Nick.

"Thanks. Thanks for guiding me through that."

"You're gonna have to place about five or ten more under supervision before I'll turn you loose to do it on your own. You know that every time one of you guys does something on my service, it's my responsibility, right? And we have a duty to treat these patients safely." He wasn't being dramatic or sappy. It was genuine Nick Givens.

"Yeah. I wanna learn it the right way. I'm ready for another whenever you have time."

This is the way medical students, interns, and residents learned everything. It is, of course, how technical skills are learned in most professions. Apprentices have been tutored under the direction of experienced professionals in black-smithing, carpentry, and other trades for thousands of years.

The difference in medicine is that an error can be very damaging to the patient. You can't just toss a mistake in the trash like a chair leg. The LA County saying that Tim Dantz mentioned during surgery on the gunshot to the chest, "See one, do one, teach one," suggests a nonchalant approach to the process. But in fact, the residents did their best, within the constraints of time, to supervise the learning of these invasive procedures. For Nick to stand there and watch me shove a long, sharp needle into a patient under his direction took courage.

"Hey, Nick, can I ask you something else?"

"Sure."

I pulled the stack of 3x5 cards out of my shirt pocket. "You know how we have all the patient info written on these little cards, and we memorize it to present on rounds?"

"Yeah."

"Well, there're so many patients, and so many details to remember, I'm struggling to keep it all in my brain. How do you jam it all into your head and then pull it out just when it's needed?"

He thought for a second. "After you've been here for a while, things start to fit together better. For instance, the smokers and drinkers…their faces and their skin look different, so you remember it. It makes sense that someone with a psych history would be on lithium or Thorazine. You start to link things together about these folks as you take their histories and examine them. Each person has his or her own story. If you get to know the patients, you'll know their stories and most of their details. We call them patients, but they're people first."

"Yeah…that makes sense. But it still seems hard to me."

"Just keep working at it. Your memory is better than you think. You'll get it, in time. I have no doubt."

Skip and I were admitting patients on 9200. There was the usual spectrum of disasters. Around 10 p.m., the ER sent up a young guy with a stab wound to the right chest and a resulting pneumothorax, an injury to the lung with leakage of air around the lung. The junior resident on the Saturday Service, Paul Takata, told Skip and me to get out all the equipment and meds to place a chest tube to release the air. We could do the procedure and he would supervise. He'd put gloves on if we needed help. We grabbed all the stuff and consented the patient. I don't remember what we told him about the planned procedure, but I'll bet it didn't match what happened.

With Paul standing by and watching, we positioned the patient, prepped the skin widely and placed drapes. We agreed Skip would be the primary surgeon and I'd assist.

"Now identify the correct interspace," instructed Paul. An interspace meant the soft indentation between the ribs. Skip did it. "Inject your lidocaine and make a two centimeter incision." Skip did that too. "Now inject the lidocaine all the way to the pleura." I was handing instruments and gauze, and chipping in with suggestions in a low voice.

"Now dissect through the muscles and into the pleural space," continued Paul.

Just then, the clerk shouted, "Dr. Takata, Dr. Givens needs you in the OR stat!"

"OK," he said. "Just finish getting the tube in. You're nearly done." And he ran out.

We looked at each other for a moment, shrugged, and returned to our work. Skip started dissecting through the muscle. The patient started groaning.

"*Lo siento, lo siento*," I said. "*Un minuto mas*." Skip injected more lidocaine. He began the dissection again, with more complaining from the patient. I had to restrain the patient intermittently to prevent him from thrashing around and upsetting the sterile field. Finally, Skip popped through the chest wall and the patient screamed. We heard the desired whoosh of air escaping. I handed Skip the tube, and he forced it through the hole, with more screaming and thrashing from the patient. We sutured the tube in place and applied a dressing. Skip had done a good job, considering our limited experience and sudden lack of guidance. I'm quite sure the patient, now out from under the drapes, felt that the stab wound we gave him was considerably more painful than the one he got out on the streets.

When we walked out to the desk to write orders and request a chest X-Ray for tube position, Skip leaned over to me and whispered, "Well, congratulations. That was our first chest tube. And I'd classify it as a punitive chest tube." He smiled and picked up the chart for the next admission.

Later that night, when Paul Takata was back on 9200, he approached me and Skip and said, "I just got called to surgery for an appy. Would one of you like to help? Things look pretty shipshape here."

Skip and I looked at each other for a few seconds. Then Skip said, "I scarfed the chest tube. You do the appy, and I'll hold down the fort."

"Are you sure about that, Skip?" I asked.

"Hell, yeah. I'm your scut monkey tonight. Besides, it's your service."

"Thanks, man. I owe you. Call me if it gets busy." Paul and I made for the elevator.

Up on the fifteenth floor, our patient was on the operating table. He was a thin guy in his early twenties. The anesthesiologist put him to sleep, and we scrubbed our hands. When we walked into the room and put our gowns on, I moved to the left side of the table, the assistant's side.

"Come on over here, cowboy," said Paul, gesturing to the right side of the table.

"Really?" I asked.

"Yeah, give it a go. I'll help you with every step."

This is why I was here: to actually do surgery, not just menial intern work!

"OK, find your landmarks," said Paul. "Scalpel." The scrub nurse slapped it into my open hand. I couldn't believe I'd arrived at this moment. Having a scalpel slapped into my hand made me feel like I was in a movie. My adrenaline was pumping. "Make an incision," he added. Up until now, my surgical experience had consisted of repairing incisions that others had made, as in the ENT clinic. This would be my first real case as primary surgeon.

The scalpel is a beautiful, gleaming, steel instrument about six inches long. Its terminal inch is a gently curved blade with a super-sharp, beveled edge. Holding it gave me a profound feeling of trustworthiness and purpose. Someone was letting me wield a scalpel! I placed the knife on the skin, pressed down, and drew the knife toward me. It was an eerie sensation, doing this intentionally to another human being.

"Deeper," said Paul. I had been too timid with the depth of my cut.

I sliced a little deeper, and the skin edges separated. Blood trickled from the edges of the wound. Paul handed me the Bovie, a thin, plastic instrument with a metal tip that delivers electric current to stop bleeding. Prior to the existence of this device, surgeons had to clamp and tie every bleeding vessel, which was very time consuming. I zapped the vessels and stopped the bleeding in seconds.

"Careful, not too close to the skin," Paul said. One had to keep the current away from the skin surface to avoid a skin burn. We spread the muscle layers open and looked through the small incision. Intestines floated around like slippery sausages.

"Now stick your fingers in there and feel around. See if you can find the appendix or anything abnormal."

I stuck my index finger through the opening and felt around. The intestines were soft and warm and wet and squishy. The probing of another human's innards through a hole I'd created was yet another strange experience. Then I detected a firm, rubbery thing about the size of my baby finger. It was clearly different from the surrounding intestines.

"I think I got it," I said, excitedly. I pulled the inflamed appendix up into the wound and we removed it. We sewed up all the layers of the abdominal wall and closed the skin. It had taken about 40 minutes. If Paul had done the case himself, it would have taken 20 minutes, tops.

"Congratulations, Dr. Debakey!" said Paul, referring to one of the greatest names in the history of surgery.

"Thanks, Paul," I said, grinning ear-to-ear.

"As they say, 'See one, do one, teach one,'" he said. "Now get outta here. I'll dictate the case, finish up the orders, and get him to recovery. They probably need you downstairs."

When I got back to 9200, Skip was busy. "How'd it go, man?" he asked.

"Great," I said, smiling. "I did my first appy here…with a lot of help, of course. Thanks for working while I was playing. What can I do here?"

"Well, there's a transvestite…uh…transsexual, whatever, who's trying to increase the size of her butt. She's been getting silicone injections back there, and now it's all infected."

"I'll take that one," I said, as I walked toward the admission room. "And Skip, when we get a break, let's walk around and go over everyone so we know what's here. I don't want to get to 7 o'clock and have the clusterfuck intern pass-on."

"Yeah, me either. That's why I'm gonna make you do it, if we have no residents. I'll just disappear like a candy ass… like that dickhead Russ."

Around 3 a.m., we got busy. At one point, I was seeing a young, Spanish-speaking-only guy with a stab wound to the abdomen. As I mentioned previously, the rules called for an NG tube to be placed in all our trauma patients. I explained this unpleasant procedure to the patient as best I could, and then attempted to insert it. Each time I tried, he would reach up, grab my hands, and pull the tube out of his nose. I couldn't convince the patient to cooperate, and I was wasting valuable time. Finally, I walked out of the room in frustration, threw the tube in the trash, and said, "Goddamn wimp. It's just an NG tube."

One of the nurses overheard me and said, "Oh, so you think it's just an NG tube? Have you ever had one shoved down your nose?"

"No, I haven't," I countered. "But I don't think I'd be that much of a pussy."

"Fine," she replied. "How about I put one in your nose?"

"I got a better idea," I said. "I'll put one in my own nose. But what's the reward? I'm not doing this for nothing."

"A dozen cookies," she said. "I'll make you a dozen cookies."

"Agreed. And if I can't do it, I'll get you a dozen cookies, or something similar."

"You're on. Let's see it."

I marched over to the supply cabinet and pulled out a new tube and some lube. I ripped open the package, smeared some lube on the end of the tube, and shoved the end in my nose. Everyone on the ward had stopped and was watching. The tube scraped roughly along my nasal passages, then hit the back of my throat. It felt horrible—I gagged and my eyes watered. The nurse smiled. I kept shoving the tube down. I gagged some more, feeling like I might puke, but kept pushing. I swallowed, and when it entered my esophagus, the rest was easy. I rammed the tube the rest of the way down and into my stomach. With the upper end of the tube hanging out of my nose, I walked over to the cabinet again and pulled out a large, irrigating syringe. I attached it to the tube and pulled on the syringe. Green stomach contents came up the tube and into the syringe to prove to everyone watching that the tube made it all the way to my stomach.

"Nice job, Harch…OK, you win," she said. "You get cookies on my next shift."

I pulled the tube out of my nose. "Now if you want to try getting a tube into that guy, knock yourself out. I'm done trying."

By 6:45 a.m., we had a moderate mess, but Nick and Paul showed up to save us from pass-on rounds. We spent the rest of the day cleaning up loose ends, and I got out of the hospital by around 5 p.m.

Billy called me as I was leaving. "Hey, I met a brother who works down in the morgue. He's a baller. Says there's a YMCA near here and thinks we can get a game. Can you make it?"

"Well, I've been up all night, but…what the hell. Sure," I said. We played full-court for an hour and a half. The new guy, Percy, was skilled. Billy had started to put together a team so we could go challenge on local courts. When we returned, I was pretty damn exhausted. I trudged back to the dorm and fell on my bed without showering. I was asleep in an instant.

Time passed quickly. The Saturday Service, known to be the worst of the services, lived up to its reputation. The days were long and the nights longer. On my third Saturday of call, we got pounded. We had lots of pass-ons from the Friday Service and a moderately busy day. When the boozing and drugging got rolling around 8 p.m., the deluge began: gunshots and stabs, beatings, motor vehicle wrecks, and routine non-trauma general surgery cases. Consults poured in from the medicine wards. The phone rang from the ER, calling us to see a Jane or John Doe, patients injured so badly that no name could be determined for them on admission. Many were scooped up off the streets and brought in without family, friends, or identification.

We joked a lot about the Doe family. It was the unluckiest tribe of people anywhere. They were assaulted and abused in the most appalling ways. All manner of Janes and Johns were dropped off or staggered in. They were always in the wrong place at the wrong time. Frequently, no one ever showed up to ask about them or take them home if they survived.

In contrast were the Dude family members. They were the assailants, the criminals, the heartless bullies. If you asked nearly any trauma victim at LA County what had happened, the reply went something like this: "Doc, I was walkin' down the street, just mindin' my own business, when this dude came up and…", or "Doc, I was just sittin' in my car, havin' a beer, and some dude walked up and…" So, it was the Dudes causing all the problems on a typical night; usually This Dude or Some Dude. And the Dudes were very busy on Saturdays.

Most of the stories weren't believable. Eventually I stopped asking how something happened, because the information was generally unreliable. And it saved time not to ask. Instead, I'd start my history by asking, "OK, where's your injury?" I didn't even want to know the who and the why unless the patient volunteered or it was a great story. If it happened to be a great story, I wrote it down in a little journal at the end of the day.

We worked all night long and, despite our best efforts, had fragmented pass-on rounds. The ICU was full of our complex, badly injured trauma patients. We had to take one guy back to the OR for bleeding early Sunday afternoon, and another from the ward later in the day for a missed injury. I ended up holding retractors for three hours during the second case. I fell asleep in the OR about five times while holding those retractors. My retracting effort would wane as I fell asleep, the view of the surgical field would deteriorate, and a resident would say, "Hey, Harch, toe in!" This meant to pull backward and downward with the retractor. I would jolt awake and pull with renewed energy and then slowly lapse back into oblivion. We finally finished Sunday night at 10:30, having started the previous day at 5:30 a.m. (a 41-hour shift).

I had made plans to get together with Lori on Tuesday evening (two days hence). Because of my schedule, I was seeing her perhaps once a week, so I was desperate to get together. But Monday and Tuesday were almost as busy as the weekend, without the all-nighter.

Late Tuesday afternoon, I'd gotten nearly all my work done by pushing hard all day long. As I was about to leave the hospital, a nurse called to say that an IV had stopped working. I hoped like hell it wasn't Lester.

Lester was a 46-year-old man who had spent years shooting IV drugs. He looked to be about 60 years old. Lately, his veins had gotten so scarred that he started skin-popping (injecting drugs under the skin). He developed multiple abscesses in his skin and was on our service for treatment. We decided not to place a central line due to the risk of infection, so we were managing his need for IVs by painstakingly maintaining them in his arms and occasionally his legs or feet. It was a constant battle that had been going on for about 10 days. Sure enough, it was Lester's IV that had gone bad, and just at the wrong time.

When I arrived at Lester's room with all the supplies to restart his IV, I was smoldering. I was completely exhausted, and my patience was gone. All I could think about was leaving the hospital and seeing Lori. And I was angry at Lester, who had landed both of us in this situation by abusing IV drugs.

Lester and I had been through this drill so many times that I didn't need to say much. This time, however, he could sense my resentment. I brusquely tied a rubber tourniquet around his arm and started searching for a vein, any vein, even something tiny. Thinking I saw a possibility, I poked the IV into his skin, with no success. I redirected, and advanced it further, not being very gentle. He grimaced, but said nothing. No luck.

I tried another spot. He gritted his teeth but again said nothing as I stabbed and probed with the sharp needle. Still no blood return to indicate I'd found the vein. I removed the tourniquet and walked around the bed to try his other arm. Three more tries with no success. I was sweating. I was in a hurry. I was angry—at him and the whole world. He understood it all. He remained silent. I went back to the other arm. I made another rough attempt without success.

Just then, I looked directly at him. He had started crying, silently. I felt like shit. All the pressure, long hours, lack of sleep, and my selfish need to get some time out of the hospital had transformed me into a heartless, cruel bastard. I was overwhelmed with guilt. I dropped my IV stuff on the bedside table and sat on the bed next to Lester. I put my arm around his shoulder and started crying right along with him. I was too depleted to even apologize.

At that moment, Kathryn, the only woman among the ten interns, walked by. When she glanced into the room, she immediately comprehended our pathetic scene: bedside table covered with used alcohol wipes and IV catheters; a crying patient with multiple, bloody, little holes in each arm; and a ragged, crying intern sitting next to him.

"Hey, let me give it a go," she said.

"You sure you want to get into this?" I blubbered. "He's a very tough start."

"Yeah, I'll get it," she said. "Just get outta here. Go on."

I got up and said, "Sorry, Lester. Thanks a million, Kathryn." And I walked out, ashamed but relieved.

Driving away, my mind raced as I replayed the events of the past few weeks: my first central line, sharing in the placement of a chest tube, the high of my first real surgery, triumph over an indignant nurse (earning me a dozen cookies), new opportunities to play basketball with Billy, a growing hope that residents like Nick Givens could see promise in me, and the frustration and embarrassment of the incident with Lester.

Lori could see the toll the internship was taking by looking at my face. I related the entire awful interaction with Lester and the fact that I left Kathryn there to solve my problem.

"John…how much sleep have you had in the last three days?" she asked.

I thought for a moment.

"About 10 hours," I responded.

"So, a little over three hours per night, on average, for three consecutive days, with the remaining time being all work. And on one of those nights, you got no sleep."

"Yeah, that's right."

"How can they expect you to act like a human being if that's how they treat you?"

"I know, I know. But it's my problem, not theirs. It just surprised me how pissed off I was at Lester for ruining my departure from the hospital to come here. I was just mean."

"Look," she said. "You need to decide if this is what you want for another four and a half years, because if you make the cut, there'll be more of this punishment. Can you live through it and still be the person I know you are, deep down inside?"

"I don't know. As of one hour ago, I'm not sure."

We were both quiet for a moment.

"I'll bet with a good night's sleep, you'll feel a lot better about everything."

"I hope you're right.... Hey, where are we going for dinner?"

I was fortunate to have someone to whom I could vent these doubts and fears. To survive, I needed her understanding, her support, and her physical contact more than ever. Not everyone was so lucky.

CHAPTER SIX

GUN PLAY

THE SUBSPECIALTIES IN MEDICINE ARE populated by different personality types. Doctors themselves acknowledge this. Describing these personality types demands gross generalizations, which is exactly what follows below.

The pediatricians are typically warm, patient, caring people who treat a spectrum of kids from babies to surly teenagers. They work long hours for comparatively low pay, and suffer the torment of overbearing parents who think they know more than doctors.

The family practitioners are a similar group, personality-wise, but they are the utility players of medicine. They treat patients from cradle to grave, and often form close relationships with two or three generations in a family. They are the bedrock for rural communities which often don't have pediatricians or obstetricians. They're the good guys of the medical world.

Radiologists and pathologists have made a conscious decision to avoid frequent contact with other smelly, bothersome human beings. They spend most of their time in dark X-Ray rooms or peering into microscopes or cutting up dead people for autopsies. They don't have to be warm and fuzzy, and some aren't.

Neurologists are a quirky bunch. They can easily come across as detached misanthropes. If you must see a neurologist for a perplexing problem, you may suffer through an uncomfortable or even bizarre office visit. An indecipherable name is proclaimed to describe your ailment, and you are told there is no treatment or cure. You are on your own. Thank you very much—that will be $300.

The internists are the thinkers and chin scratchers. They will tell you so themselves. They must acquire an encyclopedic knowledge of diseases, and they deliver most of the elder care. This is time consuming and often not very satisfying, because much of the work is focused on maintaining patients in their compromised state, rather than curing disease. The specialty generally attracts a more reserved, introspective person who may even seem gloomy. They are plagued by the general perception that they have trouble making decisions quickly or definitively.

There is a story that a general surgeon, an orthopedic surgeon, and an internist go duck hunting. Several birds approach and the general surgeon raises his gun and says, "I think that's a mallard," and fires. A bird falls to the ground. More birds fly near. The orthopedic surgeon raises his gun, fires off five quick shots, and says, "What was that?" Several birds lie dead. Finally, more birds approach and the internist says, "I think those are hooded mergansers...or perhaps Eurasian wigeons...maybe common goldeneyes... no, I'm quite sure they're white-cheeked pintails..." And the ducks are gone.

There is also a deep rift in the medical specialties concerning income, and it is the source of notable acrimony. Some nonsurgical specialists (particularly internists and family doctors) believe they are underpaid given the complexity of the job they're asked to do. They say thinking is not rewarded. They see the surgeons—or "proceduralists"— as being paid far too much for doing mechanical things that could be taught to any monkey. The surgeons, conversely, say that their training required more hours each day and more years in residency. And the teachers, the senior surgeons, were mostly assholes who made residency miserable. The surgeons also believe they work longer hours in private practice. Surgeons view themselves as the fighter pilots of medicine.

It is often possible to pick out the orthopedic surgeons as early as the first year or two of medical school. They are the athletes and extroverts. They're often the biggest and tallest people in the class. Some are academically oriented; others are not. Either way, however, the joke in medicine is that all orthopods (the slang term for orthopedic surgeons) are stupid. Do you know that to be an orthopedic surgeon requires two of three things? An orthopod must be able to read or write or lift 100 pounds. But they are happy people, perhaps because they're well paid; also because they're made that way. Cardiac surgeons are quite similar, but more obsessive-compulsive, and perhaps more likely to study.

The general surgeons are regular stiffs. They're practical; they don't mind getting dirty or treating nasty, stinky problems. If the scrub nurse doesn't have a knife ready for the incision, a general surgeon might say, "Just give me a spoon." Many exhibit a twisted sense of humor and a ribald demeanor; whether they start that way or evolve into it after seeing so much suffering and madness is a matter of some debate. They have a reputation for enjoying being awake all night, but I can assure you this isn't true. The general surgeon will, however, stay up all night if it's necessary.

Urologists fill their own little niche. They've chosen to focus on this narrow field of surgery involving the kidneys, bladder, prostate, vulva, penis, and testicles. This naturally leads to embarrassing situations and humorous stories. Urologists are serious about their medical specialty, but they don't take *themselves* too seriously, and they usually manage to stay balanced. They don't need to convince you that they outwork everyone else in the hospital. And they are some of the most hilarious people I met while at LA County. Later in my career, I met a urologist whose license plate read, "Dick Doc."

One of the first cases I admitted on the urology service was a 69-year-old man who was passing blood in his urine. In a guy his age, hematuria is often a sign of cancer, most likely in the bladder. He was a kindly old guy (yes, 69 was old at LA County).

"How are you today, Mr. Brown?" I asked.

"I'm fine, thank you," he answered.

"What brought you to see us today?"

"Well, I been peein' blood."

"How long has that been going on?"

"I don't know. A while, I guess."

"Does it burn when you pee?"

"No."

"Do you have to strain to pee?"

"No more'n usual."

"Have you ever had kidney stones?"

"No, sir."

"Lost any weight?"

"I don't think so. My pants fits the same."

On and on went the history taking. Despite a good effort, I couldn't turn up anything out of the ordinary.

"Well," I said, "let's get you checked in, and I bet Dr. Simpson will want to take a look in your bladder with a little camera."

"OK, whatever you say, Doc." I wrote orders for him to go to the ward to await a discussion with Todd Simpson, the urology resident.

Later, Todd took Mr. Brown to the OR and performed a cystoscopy: he inserted a thin metal rod (with a camera on the end) into Mr. Brown's penis and looked into his bladder. Instead of finding cancer or stones, he found a lot of stringy, rubbery grey material and an irritated bladder. It took a long time to remove the unknown material. When Todd told me about this, we decided to ask Mr. Brown a few more questions.

"Hi, Mr. Brown," said Todd. "Feelin' OK?"

"Yes, sir."

"I want to talk to you about the little operation we just did," said Todd. "We found a bunch of stringy, sticky, grey stuff in your bladder. That's what's causing the bleeding. Any idea what may have caused it?"

There was a long pause.

"Well…" admitted Mr. Brown, looking a little sheepish (but with a slight smile on his face), "I love Juicy Fruit gum… just love Juicy Fruit gum…and…uh…when I get a…especially good piece…a really good one…I rolls it up real thin in my hands…and slides it up my penis."

There was another long pause.

"Why didn't you tell us about that when you came in?" asked Todd.

Mr. Brown just looked at us and shrugged his shoulders.

"One more thing," added Todd. "How does it get up into the bladder?"

"I squeezes it back up in there."

"Well, that may be enjoyable for you, but you're gonna have to stop doing it. It's irritating your bladder and causing bleeding. And someday it'll clog up the flow of urine."

"I knows that now," said Mr. Brown. "I won't do it no more."

One afternoon, I had gone over to the dorm to change my dirty greens. On my return to the hospital, I crossed the plaza and went down the stairs. Outside the back door of the hospital, a short distance ahead of me, were three very sketchy-looking guys about 30 years old. They were dirty, wore ragged clothes, and had long, greasy hair. They were nervous, like meth addicts. They were nearly blocking the entrance. I had to make a quick decision about whether to turn around and walk a long way to another entrance, or walk between them. There was no one else in sight to depend on if I had a problem.

I decided I'd pretend I had no fear at all. As I reached them, one stepped aside just a little.

"Howdy," I said, passing between them. They said nothing, but let me pass. The limited security around the hospital continued to be a concern for everyone, especially the female staff and patients. My brother was a medical student at Johns Hopkins (in Baltimore, Maryland) a few years back when fellow students had been stabbed on two separate occasions outside their hospital. One of them, stabbed on the front steps of the hospital, had died. Our hospital was situated in a similarly bad part of a major city.

When I reached the urology ward, Jim Munson and Marty Goldman were there. Jim was my fellow intern for this rotation, and Marty was one of his buddies, both headed into urology. Goldman was an enormously sarcastic, funny guy, whom I'd met recently through Jim. Nothing ever seemed to bother him.

"Hey, Harch, what's happenin'?" asked Marty.

"Well, nothin' right now," I said. "But I'm on call for general surgery tonight."

"Oh, fuck your ass," said Marty. "You asked for it, though, you masochistic, shit-sniffing, chitlin surgeon."

"Yeah," said Jim. "All we have to deal with are dicks, pussies, and piss."

"Hey, let me ask you guys something," I said. "I just walked over from the dorm, and there were three really scummy-looking drugees outside the back door. I was a little worried about getting mugged or stabbed. Does that ever bother you, walking around this place?"

"Shit, yeah," said Jim. "I'm always thinkin' about it, watching every scuz bucket around me. Especially in the parking garage. That place is scary."

I looked at Marty, who was shaking his head.

"Doesn't bother me at all," he said.

"Really?" I asked, not believing him. He was a good-sized guy, but not particularly tough-looking. He was pasty white, with prominent facial features dominated by a big nose. He had a pair of glasses on with wide, plastic frames and very thick lenses, which made his eyes look about twice their actual size.

"No," he continued. "I don't spend any time worrying about all those dirtballs."

"Why not? What's the secret to your studly courage?"

"Well…" said Marty, reaching down into the V-neck of his scrub shirt. He slowly pulled out the butt of a handgun. As the barrel followed the gun out of his shirt, it kept coming and coming, until he had removed a .357 magnum with an eight-inch barrel. It was a gigantic weapon, at least 12 inches long. It had to be the largest handgun I'd ever seen.

"Goddamn!" I said. "Do you always carry that thing?"

"Yep, everywhere I go," he said calmly. "Even in the OR."

"Why do you carry such a big-ass gun?"

"Well, when a mother-fuckin' bad guy pops up, you want some knock-down power. And the long barrel means straight shooting." He pointed it at the wall, mouthed the word *pow* as he flexed his thumb, then gave it a little kiss and tucked it back in his shirt.

"But how do you get away with carrying it?" I asked. "Isn't it illegal?"

"Maybe for most people, but my dad was a sheriff in our rural county, and he deputized me a long time ago. I have the right to carry this bad boy anywhere I want."

My work on the urology ward finished about 5 p.m. I made it to dinner and reported to 9200 for general surgery backup call. It was steady until about 9 p.m., then things slowly started to unravel. Over the next three hours, we received the following cases: stab wound to the abdomen, gunshot to the chest, bowel obstruction, wound dehiscence (the abdominal incision didn't heal and came open), woman beaten and raped and burned by two assailants (who also dislocated her hip), and a guy with a cold leg (a very serious emergency because blood supply has been stopped).

My shoulders sagged when the phone rang again. The ER had a guy who took a shotgun blast to the upper chest and face. No one from general surgery had seen him yet, but they knew he had to come here, so they were sending him up. The elevator doors opened, and out rolled Mario Rodriguez, sitting partially upright on a gurney. He had dried blood all over his face and neck, which were covered with little punctures.

"Mr. Rodriguez, how are you doing?" I asked.

"OK," he mumbled, with difficulty.

I took a rudimentary history, but his answers were hard to understand because of the pellets that had pierced his lips, tongue, and mouth. His eyes were swollen shut. I tried to pry his lids open, but could see only bloody, puffy, pink tissue in each little slit of his eyes. His lips and tongue were bulging with blood. There were 20 little holes in his neck and more on his chest. I was starting to become concerned that his upper airway might get obstructed and he might be unable to breathe.

I looked at the X-Rays done in the ER. There were pellets in his brain, and the only way they could have gotten there, in my judgment, was to have passed through his eyes. I asked the clerk to call the eye doctors for an emergency consult.

Now we were hopelessly behind. There were simply too many things to do at once. I got called to the phone to hear about another stab wound coming from the ER. Halfway through this discussion, a sleepy-looking doctor walked slowly off the elevator, rubbing his eyes. "Did someone call for an ophthalmology consult?" he asked.

"I did," I said, interrupting my conversation. "The guy's in bed two right over there. Thanks." I went back to my phone call.

"What did the eye exam show?" the ophthalmology resident asked.

I stopped my conversation again and said, "His eyes were swollen shut, and I couldn't see anything."

"Do you always call consults without examining your patients?" he asked.

That question sent me over the edge. "Hold on a second," I said into the phone, which I slammed down on the desk. I jumped up and stomped over to the resident, getting right up in his face. "Look, you fuckin' asshole. We're up to our necks in alligators here while you're getting your beauty sleep. We got vascular occlusions. We got dislocated hips, burns, and stab wounds. We got potential airway problems. This guy has pellets in his brain that must have gone through his eyes. Unless you want to end up on the floor with me right now, get your sorry ass in there and do a consult." I felt like I might explode.

"You can't talk to me like that," he said, backing up a little.

"The hell I can't," I said. "And my next move, after I kick your ass, is to drag your staff out of bed to do the consult you won't do."

We were standing in the middle of the admitting area face to face. The clerk and my student were watching closely. The ophthalmology resident stared at me. I stared back, as menacingly as I could. He turned slightly to one side and walked into the patient's room. I returned to my phone call.

When I hung up the phone, I calmed down a little and started worrying. This was a consulting resident who was senior to me. I'd really lost it there and threatened him with bodily harm. By morning I'd probably be in the chief's office trying to explain why I hadn't kept my cool. What did this mean for my future here? Why hadn't I modeled equanimity under duress?

After a few minutes, the resident walked out of the room and, seeming embarrassed, said, "Where are the films?" I handed them to him. He held them up to the lights. "I couldn't get much of an exam either. And I am concerned about possible pellet injuries to the globes. I'll speak to my staff and get back to you."

"Thanks," I said. He walked off the ward, and I didn't have time to worry about it any further.

By midmorning, I was back on the urology ward and there was no call from the chief's office. Just give it time, I thought. I went down to my mailbox and found a letter from the Department of Surgery. It was too soon for a letter related to last night, but I was nervous anyway. The letter announced a meeting to discuss the intern cut. The thought of appearing in front of the chiefs of surgery was terrifying. Was there any way to prepare?

Late in the afternoon, Skip passed me in the hallway. He said, "Hey, I heard you ripped the ophthalmology resident a new anal sphincter."

"Let's not talk about it, Skip," I said. "I'm already on thin ice around here, and that could be the last straw. I'd rather you don't repeat it."

"Suit yourself, but everybody already knows," he said. As he rounded the corner, he added, "I love it! I bet you made that little pussy brown his pants."

I got a call from Todd, who was in the ER. "I got a case for you: some real sharpshooting," he said. "This guy was trying to leave Walmart without paying for two cassette tapes. The security guard told him to stop, but he didn't. The guard followed him out of the store and again told him to stop. When he kept walking, the guard reeled off two shots. One passed through his anterior thigh, then through the shaft of his penis. The second shot went straight through his penis just below the glans, without hitting anything else."

"That's a tall price to pay for two cassette tapes," I said.

"Yeah, for sure. He couldn't repeat those shots if he had 100 tries. Anyway, I need you to admit him, clean him up, and apply a fresh dressing. Put him on antibiotics. We'll wait a few days for the swelling to go down, and then we'll try to repair the damage."

The external part of the penis, the part the world sees, is made up of three long, thin tubes. The smallest of those tubes, the urethra, is on the underside of the penis, and it carries urine from the bladder to the outside. Sitting just above this structure are two identical tubes of spongy tissue, the corpora cavernosa, like a double-barreled shotgun. When the male animal becomes sexually stimulated, blood flow increases into these reservoirs, and the venous outflow is closed off. So as more blood flows in and very little is flowing out, the tubes fill with blood and become firm, just like the air reservoirs in an inflatable raft. If the stimulation ends, or an orgasm occurs, the little closed gates of the veins open wide again, and the blood flows out, resulting in the usual soft, limp state of the penis. Any penetrating trauma to the penis risks damaging the integrity of these three main structures. The outcome could be urine leakage or inability to achieve or maintain an erection.

Soon enough, a 22-year-old guy showed up on a gurney with a very long face. His name was Randy.

"Hi, Randy. I'm Dr. Harch," I said. "How you doin'?"

"Not too good. That guy fucked me up."

"Sorry you got shot."

"He didn't have to shoot me over two cassettes. "I woulda given 'em back."

"Well, we're hoping we can fix you up with some surgery."

"I don't know, man. It's pretty bad."

When I finished interviewing Randy, I started his physical exam. As I pulled up his gown, I observed two bullet holes on the front of his left thigh—bullet entry and exit sites—which didn't look too serious. His penis, however, looked bad. It was swollen and purple, much like a medium-sized eggplant. Fortunately, Todd had been able to get a catheter up through the urethra and into the bladder. If this hadn't been possible, it would have been a much more complicated problem.

It was problem enough, however. There were bullet holes on either side of the penis at two different levels. The tissue was ragged, and the holes oozed small amounts of bloody fluid. I was certain that both corpora cavernosa had been badly damaged. He was lucky that his penis hadn't been completely shot off, or that the blood supply hadn't been compromised so much that the tip would die. Looking at the damage, it was hard to believe that someone could fire two shots and hit this relatively protected target while causing almost no damage to any other part of the body.

Randy was staring down as I examined him. "Do you think it'll ever work again?" he asked.

"I don't know," I said. I wished I could tell him yes, but knew the answer would likely end up being no. "They're planning to operate, so maybe they can fix it." He just shook his head. I cleaned him up as carefully as I could and applied new bandages.

For the next few days, I changed his dressings in the morning and evening, and the swelling gradually diminished. The day before his surgery, we were in the middle of a dressing change when he looked down and said, sadly, "Man, that dude really ruined my pride and joy."

Todd and one of the senior faculty urologists did take Randy to surgery and repaired what they could. Randy healed up and was eventually discharged. I have often wondered two things: did Randy's penis ever work properly, and did the security guard at Walmart get commended or fired?

October 12 was significant for two reasons: it was the last day of my urology rotation and it was the day of my interview to discuss the intern cut. As my time slot approached, I had trouble focusing on my work. I'd arranged with Todd to get about 45 minutes off so I could guarantee a timely showing. I waited outside the chief's office, nervously pacing.

The door opened and Ed Park walked out. I hadn't gotten to know him much over the last four months. He'd been on different rotations, and we hadn't had call nights together.

"Hi, John," he said. "Don't go in yet. They need a few minutes to talk about me."

"How'd it go?" I asked.

"I have no idea," he said, with his stilted Korean accent. "That is the problem here. You work your butt off every day, and no one says anything. No way to know what your chances are."

"I agree. It sucks."

"See you later," he said solemnly, and walked away.

I paced the hallway for another five minutes. The office door opened, and Betty, Dr. O'Donnelly's secretary, said, "Come on in, Dr. Harch." She showed me to an inner meeting room. There sat Dr. O'Donnelly, Dr. Rollins, and

Dr. Everett. They were the three chiefs of the program. I shook hands with each of them.

"Please sit down, Dr. Harch," said Dr. O'Donnelly. "How are you today?" he asked.

"Fine, sir," I replied, my heart racing. I hoped they couldn't sense how nervous I was, but it must have been obvious.

"How have the last four months gone for you?" he asked.

"Pretty well, I think…it's difficult…there's so much to know," I stated.

"Yes, there is," he said. "You've been working hard. We've seen that."

"Thank you, sir," I said.

"And you're good with patients, according to the residents," said Dr. Everett. He was a big bear of a man, soft-spoken and kind when I saw him interact with the interns and residents. I got the feeling he might be pulling for me, even though I had no justification for it.

"Thank you," I responded.

Dr. Rollins was just sitting there, staring at me with his arms crossed, as usual. "You need to read more," he said.

"Yes, sir, I realize that…I…I'm trying to find the time…" I stammered.

"You have to make the time," he persisted.

"Yes, sir."

I was thinking that now would be the time to attack me for stopping the Pitressin drip on that call night two months ago or, more likely, to reprimand me for the loss of control with the ophthalmology resident. Rollins would be just the guy to do it. To my surprise, neither happened.

"All ten interns are capable enough to make this cut," said Dr. Rollins. "Do you think you have the physical endurance and the willpower to continue here for another four and a half years? Because as hard as internship is, residency, in some ways, is harder."

"Yes, sir, I know I can do it," I said. But I was thinking about my discussion with Lori, and whether I wanted to stay.

"That's what everyone says," said Rollins. "You'll need to back it up."

"Yes, sir," I repeated. I wanted to say, "You little shit. Is this how you get a hard-on, by intimidating anyone you think is beneath you?"

"Well, whatever happens, keep working hard," said Dr. O'Donnelly. "And remember that you represent the Department of Surgery in every interaction that takes place here." Was he trying to communicate more with this comment? I looked directly into his eyes but couldn't tell.

"Yes, sir, I understand."

"Any other questions for Dr. Harch?" asked Dr. O'Donnelly, looking at the other two.

With a sympathetic look on his face, Dr. Everett shook his head. Dr. Rollins just sat there looking through me.

"OK," said Dr. O'Donnelly. "That will be all. Thank you for your time. We'll be notifying you of our decision in the next few days. You can return to your work."

"Thank you," I said, nodding to them.

As I stepped into the hallway, I ran into Mike Miller, the other graduate from USC (like Skip). He was next in line for an interview. He appeared totally relaxed and confident. Any positive feelings I might have had were immediately erased as I remembered that multiple spots were probably taken.

"Hey, John," he said, with a big smile. "How was it?"

"I guess I'll find out in a few days," I said. "Good luck." But I didn't really mean it.

Back on the urology ward, I was ruminating. What did Rollins mean about reading more? Was everyone else ahead of me on that? Was Russ setting the bar high by dumping his scut work on others so he could stick his nose in a book? And the question about endurance and willpower; why ask me that if they've already decided not to keep me? Was Rollins just torturing me?

Todd walked onto the ward. "Hey, Harch, I need you to admit a 71-year-old guy with newly diagnosed prostate cancer. He's scheduled for surgery in two days. His son is a physician here in the hospital and he'll be dropping by soon."

"Sounds good," I said. I went through the curtains in the exam area and introduced myself to the new patient. He was from somewhere like Croatia and didn't speak much English. After I'd asked a series of simple questions about his medical history, there was a tap on the wall and a young doctor in a white coat pulled the curtain back. We both froze. The patient's son was the ophthalmology resident I'd threatened two weeks ago. I couldn't believe it, and neither could he. He was horrified that the lunatic intern was going to be involved in his father's care. And I could tell from his face he was worried this could be my chance to get even with him.

"Excuse me for a minute," I said to the patient. I tapped the resident on the arm and motioned for him to follow me. When we were out of his father's earshot, I said, "Look, I know I'm the last guy you wanted to see here as one of your dad's doctors…but I just want to assure you that I'll take really good care of him. Let's just forget what happened between us and try to be professional as we go forward." I stuck out my hand.

He looked instantly relieved and grabbed my hand, shaking it. "Yeah. Good idea. I just want everything to go right for my dad. My mom died three years ago, so he and my sister are all I've got left. I'm really close to him."

"No problem," I said. "Let's get back in there. He's probably wondering what the hell we're talking about."

Looking back at this bizarre coincidence, I know this guy was totally shocked. But was it possible that, on reflection, he might have been reassured to know that I was the kind of doctor who would push the system to get what his father needed, even when consulting doctors are reluctant to do their jobs?

Late that afternoon, I got called to 9200 early by Craig Kelly, the resident on call. He was the one who checked out Tammy (the lady with the vascular problems and dead, infected stumps) to me in the ICU two months ago. He had also made the rude comment about UCLA graduates not being kept. He always acted lazy and impatient.

"Hey, I know it's early to get you up here," he said, "but I need to sort something out while the urology resident is still here in house. We just admitted a guy to 9200 with a bunch of little stab wounds to the back. His friend, or partner, or whatever you want to call him, was admitted to the jail ward with bites to the dick."

"Alright…" I said.

"Anyway," said Craig, "there's a dispute over what happened between these two fruits, and the cops are involved. I don't have time for stupid shit like this. I know you're rotating through urology right now, so you're the perfect person to take care of both these guys and keep the cops out of my hair."

"No problem," I said. "Give me the names. By the way, what ever happened to Tammy, the gal with the infected amp stumps?"

"Oh, she died. The names of your guys are in the book. I'll be in the residents' library." He walked off.

I started with Chaz Olsen, 42 years old. He was the guy on our ward with stabs to his back.

"How are you, Mr. Olsen?" I asked.

"Oh, honey, don't call me Mr. Olsen. Makes me feel old. My name is Chaz."

"Okay, Chaz. What happened today?" I was breaking my rule about not wanting the details, for obvious reasons.

"Well, Harold, my roommate, and I got into an argument today. At one point, he got so mad he knocked me down and started stabbing me in the back with a little knife. I was afraid he might kill me, so I had to think of something. I reached up...pulled down his pants...and bit his penis."

"What happened next?"

"Well, we realized we were both hurt, so we called the police."

"And they brought you here and arrested Harold."

"Yes, that's right."

"What kind of knife was it?" I asked. "How long?"

"It's a little pen knife, about three inches long."

"Do you have any injuries other than the stabs to your back? Did you get hurt when he hit you and you fell down?"

"No, I think I'm alright otherwise."

When I examined him, all I could find were about 10 small stab wounds scattered across his upper back. No bleeding, no hematomas. Breath sounds were clear on both sides. I checked his chest X-Ray: no pneumothorax. Chaz was going to survive without any intervention.

I called Todd and asked if he'd meet me on the jail ward. I suggested he bring Jim along.

I got off the elevator on the thirteenth floor, the jail ward. I waited a few minutes for Todd and Jim to arrive. We pressed the buzzer, and the deputy looked at us through a small, wire-reinforced viewing window. He pressed a button, and a three-inch-thick steel door slowly slid open. We walked in and the door closed behind us with a loud *ka-chung*. The deputy did a quick, obligatory pat-down of all three of us to make sure we didn't have weapons. I wondered what Marty would do with the cannon in his shirt if he came up here for a consult.

"We're here to do a consult on the guy who got bitten on the penis," I explained.

"Oh, yeah," said the deputy. "We got that faggot over here in the holding area." He handed us a chart. The name on it was Harold Wunder. He was sitting on a gurney with his hands cuffed in front of him.

"Hello, Mr. Wunder," said Todd. We introduced ourselves.

"Hi, doctors. I'm really glad to see you," said Harold. "I hope you can help clear this up. They're treating me like an animal."

"Well, we'll do our best," promised Todd. "Tell us what happened."

He lowered his voice and said, "Chaz and I had a disagreement earlier today. But we ironed out our problem and made up. He was giving me a blowjob... and I guess he was still mad... suddenly he started biting me. I reached over and grabbed a little knife and stabbed him in the back until he stopped biting. That's it. Purely self-defense. I'd like to just forget the whole thing."

All three of us looked at him with straight faces—medical faces.

"Have you been able to urinate since the injury?" asked Todd.

"Yes...a little while ago."

"Any problem?" asked Todd.

"No, it was fine."

When we examined him, we did find several tiny breaks in the skin and some superficial bruising on his penis, but no obvious injuries to the major structures. We reassured him there was likely no significant injury and said we'd talk to the deputies.

We moved into an adjacent room for Todd to put a note in the chart. A different officer walked in and said, in a very official, no-nonsense tone, "Doctors, I'm Detective Grady, and I've been assigned to investigate this case. We've taken statements from both individuals involved and gathered evidence from the scene. We've come to the point that we need one crucial piece of information, and we're hoping you can provide it."

"Okay," Todd responded. "What can we do for you?"

"We realize this may be circumstantial evidence," confided Grady, "but we need to know with certainty if our suspect had an erect penis when the biting took place."

The detective was looking at the three of us. I looked straight back at him because I knew I'd crack up if I so much as glanced at Todd or Jim. Neither Todd nor Jim dared look at me.

"Well, I doubt we'll be able to say anything definitive about the state of Mr. Wunder's penis at the moment of the crime," said Todd.

Grady looked crestfallen. "Are there any tests you can do to sort this out?"

"Not that I can think of," said Todd. "You're going to have to decide which story you believe. But you also have to consider that neither of them has told you the real story."

When this possibility dawned on Detective Grady, he was even more disappointed. "Well, thanks guys." He shuffled off, presumably to solve other similarly heinous crimes.

When the elevator doors closed for the return trip to the fourth floor, we laughed all the way down.

CHAPTER SEVEN

ROOM OF DOOM

T HE NEUROSURGERY ROTATION WAS A
month generally despised by interns because of dis-
heartening cases and infrequent opportunities to get
to the operating room. The workload would also likely be
horrendous, and all this in a nightmarish setting.

There were two neurosurgery services. One received two
interns, while the other got one intern. Paradoxically, the
"one-intern service" almost always had more patients to care
for, sometimes more than twice as many. Nonetheless, no
effort was ever made to relieve the poor bastard who was
alone and getting beaten down by a heavy patient load.

I soon discovered I was the lonely intern. I had 17
patients, compared with the eight patients that would be

shared by my two colleagues, who were already grinning and preparing for an early exit from the hospital that day. The final bad news: no medical students to help me.

A clerk handed me a list of the patients. She told me that the neurosurgery chief resident, Walter von Eichler, was in the OR and would have to meet with me later. By the way, she added, there was a brand new post-op patient whose operation hadn't gone well. He was in an adjacent room, and Dr. von Eichler wanted me to assume his care immediately.

I'd heard about von Eichler. The interns called him Walter von Walter. He was a rather odd guy, as were many of the neurosurgeons. He claimed he was descended from a long line of Prussian noblemen, some of whom were physicians, and it was his destiny to be a neurosurgeon. It was rumored that on each call night his mother would show up with a brown bag meal accompanied by a fresh pair of underwear.

A nurse stepped out of a side room. "Are you the new intern?" she asked.

"Yes, I'm Dr. Harch."

"This patient just came out of the OR. He has a bad head injury. They drained some blood out, but he had a lot of brain swelling, and he's not doing very well."

"Why is he here on the ward, instead of in the ICU?"

"The ICU is full, and...I guess...they don't think he's gonna make it, anyway."

I couldn't believe it. I'm on the service for three minutes and they dump a dying patient on me, with no ICU support. And I don't know a damn thing about neurosurgery. And

132

not a hell of a lot about resuscitating critical post-op patients either.

I hurried into the room to assess the patient. I said to the nurse, "Could you try to reach Dr. von Eichler and ask him what he wants me to do? I need to know if I'm supposed to do a full-court press on this guy, or just let him die. And has anyone spoken to the family?"

"No one knows if he has any family. He came in as a John Doe."

I looked at the patient. He was unresponsive, had a big bandage on his head, and was intubated and connected to a little portable ventilator. A ventricular drain, or bolt, protruded from his bandages, an attempt to let out extra brain fluid and relieve the pressure. He couldn't have been more than 25 years old. I had no idea how to proceed with this poor guy. If I did too little, or too much, or made a wrong decision, would he die? Would I be criticized, blamed?

I took his blood pressure. It was 60 systolic—dangerously low. I told the nurse to turn up his IV fluids. I checked his breath sounds and heart tones; all seemed satisfactory, but the patient was dying of his head injury. After a few minutes, the nurse returned to say that Dr. von Eichler was in the OR, couldn't be disturbed, and didn't have much to say about the dying patient.

Couldn't be disturbed? Didn't have much to say about the dying patient? He's supposed to be in charge of this service! What the hell kind of guidance is that? It was a clear signal to me that I would be making a lot of decisions myself on this service, so I might as well start right now. To hell with the worries about being correct or incorrect. Someone had to act.

"You sure there's no ICU bed?" I asked.

"Yes, I'm sure."

"OK, then. Continue the fluids, and get a blood gas and a chem 7." The blood pressure was now slightly higher, after receiving the first bolus of IV fluids.

Since I had no resident or med students to round with, I gathered up some charts and started rounds with the supervising nurse. We went from bed to bed, reviewing a series of pitiful cases. One was a 17-year-old who got drunk and fell off a balcony, landing on his head, sustaining a severe brain injury. He was lying in bed staring toward the ceiling blankly, with a feeding tube hanging out of his nose. Another was a 35-year-old who'd broken his neck in a motorcycle accident and was quadriplegic. He'd already had an operation to stabilize his neck fracture, but his paralysis was unimproved. He was strapped upright in a chair being fed by a nurse assistant. He was awake and alert, but appeared profoundly depressed. There were also several older stroke victims sitting in chairs at their bedsides, gazing off into space.

There was one room dedicated to patients whose injuries were too severe to allow them to come off their ventilators, but they couldn't stay in the ICU any longer due to the critical need for the beds. These people had been given tracheostomies (an opening in the lower neck directly into the trachea) and placed on compact, portable ventilators, like the one supporting the critically injured guy I'd just inherited.

The nurses were supposed to suction the excess sputum from the tracheostomies about every 30-60 minutes, depending on how much bubbling and gurgling could be heard with each ventilator breath. Right now, there was a lot of bubbling and gurgling. The scene was truly discouraging. I discovered that other interns had nicknamed this room the Darwinian Challenge or Room of Doom or Intensive Neglect. Others called it the Isolation Room because it isolated the patients from health care.

Each neurosurgery patient had individual needs. The ones with high temperatures required fever workups: a chest X-Ray to look for pneumonia, urinalysis to identify possibly infected urine, blood cultures, sputum cultures, daily blood tests, removal and replacement of intravenous lines that could be infected, and inspection for bedsores. The list of work on my clipboard grew as we reviewed all 18 patients. Intermittently, I would hustle back to check the post-op patient, who now had a worsening (falling) blood pressure, along with a slowing heart rate. These, I knew, were signs of impending death. Since the brain is contained in a rigid, bony vault (the cranium), with a hole at the bottom where the spinal cord exits, the rising pressure eventually begins to squeeze the brain out this small emergency exit, causing death in a short period of time.

Over the next few minutes, that is exactly what we witnessed. The blood pressure continued its decline, and then the patient's heart rate fell to 50, then 40, then 30. Finally, the patient's EKG monitor went flatline. We did not start

CPR, since there is no point in resuscitating the heart and lungs when the patient is dying of brain injury. We turned the ventilator off. I'd been on the neurosurgery service for about 90 minutes and already presided over one death. It seemed like a bad omen. And I'm ashamed to say I was slightly pleased that my list was back down to 17 patients.

I walked over to the neurosurgery ICU. All five beds were occupied, and all five patients were intubated, on ventilators. Three of the five belonged to my service; two of my three were critical, with their survival in question. In bed one was a 21-year-old guy, recently married, who had a sudden, massive hemorrhage in his brain from a ruptured aneurysm. Von Eichler had been able to drain the blood in the OR, but the patient remained comatose, on a ventilator, with low expectations for survival. I stared at him uneasily...a previously healthy 21-year-old...living his life...just married... now suddenly not expected to survive....

In bed three was a 23-year-old mentally retarded male whose mother sent him to the local market for a loaf of bread. He didn't return home, and police eventually found him in a nearby field unconscious, with a large rock lying next to his smashed head. Paramedics reported that the rock had brain matter on it. Inexplicably, he also had several fingertips missing. He was taken to the OR, but not much could be done for him, and he was placed on a ventilator in the ICU, where he had remained for the last few days. I imagined his mother, sitting at home, struggling with guilt and sorrow.

Bed four contained a 34-year-old male who recently broke up with his boyfriend. He became depressed and then psychotic. Convinced he was the anti-Christ, he drove his car over a cliff in a suicide attempt, breaking his neck and causing total paralysis of his arms and legs.

With a gargantuan list of scut work to do, I found that the day raced by. The other interns would pass me in the hallway with ashamed looks on their faces, but didn't offer any help. It was a dog-eat-dog attitude at the county hospital, and unless you had something definite to gain (or someone was perilously close to physical or emotional breakdown), each intern was expected to carry his/her own load. Furthermore, to offer help would establish a precedent; would you then offer help each day? And how long would you stay in the hospital each day to get the other person caught up? Would you help even on days when you had been on call the entire night previously? It was much simpler for all of us to just mind our own business. I understood this, so when the other interns split the work on their eight patients and disappeared from the hospital around 2 p.m., I knew I just had to put my head down and press on. I finished at about 10 p.m. and headed for the intern's dorm to get some sleep.

I replayed this tape each day. On the third day, I was able to finish by 8 p.m. The general surgery interns hadn't yet been called in to get the news about the cut, so we were getting increasingly edgy. I beeped Billy to see if he needed a break from the hospital for an hour or two. He wanted to get away too.

We drove over to Hollywood and got a table at a little jazz club. I ordered a beer. Billy didn't drink alcohol, so he got a soda. We sat quietly for a minute.

"What do you think's gonna happen?" I asked.

"I don't know, but I think they'd be crazy not to take us," he said.

"I've said it before, and I still believe it," I said. "I'm from the enemy school across town, and you're from across the country. Neither of us has an in here, while others have history or connections."

"I'll lose all respect for the chiefs if they keep Russ and let either of us go," he said. "He's lazy, and he shits on his fellow interns."

"Yeah, we all know that," I said, "but I'm not sure the senior staff knows it."

"I bet the residents have noticed," he said.

"It's just so hard to know what the chiefs are thinking," I said.

"Yeah, how about this," he said. "On my very first night of call, I was POC for the ICU. Around 10 p.m., I was sitting in the call room across the hall from the ICU. That super-hot nurse, Cindy, knocks on the door, opens it, and sits down on the bed next to me. She asks me some questions about a sick patient and kind of hangs around. I'm real professional, answer all the questions, and she leaves. Then she comes back two more times in the next two hours, acting all friendly."

"Whoa," I said, "she's after you."

"Well, I'm not so sure," Billy countered. "I got the feeling it was some kind of test. Can you imagine if, on my second day of internship and my first call night in the hospital, I got caught messing around with an ICU nurse in the call room? Or let's say I incorrectly assume something, make a move, and she reports me for assault?"

"Yeah…I get what you mean," I said. "What did you do?"

"I just pretended it was all business. Answered the questions and said, 'Anything else?' And she said no and went back to the ICU."

"Amazing. Has she done anything similar since then?"

"No, but she's still kinda friendly."

"Hey, what do you think about Rollins?" I asked. "I think he hates me."

"He treats me the same way," he said. "I think he hates everyone. He just stares and criticizes."

"Well, all I can say is I really dread searching for another spot somewhere if I get cut," I said.

The following afternoon, I got a beep. It was Betty, Dr. O'Donnelly's secretary. I called the office immediately.

"Hello, Department of Surgery," she said.

"This is Dr. Harch. You beeped me?"

"Yes. Dr. O'Donnelly would like to see you in his office. Are you available?"

"Yes, I'll come right up. Thank you." Well, this was it. By the time I got upstairs my heart rate was up 30 beats, and I was sweating. Everything I'd worked for and much of my future was hanging in the balance. I hoped Dr. Rollins wouldn't be involved in the meeting.

When Betty ushered me into Dr. O'Donnelly's inner office, he was sitting behind his desk, alone. I tried to read his face. It didn't look grim…maybe good news. He got up, walked around the desk, and said, "Dr. Harch, we've watched you very closely these past four months." He paused. My pulse pounded in my head. "You've performed well in nearly every metric we look at. Would you be willing to stay around for another four and a half years?" He extended his hand.

Four months of pent up anxiety rushed out of me. My thoughts were racing as I grabbed his hand and shook it. "What about Billy?" I wanted to ask. "What about Skip?"

"Yes, sir," I said. "I'd love to stay. Thank you." Love might have been an exaggeration.

"We think you'll make a fine resident and a fine surgeon, if you keep working hard."

"Thank you, sir," I said, backing out of his office. "Thank you."

I smiled at Betty on my way out, and she gave me a big, slow nod and a smile back. In the hallway, I wanted to jump or scream or something. But it occurred to me that Dr. O'Donnelly had five other uplifting meetings like this today, and four demoralizing ones. And there were four very smart, dedicated doctors who were about to be crushed. They could be anywhere around here. I better keep my mouth shut.

I hurried to the nearest phone where I could have a little privacy. I dialed Lori's work number.

"*Motorcyclist Magazine*, can I help you?" asked the receptionist.

"Lori Kimball, please," I said.

I could hardly stand the wait.

"This is Lori."

"Lori, I made it!" I blurted out, in a low tone.

"What? Who is this?"

"It's me, John. I made the cut."

"Oh, my God! Congratulations, honey! You must be so relieved. That's fantastic."

"Yeah, I can't believe it…"

"Well I can. They'd be stupid to let you go." Her support was unfailing, despite months of my anxiety and skepticism. Her comment made me think, "Yeah, I guess I do deserve this."

"What about Billy and Skip?" she asked. "Did they make it?"

"I don't know. I just came from the chief's office. I haven't had time to contact anyone. I'll let you know later. I'll try to get out of here at a decent time so we can celebrate tonight. Bye."

I wanted to beep Billy and Skip. Had they been notified yet? What if they hadn't been accepted? Were they hesitant to call me because they were worried I'd been cut? I took the stairs down to the neurosurgery ward, trying to decide whether to call them. I resumed working while I considered what to do. After about 45 minutes, I couldn't stand it any longer; I couldn't think about anything else. I beeped Billy. He called me in about 30 seconds.

"My brother," he whispered. "Have you heard?"

"Yes, my man. I'm in," I said quietly. "How about you?"

"I'm in too."

This was another huge boost to my morale, because it meant we could sustain each other through the difficult times ahead.

"Amazing news, buddy," I said, incredibly relieved. "Congratulations. What about the others? Have you heard?"

"I heard Russ got cut, but I'm not sure."

"Wow! I'm shocked," I said. I had to let this sink in for a moment. "Maybe there is justice in this world. How about Skip?"

"Don't know."

"Okay. Talk to you later."

I beeped Skip. No answer. A few minutes later, he called. "What's shakin', Yogi?" he said. "Do you have any news?"

"As hard as this is to believe, they kept me," I said. "How about you?"

"I have to assume some kind of mix-up occurred. I'll be underperforming here for a full five years!"

"Fantastic, Skipper! What about the rest?"

"Miller's in," he said. "Kathryn's out."

"Damn, that's too bad. She's the nicest person around here and a really good doctor. I'm sorry to hear that. What about the others?"

"Billy's in," he said.

"Yeah, I know. I'm totally stoked about that. I wouldn't want to stay here without you and Billy. What about the others?"

"Pearson and Park are in; Liu is gone," he said. Chen Liu had been a solid performer to this point, but I wondered if his meek personality had eliminated him.

"And get this," Skip continued. "Russ is out. Good fuckin' riddance."

"I agree. Is that everybody?"

"Uh...Riley. It looks like he's one of the four to be cut, but in fact, he owes the military two more years, so he'll disappear at the end of this year and come back when he's done."

"Oh, that's good news; I like Riley. That means Dr. O'Donnelly actually had to cut only three of us. Alright, see you later." I hung up the phone. All the planning, all the hard work, and three people released. What would I say when I ran into them? Nothing might be the best choice.

I labored on in neurosurgery. Walter von Walter would show up occasionally for rounds, make odd comments, and disappear into the OR, but only after dumping a ton of new work on me. In defiance of randomness, the proportion of patients on each service never evened out. By the end of the eighth day of my four-week stint, it was apparent to everyone that I was being worn to a complete frazzle. It would have made sense to simply shift one of the other interns to my service, but that was too logical, so it was never considered. Meanwhile, I was spending every third night on call for general surgery. I had yet to get a moment of sleep on any of those call nights.

One morning, as I was making rounds, one of the residents announced that since I was getting so hammered, a decision had been made to recruit some help. I was ecstatic. One of the other interns? An intern from another service? No, they would be assigning me some medical students. In fact, five medical students!

Wow! Two good medical students were almost equal to one decent intern (it strikes me that this thinking is a little like weighing the relative value of chess pieces). Five med students…they could draw blood, run to the lab, order and fetch X-Rays, write notes, start IVs. I was nearly delirious about the possibilities.

At about 8 a.m., the cavalry strolled in: three male, two female, all enthusiastic looking. I introduced myself, and gave them a little briefing on the service and the patients. From the looks on their faces, I think they were a little stunned by how haggard I appeared.

I was excited at the prospect of doling out the list of scut work I'd already accrued that morning, with the expectation that six of us could knock down 12 or 14 hours of drudgery in, say, four-to-eight hours.

"Steve," I said, "I want you to go draw a CBC and a chem 7 on Mr. Jones."

He peered back at me and said, "What's a CBC?" My heart fell. The other students gave me the same deer-in-the-headlights expression.

"Do any of you know how to draw blood?" I asked hopefully.

"No," they answered in unison.

"Is this your first rotation?"

"Yes," they answered with big smiles.

I covered my face with both hands and considered crying. This also meant they didn't know how to do the paperwork or retrieve lab results or order X-Rays or write notes or anything. I wanted to scream, because the magnanimous act of giving me five new students had just doubled my workload. They all had to be trained.

I looked across the room between my fingers, assessing how best to proceed with these fresh-faced newbies. When I finally dropped my hands, the students stared at me like golden retrievers. I had to hope that if I put in the time, this group could pay dividends somewhere down the line.

"Look," I explained, "there's a ton of shit to do around here, and everything requires a process that you'll have to learn. I can't teach you everything immediately, so let's start this way. I'm going to go around like I usually do, knocking down my work. I want you to follow along and watch carefully. After a few hours, you should pick up a lot of the mundane stuff, like filling out lab slips. The blood drawing can come later."

I took a big breath and moved forward like I'd been shot out of a gun. We entered the ICU. At the bedside of the comatose 21-year-old, I pulled a tourniquet out of my pocket and quickly tied it around his arm. I pulled blood tubes from the other pocket, swabbed the arm with alcohol, and plunged a needle into a vein. I filled the tubes and handed them to one student. I had another student apply pressure to the vein, while I and the other four went to the nurses' desk. We placed the patient's ID card in the stamper, stamped enough sticky labels for the blood tubes, stamped the appropriate lab request forms, filled in the necessary blanks, slapped the labels on each tube, and signed and dated the forms. I dropped everything in a plastic lab bag, handed it to one student, and said, "Hold this."

We raced around all day in this fashion, and by about 4 p.m. they had learned the basics of scut work and were already jumping in to label things, deliver things, and fetch things. Fetching things was the most common and time-consuming duty required of interns at LA County, so my world was looking a little brighter.

It was also apparent that they were now on overload. For new students, the wretched stories and the hopeless appearance of these patients was a heavy burden to carry on the first day. I handed them one last set of things to deliver downstairs and told them to go home. Tomorrow we would learn to draw blood and start IVs, if time allowed.

When I looked at my list, there wasn't too much left to do. We had gone at a ferocious pace, and after about two to three hours, they had begun to save me some time. Helping them learn to do procedures on live people would still be a slow process, but now it seemed possible.

A few days later, after working most of the day on the neurosurgery service, I spent a horrendous night on call with the Saturday Service. We didn't get a minute of sleep, and we ran our asses off with every kind of trauma and general surgery emergency imaginable. The entire team got whipped. We left an embarrassing mess for the Sunday Service in the morning. By about 7:45 a.m., I made my way down to the cafeteria to get some breakfast, then staggered up to the neurosurgery floor to start rounds. I'd given the students the day off, since it was Sunday (a benevolent decision that I now regretted). I was not a pretty sight when I entered the ward. I was unshaven and my hair was a greasy mop. My greens were splattered with blood and some vomit, too. I'm sure I didn't smell very good. I was about half-awake and moving slowly. I desperately wanted to get my work done and just go home (home, pathetically, being the intern's dorm).

The moment I arrived, a nurse rushed up to me and announced that Mrs. Thomas wasn't taking her feedings well. Mrs. Thomas was a 75-year-old lady who had suffered a stroke about 10 days ago, leaving her unable to move her right arm or leg. Since her admission, this poor lady had done little but sleep or slump silently in a chair.

Given my state of exhaustion at the time and the events of the preceding night, the nurse's animated declaration seemed tantamount to saying that a car had gone over a cliff and she was concerned that the paint might be scratched. I really didn't give a shit. But I dragged myself into the room and observed Mrs. Thomas sitting in a specially designed chair to help the semiconscious sit upright. Her face showed no emotion. Her eyes were half open. There was a young nurse's aide sitting beside her, spooning something that looked like gruel into her mouth. After each spoonful, the gruel would dribble out and run partway down Mrs. Thomas's chin, where it was patiently scooped up by the aide and reinserted into Mrs. Thomas's mouth, just as you'd do with a baby. Every now and then, the aide would get just a little more from the bowl and try to force it in.

I stood at the foot of the bed, watching with my arms folded. I was immensely pissed off at how tired I was, and frustrated knowing I had another 15 days of this torture ahead. I was even more annoyed because it was my responsibility to magically make this bleak situation better. The nurse looked at me with anticipation, the aide still spooning.

I reached down and lifted the vital sign sheet up to where I could read it. Yep, all the vital signs looked good through the night, right up to about an hour ago. I set the vital sign sheet down and reached over to Mrs. Thomas, slowly placing the pad of my left index finger on her forearm, then removing it. That was all the examination I needed to do. I recrossed my arms and cleared my throat, blinking slowly.

"Stop," I said. "Stop feeding the patient."

The aide looked at me vacuously, mid-chin scrape, and stopped.

In a monotone, I said very slowly, "The reason Mrs. Thomas isn't taking her feedings well this morning…is because…she is dead."

The pause that followed was disturbing, but I confess I relished it in my miserable state. The aide now looked more closely at her patient. Suddenly, she dropped the spoon and the bowl, let out a gasp, and ran from the room, followed closely by the nurse. I didn't have the energy to follow them, nor the frame of mind to apologize or comfort them. I performed a brief exam on the lady, who was cool to the touch, and already beginning to get a bit stiff from rigor mortis, and went to the chart to pronounce her dead. I had six hours of rounds to finish.

As a matter of self-defense, I offer a brief discussion of black humor and sleep deprivation. The two subjects are distinct, but the event described above combines them so perfectly that I must consider them together.

Black humor occurs in extreme circumstances or with unusual aggregations of humans that persist for prolonged periods (war, confinement, geographic isolation, natural disaster). It is defined as a form of humor that regards human suffering as ludicrous rather than pitiable. It utilizes the morbid and grotesque to convey the absurdity of life. Often, it makes light of subject matter typically considered taboo.

Seeking and finding amusement in the misfortune of others seems cold and heartless, but it provides a cathartic release for stressful life situations. This was portrayed very nicely in the television series *M*A*S*H*, which brought together war and the medical care of severely injured soldiers. Surviving day after day of senseless carnage was made easier by a sarcastic give-and-take between the odd characters thrown together by the Korean War.

So it was at LA County-USC. Five years of long hours, nonstop violence, pressure to perform, and nonsensical human behavior (both outside and inside the hospital) led us inevitably to our own unique form of joking.

Next, consider the physical, mental, and emotional effects of severe and chronic sleep deprivation. You might have experienced a night when an unusual event occurs, such as a phone call at 1 a.m. informing you that a family member has died, or that someone is stranded somewhere and needs help. The response causes you to stay up most of the night to deal with the crisis, and you may get an hour or two of sleep. The following day you are initially a little exhilarated by having handled an all-nighter and remained functional, but if you must work all day, you eventually start to wear down. By the end of the day, you're on empty, with lightheadedness, nausea, and a headache. When you finally lie down, you discover, amazingly, that you can't fall asleep. When you eventually do sleep, the alarm awakens you way too soon, and you are disoriented and dog-tired. You may recall a similar pattern when staying up most of the night before a big test, only to fall asleep and then awaken just before the test, in a frantic, confused state.

What most people don't experience is 10 or 12 days like that each month, a common occurrence in internship and residency before the implementation of work-hour restrictions in 1989 and 2003. And many nights when we managed to get to sleep by 10 or 11 p.m., we were shocked awake every 45 to 60 minutes by ICU nurses requiring specific orders on sick, complicated patients. If you are a good intern or resident (by conventional standards), you must arise the following day at 5 a.m. to make rounds at 6 and appear prepared when formal rounds start at 7. Pile on attempts to read the medical literature in your "spare time," and the hours to sleep become perilously scarce. As the days turn to weeks, and the weeks drag into months, the physical and psychological toll accumulates. You begin to get exasperated—at the nurses who call you, at the resident who gives you more work, at the patients who arrive in numbers too large to deal with, at people who've made stupid decisions resulting in a need for your services. You develop a smoldering anger at your girlfriend, your spouse, your kids, the guy in the car behind you who just honked because you fell asleep at the stoplight. You hate the poor bastard who can't get your sandwich order correct.

You are unable to accomplish routine tasks that most people do every day: cashing a check at the bank, dropping a package at the post office, arriving on time (or at all) for a date. Your battery runs low. Your personal hygiene may suffer (no time for a shave, no time for a haircut). You may find it impossible to exercise, which accelerates the physical decline. Sometimes the exhaustion leads to isolation; you just don't want contact with anyone. Then come the outbursts, the snide comments, the biting sarcasm. Ultimately, the problem leads to strained work relationships, unhealthy personal interactions, and divorce. And black humor. All these are things you wish you could undo, but you can't.

Amidst all of this you are expected to soldier on in the hospital without complaint, arriving on time each day—better yet, early—and staying until all the work is done. It's a very unhealthy environment.

These are my excuses for some of the shocking things we said in residency. The black humor helped us survive, and it links us together to this day.

Late one night, while on call for general surgery, I decided to mosey down to the fifth floor to check on my mostly vegetative neurosurgery patients. The ward was dimly lit. A single, middle-aged, very overweight nurse sat at the desk writing on the vital sign sheets. I looked in the rooms. One patient was slipping out of bed, her head nearly touching the floor. I pulled her back into bed and put the blanket back on her. In the Darwinian Challenge room respirators were running and tubes were gurgling loudly. Everyone in there needed suctioning.

I walked out to the nurses' desk fuming. I grabbed one of the vital signs sheets. Blood pressure was 120/80 (a perfect reading). Heart rate 80. Respirations 20. I picked up another: exactly the same numbers on the next patient. I looked at the nurse, who pursed her lips a bit and tilted her head to the side as if to say, "So what if I'm making up vital signs? That's how it works here. It's none of your business."

"Where the hell is everyone?" I asked.

She jerked her thumb over her shoulder, directing me to the darkened break room behind her. I walked back there. Four nurses were leaned back in chairs, feet up, sound asleep. I was outraged. They were being paid! I reached over and picked up a pan from the sink, along with a wooden spoon and started beating on the pan. All four of them sat bolt upright, saying, "What the hell…" or "dayamm!"

"Goddammit, get up and do your job!" I said. "Those vent patients are drowning in their sputum! And people are falling out of bed! This is a disgrace!"

I expected defiance, but to my surprise, they slowly got up, muttering, and went back to work.

CHAPTER EIGHT

"ARE WE IN A CHURCH?"

MONDAY MORNING MEANT AN ELEVATOR ride to the twelfth floor for another Kafkaesque experience in internship: a month on the burn ward. This meant long operations and aggressive care, some of it for hopeless cases.

Our work began with rounds on the first day. My senior resident was a guy named Ron Peterson. He and I and the team entered a room with four patients. They had varying sizes of burns, with thick, white bandages to match. Some faces and heads were wrapped, some torsos, some extremities.

Some had had surgery; some were awaiting surgery. No one looked happy. No one laughed. Very few smiled, ever.

We walked down the hall to the "dressing room." The nurses had a five-year-old boy in the whirlpool, trying to soak the bandages on his chest and arms so that removing them would be less painful. He had suffered grease burns from a deep fat fryer pulled off a stove. He was a lucky one— no facial or scalp burns. He was already crying. When the bandages were slowly peeled off, he began shrieking and wailing, but remained rigidly still, since thrashing would only worsen the pain. Despite the various forms of horror I'd witnessed the past few months, I nearly became nauseated. This poor kid was in absolute hell, with no escape.

Later that afternoon, we got our first new case. Edward, a 30-year-old black man, was cleaning his garage floor with gasoline and a mop. Without thinking, he stopped for a break and decided to have a cigarette: *ka-boom!*

He was lying on a stretcher moaning, clothes partially burned off, hair and moustache singed badly, working hard to breathe. Pieces of his skin could be seen hanging between shreds of clothing. Ron and I started to strip off his clothes as well as the loose, burned skin. There was something I noticed on the burn ward. No matter the ethnicity of the patient, once you peel off the paper-thin layer of burned skin, we're all exactly the same color: pink.

Our exam revealed that roughly 50% of Edward's body had been burned. A general rule of thumb is that the sum of the percent burn and the patient's age yields the mortality (likelihood of dying). Inhalation injury (breathing of hot, toxic smoke) is known to increase this number. Thus, Edward's expected mortality would be well over 80%.

We intubated Edward and quickly moved him to the ICU. About two hours later, the director of the burn service, Dr. Zelinsky (commonly referred to as Dr. Z), walked in. He was in his fifties, energetic, friendly, but very serious. Dr. Z moved to the bedside. He turned first to me and, in a low voice, said, "Before we can proceed to fully treat this patient, we need to be sure he understands the severity of his injury, what he faces in the next days and weeks, and how he wants to be treated. How shall we determine this?"

I looked at Edward. His eyes were swollen shut. The breathing tube was sticking out his nose, and anyone with a breathing tube in place can't speak because the tube occupies the space between the vocal cords. Massive bandages covered his swollen body. The rhythmic *whoooosh phoooo, whoooosh phoooo* of the ventilator joined in chorus with the beeping of the heart monitor. I was unable to answer Dr. Z's question. Ron watched patiently, his arms folded.

"Mr. Edward Johnson?" Dr. Z began. "Can you hear me?"

The patient nodded slightly.

"I'm Dr. Zelinsky. Is it okay to talk about your burn?"

Another nod.

"Before we go any further, I need to make sure you are alert enough to follow the rest of this important discussion. I need to ask you a few questions. Where do you think we are right now? Are we in a church?

A head shake side to side.

"Are we in a grocery store?"

No.

"Are we in a hospital?"

Nod.

"Okay. Is it 1962?"

No.

"Is it 1982?"

Nod.

"Very good…now, Edward, you have a very severe burn injury. We estimate that about half your skin is burned… and your lungs are injured from the explosion. Do you understand me so far?"

Nod.

"The severity of your burn indicates that your chances of dying are rather high…maybe as high as 75 or 80%. Do you understand?"

Long pause. *Whooooosh phoooo, whooooosh phoooo, whooooosh phoooo.* Then a slow nod.

"We'd like to treat your burn. It will require several operations to remove the dead skin and place skin grafts. You'll be here for some time. Do you want us to go ahead with this… to give you a chance to live?"

Another long pause, then a nod.

"Okay. Very well. We'll get to work."

I spent the rest of the day, and evening, changing dressings, drawing blood, checking labs, replacing intravenous lines, and evaluating another new burn that was less serious. I left for the intern's dorm at 11 p.m.

I arrived the next morning at 5:45, quickly visiting all the patients before formal rounds at 6:30. We walked bed to bed, piling up a list of things to do. I sent the medical students off to begin some of the scut work, then reported to the operating room at about 7:30.

The team was just moving a 22-year-old woman from ICU to the operating room. Five days ago, she was in a bad car accident and was severely burned before rescuers could pull her from the vehicle. Her burned skin was starting to get infected.

Mrs. Santino was the burn OR director. She was short, abrupt, and stubborn—a bureaucratic nurse who controlled this small area of the hospital. She thought it was her job to get things done her way, not the best way for patients. Ron was already arguing with her over details of the operation, and she was slowly raising her voice with its heavy Filipina accent.

"We're going to need more Surgicel than that today," said Ron, "or the bleeding will be hard to control."

"No," replied Mrs. Santino, "it is too expensive. You will have to use lap pads."

"Then our blood loss will be excessive," said Ron. "That's no good for the patient…or the blood bank."

"The Surgicel will not help that much…and it's too expensive. It will hurt my budget."

"I don't care about your damn budget. I'm trying to do what's best for the patient. Just get us some more Surgicel."

"No, I will not."

"That's bullshit, Mrs. Santino. And you know it."

We got to work, cutting off the dead, infected skin.

"Mrs. Santino, this excision knife is dull," said Ron. "It's hard to make an accurate cut. How long since it was sharpened?"

"It was sharpened last month," said Mrs. Santino.

"We use it almost every day, here. We should order another one and send this one out for professional sharpening."

"That is too expensive."

Dr. Z took the knife and made a pass, excising some burned skin. "He's right, Mrs. Santino. It's kind of dull, and our cuts are less accurate. I think we should get another one and rotate them out for sharpening."

Normally, an exchange like this might have infuriated Mrs. Santino, but she worshipped Dr. Z and always tried to keep him happy. He appreciated her efforts to keep costs down, but patient care was paramount to him.

"I will do it," she said curtly, but she wouldn't look at Ron. She had lost this battle, but there would be many more that she would win.

The OR had to be kept very warm because the patient was naked and completely exposed; she could easily become dangerously cold. The case was long, bloody, and tedious. We sweated like pigs, and our greens became soaked. We had another arduous case that afternoon, and around 6 p.m., I finally emerged from the OR, feeling like a wrung-out rag. We finished the rest of our work at 11:30 p.m.

A few days later, we received a brother and sister, aged five and six, who belonged to a Gypsy family. They had climbed into an abandoned car, closed the doors, and were playing with matches. Once the car interior started to burn, they panicked and couldn't immediately open the doors. Someone finally pulled them out, but not before they received very extensive burns and inhalation injuries.

Dozens of visitors arrived, all claiming to be family members. They gathered in the hallway, opened any unlocked doors, and entered other patients' rooms inappropriately. The parents wanted to be in the treatment areas all the time, asked repetitive questions, and impeded our treatment. Different family members demanded their own individual progress reports many times a day. They seemed to live in their cars, and a sizeable Gypsy encampment grew in the parking lot. They set up a large religious shrine in the hallway on the twelfth floor. Every loose item in the area disappeared, as well as some things that were bolted down, including an actual metal sink in an adjacent washroom (almost, but not specifically, the proverbial kitchen sink). Toothbrushes, brooms, dustpans, curtains, telephones, beepers, clothing, dressings, toilet paper, and soap all vanished.

One afternoon, I smelled something burning in the hallway. I walked down to the Gypsy shrine to find them cooking hot dogs over a fire they had built on the linoleum floor! I called security, and an argument erupted between our fire personnel and the Gypsies. When told that fires are strictly forbidden within the hospital, they responded, "But we are Gypsies! We live by our own rules. No one tells us what we can or cannot do." They also missed the irony of setting fires in the hallway on the burn ward. To our relief, security banned most of them from the hospital. Only the immediate family could visit thereafter.

Treating badly injured children is emotionally exhausting. The doctors and nurses will do almost anything to minimize discomfort and maximize the chances for recovery. When kids fail to improve, we often feel a sense of personal failure, and it can be very depressing. Unfortunately, one of the burned Gypsy children got severely infected and died after about two weeks; the other lived only after many surgeries and a long, difficult, painful hospital stay.

One afternoon, we saw numerous recovering patients in the outpatient burn clinic. One was Daniel, a seven-year-old boy who'd been very badly burned a year earlier in a house fire. He'd had multiple operations and a prolonged, complicated recuperation.

I first saw him from across the room. His face was almost unrecognizable as such. It appeared to have melted and then hardened in that new shape. His eyes were barely visible behind two little slits. His nose, although reconstructed, was small and flat, with nostrils pointing straight out. His mouth was a tight, little, immobile, horizontal diamond. He had essentially no lips. His chin melded gradually into a flat, vertically ridged neck that flowed onto his upper chest. I tried hard to suppress the thought, but this poor little boy looked like a fish. It was a struggle not to cry.

Ron walked me over and said, "Daniel, I want you to meet Dr. Harch, my intern." And out of this distorted, misshapen figure came the sweetest, clearest, most confident little voice, "Hello, happy to meet you." And he stuck out a small hand missing two fingers and grasped my hand as best he could, shaking it. With that little hand in mine, I felt an emotional tidal wave of sorrow tangled with hope.

It is safe to say that people like Daniel desperately want to be treated like everyone else. This is also true of those with cancer. Although their medical problem may be plainly obvious, and impossible to ignore, they desire normal friendships, normal interactions, and truth. Often, family and friends of these sick or injured people don't know what to say or how to act around them, so they avoid them altogether. Patients have told me that the resulting isolation is worse than the disease.

About two weeks into the rotation, things spiraled downward. We received a series of extensively burned patients in a short period of time. One of them was a guy burned in the explosion of a PCP lab. This sort of thing was common enough that it threatened the viability of many burn centers around the country, mainly because the burns were massive and nearly 100% of the patients were uninsured. It led to the macabre statement sometimes heard on the surgical services: "Most people who are burned deserve it."

Deon, a 20-year-old, was helicoptered to our hospital in very bad shape. He was in severe respiratory distress. Most of his clothes were burned or blown off. His hair was completely burned away. When Ron came out of the OR, I was already putting a breathing tube in Deon. The burn diagram showed a 90% burn. His inhalation injury was extreme, and the ventilator settings needed to support his lungs were already rather ominous.

Over the prior three weeks, I'd watched as we treated patients with a variety of burns. Many had lived and some had died, including Edward Johnson, the guy who'd cleaned his garage floor with gasoline. None were as badly burned as Deon. In fact, his estimated mortality was 110%, not counting the severe effect of his inhalation injury.

I believed that some of the initial discussions with patients hadn't been accurate enough to allow a truly informed decision about treatment. I knew that if I were a badly burned patient, I would want a more comprehensive explanation of how difficult the treatment would be and an honest appraisal of my chances of living or dying.

Ron had to return to the OR as soon as we got Deon intubated. I was the most senior person left on the ward. I usually preferred to leave the "Do you want to be treated?" discussion to Ron or Dr. Z, but I feared that Deon might deteriorate quickly and wouldn't be able to participate in this essential process. I looked at the ICU nurse, whose expression indicated she understood my concerns.

Cradling his right hand, I said, "Deon…" He was minimally sedated because we'd had to rush his treatment to this point. He nodded. I went through the sequence of questioning to determine his mental capacity. He was entirely clear and alert.

"We need to talk about your burn. I need to get an idea about how much treatment you want us to provide."

A nod.

"This explosion has burned about 90% of your body. Your lungs are badly injured too. According to what we know, your risk of dying from this problem is…about…" It was hard to say it, but I did. "100%."

In fact, his risk of dying was far greater than 110%, but saying that seemed both nonsensical and cruel. Saying "100%" was cruel enough.

I looked back at the nurse. She nodded in agreement. We let the bad news sink in.

"Are you following me?" I asked.

A nod.

"Now, sometimes young people like you are strong enough and healthy enough that they surprise us. And there is a small chance you could survive. But it will be a long, tough battle. You'll need multiple operations, and if you do make it, you'll be here a long time. And there's a very high risk of infection and scarring."

There was a long pause. I felt uneasy because he couldn't ask me questions that were doubtless critical; questions that were racing through his brain right now.

"Do you understand?"

A slow nod.

"So, the decision regarding what we do is up to you. We can go all out with operations, antibiotics, skin grafts, blood transfusions...that's what we do here...or you can decide not to receive any treatment."

There was another long pause: Deon was thinking, while I was worrying about conducting this critical conversation.

"I need to add that if you decide not to aggressively treat this burn, we will use morphine to keep you comfortable. We'll do our best to keep you pain-free." I waited about five long seconds. "What do you think?"

Deon began to shake his head side to side, as much as the endotracheal tube would allow.

"Let me get this straight. You don't want us to do all the stuff we usually do here to try to fix you? Because if you do, we will treat you."

Deon shook his head back and forth three times, very deliberately.

"And you only want us to give you pain medicines to keep you comfortable?"

Two definite nods up and down. I squeezed Deon's hand.

"Then that's what we'll do. We'll give you some more pain medicine right now."

I looked back at the nurse, concerned. If she didn't approve of the way things just transpired, it could have serious repercussions for me. Her expression suggested approval, and then, as I turned to go, she gave me a subtle wink.

Sometime later, Ron and Dr. Z emerged from surgery. I related my discussion with Deon, which was now documented carefully in the chart. Dr. Z looked a bit stricken, and went to the bedside. He attempted to repeat the discussion, but Deon was drifting away, and all Dr. Z could get was sluggish "no" headshakes to any talk of "saving your life." Fortunately, the nurse confirmed the clarity and certainty of Deon's responses, and the matter was dropped.

We placed Deon in one corner of the ICU, medicated him generously, and provided basic ventilator support. He slipped away and died in about two hours.

I escaped the burn ward late that afternoon and drove to Hollywood to take Lori out to dinner. I told her what happened with Deon.

"You know, I feel kinda uncomfortable because it seems like I played God today with someone's life," I said. "I've never been in that role before, since I'm near the bottom of the totem pole."

"Someone had to do it," said Lori.

"Yeah, but it's a weird feeling, because he was dead not long after we spoke."

"He was gonna die no matter what you did."

"Yeah, but not without a lot of suffering, if we had treated him aggressively."

"Then I'd say you did him a big favor."

I had to agree.

Lori was quiet for a few seconds. "I applied for a new job today," she said.

"Really? I thought you liked it at *Motorcyclist*."

"I do like it, but this would be a big step up for me because I'd be in control of so much more. I'd be hiring my own staff of writers, an art director, freelancers, and deciding on all the editorial content."

"What kind of magazine is it?"

"It's called *Intro*. Half the magazine is ads for single people looking to meet one another. The other half, which I'd be the editor of, would be any articles that would be of interest to single people, like health, travel, celebrity interviews, humor…stuff like that."

"I've never heard of a magazine like that."

"They're trying to take the sleaze factor out of personal ads. How else can most people meet someone they want to date?"

"Yeah, like all the poor bastards stuck at the hospital all the time. That's why most of them end up dating other doctors, nurses, or hospital staff."

"Exactly."

"Where's the magazine located?"

"Oh, they're close by…about the same distance from here as Peterson Publishing."

I was relieved she wasn't considering moving away, but I didn't say it.

"I hope you get the job."

One night, we took a cadaver to the OR and spent about five hours shaving off his skin to use for grafts on some of our badly burned patients. We got about two hours of sleep and were back on the burn ward at 7 a.m., feeling like limp spaghetti. Including my two call nights for general surgery that week, which were both sleepless, I suddenly realized that seven days had gone by with very little sleep. I sat down to calculate just how much I'd worked. Shockingly, it added up to 141 hours, which translated to an average of fewer than four hours out of each day to walk to the dorm, sleep, wake up, shower, and return to the ward.

Fortunately, hard work was familiar to me. My brothers and I started delivering newspapers at the age of 11, and worked nearly any job we could find in the years that followed.

When I returned to California after my freshman year at Northwestern University in Illinois, I was desperate for a job. Even though I received scholarships, there was enough of a financial shortfall that I had to squirrel away as much money as possible each summer. I went to see an old family friend named Charlie, who owned an aluminum foundry and was the kindest man I knew. Charlie looked at my skinny frame and said I could paint the outside of the old, decrepit factory building that housed his business. It was a building that didn't need to be painted.

As I worked, I peered through the grimy windows of the foundry. There were three blast furnaces going full tilt, creating a deafening roar as they melted aluminum at 1,100 degrees. Guys drove tractors around furiously, mixed oil and sand for the molds, poured molten metal, or ran band saws or grinders. It was filthy, hot as hell, and hazardous.

After three days of painting, I announced I was done. Charlie paid me.

"Do you have any other work?" I asked.

"That's all I've got," he replied.

"Can I work in there?" I asked, pointing through a window.

"No, you don't want to work in there," he said, shaking his head emphatically.

"But I really need a job, Charlie."

"Believe me, you don't want to work in there. It's dirty and dangerous." Then he added, "And your mother would never forgive me if you got hurt."

"I'd like to give it a try," I persisted. "Please."

He looked at me carefully, rubbing his chin. I knew I'd put him in a tough spot. "Well, if you really want to try it, come back tomorrow morning at 7. Wear old clothes. But you can quit anytime you want to. Anytime. I mean that."

The next morning, I showed up just before 7 in tattered jeans and an old shirt. A big, burly, young guy greeted me, handed me a filthy apron and advised me to remove my shirt to avoid "getting cooked." On the far left, sand molds were being made and sent down a conveyor belt.

The burly guy handed me some ear protection, gave me a pair of asbestos gloves, and demonstrated my job. After the molten aluminum was poured into the molds, the molds were pushed down the conveyor belt. I was to lift the entire mold (metal base, metal frame, burning oily black sand, and smoking 500-degree aluminum part inside) and throw it on the floor. I would separate everything and return the steel frames to the mold makers. The parts would be wheelbar-rowed to the next stage of processing.

"Oh, and one more thing," he added. "Don't let any hot sand get in your gloves or inside your apron; the bosses don't want to take you to the hospital."

I can do this, I thought. I put on my gloves, walked confidently over to the first mold, and lifted it up. It weighed about 100 pounds. I pitched it on the floor, turned and grabbed another, threw it, and moved to the third. My small work space was immediately filled with noxious, white smoke. I was already sweating profusely.

I looked down the belt. It was full of molds, and they seemed to be backing up. The mold frames and bases had to be picked up off the floor and the oily sand removed. I picked up my pace, getting some hot sand down my glove one time, but managing to whip off the glove in time to avoid a burn. Some of the molds were less than 100 pounds; some were far more. After 20 minutes, my back was killing me. I was getting exhausted quickly, but I worked as hard as I've ever worked. After what seemed a very long time, I estimated it must be near break time, which I knew was 10 o'clock. I leaned to one side to see the clock on the far wall—it was only 8:35!

When I saw the time, I stopped working, stood straight up, and had one of those seminal moments that come along infrequently in one's life. I was pretty sure I couldn't make it to 10 o'clock, not to mention noon or the end of the day. And if I did make it, did I want to return here each day all summer and continue this agony? I seriously considered walking out right then. But I would be quitting, and then I would have established a pattern of quitting. And I didn't want the other workers or Charlie to see me quit, to know I couldn't hack it. I knew they were watching, waiting for me to quit, expecting me to quit. I felt miserable, but after standing there for another few seconds, I told myself I had to make it to 10. It was a matter of pride.

Somehow, I did make it to the 10 o'clock break. I shuffled over to the break area and plopped down on a bench, saying nothing. Someone brought me a glass of water and a donut, which I consumed. Someone else asked if I was okay, and I nodded. After 15 minutes, everyone got up, and to their complete astonishment, so did I, and I walked back in feeling a little better. I continued the drudgery (it now seemed somewhat easier) and I made it to lunch. After lunch, strangely, the molds came down the belt more slowly, then much more slowly, and I kept up a lot better. I was still tired as hell, and sore, but made it to the end of the day. When I blew my nose into a Kleenex, what came out was black.

I returned the following day, and the molds came down at a much slower, steadier pace all day long. I realized— and the other workers later admitted—that they had been busting their asses the prior day to try to break the wimpy college kid. By afternoon, they were all so exhausted they had to slow way down. And they were still tired on that second day. The foreman and Charlie were happy, however, because they had a new grunt worker, and they had a record day of production.

That first day established a baseline for me. Any job thereafter seemed easy in comparison. I could always look back and think, "This is nothing compared to my first few hours in the foundry." And it gave me confidence: you can't drive me away with hard work, even if that's your sole intention.

As the burn rotation neared its end we had all become completely frustrated with the stalling and foot dragging by Mrs. Santino in the OR. On a few occasions, I'd been close to exploding at her. Then Ron told me a great story.

There was a second-year resident named Larry Betz. He was a short, mercurial, fearless New Yorker. During his internship, he'd been "written up" by nurses for various episodes of bad behavior 150 times. Most interns were written up at most two or three times in a year.

When Larry rotated through burns as an intern last year, he'd immediately butted heads with Mrs. Santino. The situation deteriorated rapidly, as with the irresistible force and immovable object. One morning, they brought a very sick, burned patient to the OR for excision and grafting. Larry had to cut off all the dressings. When he asked for bandage scissors, Mrs. Santino handed him a tiny, flimsy pair of suture-cutting scissors. She didn't want to unwrap the large, sharp bandage scissors, which she was "saving" for who knows what. It would have taken Larry an hour of struggling to cut off the bandages. He demanded a good pair of scissors, and she refused, citing shortages of equipment and the need to conserve what they had.

Larry became enraged. He stepped forward toward Mrs. Santino and said, "Mrs. Santino, you know what I'm gonna do right now? I'm gonna walk over to that cabinet and get out a big skin excision knife. I'm gonna cut your head off, stick my thumb in your mouth hole and these two fingers in your eye holes. Then, I'm gonna roll your head down the hall, like a bowling ball."

Mrs. Santino looked at him in terror, her eyes bulging. Larry stepped right up into her face and yelled, "Like a fucking bowling ball!" With that, Mrs. Santino screamed, dropped the instruments she was holding, and ran down the hallway shouting, "*Ave Maria! Ave Maria!*"

Larry was in the chief's office in about 30 minutes, having to explain this latest loss of control. Larry became an absolute hero to me the moment I heard that story (and remains so in my mind), but before the year was out, he was deselected from the general surgery program. It was deemed too big a risk to have such a volatile guy in stressful, critical situations. He did get accepted to our Urology program, however, and I would run into him from time to time. I'm certain he remains fearless to this day.

CHAPTER NINE

RESPITE

SURPRISING THOUGH IT MAY SEEM, we did have planned vacation days. Our contract expressly stated, "All postgraduate physicians are entitled to 24 days paid leave each year." I guess that technically the directors of the residency considered a work week to be six days because the 24 days worked out to be exactly four weeks off. Thus, in our internship year, we had 13 rotations of four weeks, and one of the rotations was vacation. Unfortunately, this meant that all four weeks off had to be taken in one block. Most of us worked all the other days of the year, so the four weeks off were a strange transition from the daily grind as an intern to life as a normal human being. It reminded me of the book *All Quiet on the Western Front*, in which the German soldiers suffered deprivation and terror in the trench warfare of World War I, then were sent home on leave every few months. The stark contrast left the soldiers feeling detached and dissociated in their own communities because their families and friends couldn't possibly understand their battlefield experiences. I realize that equating our internship to war is a dramatic overreach, but in small measure, it seemed that way to us.

The isolation from routine life during working months had comical consequences in the vacation month. I remember taking my car in for servicing one day. As I sat in the waiting room with other people, I noticed a young, muscular guy reading a magazine. His forearms were covered with big, cord-like, juicy veins; the type you could puncture for an IV or blood draw with your eyes closed. Since every day at work was a battle to maintain IVs in fat people, drug addicts, and others with disappearing veins, this was a magnificent sight. I sat there staring as though his forearms were a *Playboy* centerfold. Perhaps he felt my stare, because he looked up and saw me transfixed. I looked away, embarrassed.

With 28 long, luscious vacation days waiting, it was imperative to set priorities. The first order of business for most of us was to get to our loved one's place and jump in bed, followed by the second order of business, which was sleep. These two priorities were wonderfully intertwined. Lori would often leave me slumbering in her bed late into the morning. Further down my priorities list were eating properly, exercising, seeing family, and catching up on life's

175

mundane chores (e.g. renewing a driver's license, going to the bank). But there was one more responsibility hanging over us.

The American Board of Surgery (the certifying body for general surgeons) sought to validate the academic progress of all residents-in-training. Therefore, they designed the In-Service Training Examination, which in those days was administered annually to all residents. Failure to score above a set minimum could set you back a year or get you dismissed from the residency program. Senior residents had to achieve their minimum level or not graduate. Studying for this exam began in internship and continued for all five years. Since our rotations were so busy, we crammed much of this study into our vacation month. The range of information to consume was vast and intimidating.

Honestly, I don't remember much about this first vacation month of my residency. But I do recall that Lori's parents invited us to join them for a couple of days in Palm Springs, all expenses paid. We happily agreed to go, eagerly anticipating the indulgence. It also gave us the opportunity to celebrate Lori's recent hiring as the new editor of *Intro Magazine*.

Lori's dad, Dave, was a devout Catholic. Her mom, Pat, was also Catholic, but not so devout. Arrangements were made for us to have separate rooms at the hotel, for obvious reasons. The weather was great. The meals and accommodations were excellent. We lay by the pool soaking up the sun. We were even treated to massages. After the merciless grind of internship, it was paradise.

On the second day, we were suffering. After all, it was vacation, and more than 36 hours had passed without any sex. In the afternoon, I announced I had to go study for my exam, and Lori stated she had editing to do for her work. The ungrateful, devious pair of us snuck off and met in her room. Dave and Pat must have known what we were up to, but since we were both 27 years old, they looked the other way, probably thinking they had done their best to prevent the sin of premarital sex.

Billy's vacation six weeks earlier had a more complicated ending. Toward the latter part of his month, he had travelled to Houston with a girlfriend to visit friends. There were no cell phones then, and he hadn't left any phone numbers to call in case of emergency. When he arrived back at his dorm room at the hospital, he checked the messages on his phone recorder.

"Billy, this is Terry," said his sister's voice, urgently. "Daddy's got a tumor! Call me!"

Then a follow-up message from his mother, in a more restrained voice: "Billy, could you call me at home? We need to talk."

He called his mom immediately. His father had been found to have a tumor in the head of his pancreas and was scheduled for surgery in a few days. The irony was that William Wenzel Goodwin II, Billy's dad, had specialized in surgery for pancreatic cancer. Billy's full name was William Wenzel Goodwin III.

In a move that surprised us, Dr. O'Donnelly allowed Billy to fly to Washington, DC, at the time he was scheduled to start the Tuesday Service. The chief filled the gap with another intern. Billy arrived home the evening before his dad's surgery, which was attended by several bigwig surgeon acquaintances of his father. The tumor was found to be malignant, and was unresectable. Billy stayed long enough to cry with his father and the rest of his family, and then jumped back on a plane the third day.

When Billy returned to Los Angeles, he stayed up most of the night studying the charts of his patients so he'd be familiar with them for staff rounds that week. It was a one-intern service, so he was responsible for all of the presentations. Two mornings later, the Tuesday Service staff walked around the wards to receive the narratives for all the patients. Billy led the way, with attending physicians listening, and his senior resident, Nick Givens (my favorite), observing. As Billy finished discussing the last patient, the group rounded the corner into the main hallway. One of the attendings, a kindly older black surgeon, Dr. Middleman, looked at Billy's nametag.

"Goodwin, eh?" he said.

"Yes, sir," said Billy.

"I trained with a William Goodwin at Howard University years ago," said Dr. Middleman. "Any relation to you?"

"Yes, sir," said Billy. "That's my father."

"Well, how's he doin'?" asked Middleman.

"Unfortunately, sir, he was just found to have unresectable pancreatic cancer."

"I'm really sorry to hear that, Billy," said Middleman. "Would you please give him my regards?"

"Yes, sir. Thank you."

A week later, the scene was replayed for staff rounds, except that Dr. Middleman wasn't present. Another attending, Dr. Ted Ryder, who hadn't participated the prior week, was in the group. As they rounded the same corner near the end of patient presentations, Ryder tapped Billy on the shoulder.

"Hey, Billy," said Ryder, in his slow, deep, throaty voice. "I hear your dad has unresectable pancreatic cancer."

"Yes, that's correct, sir," responded Billy, sadly.

"Well…" said Ryder, "I guess that means he won't be seeing you graduate from this program."

Billy just looked at him. The news about his dad was only 10 days old, and all the emotions were still raw. Billy contemplated saying, "Well, motherfucker, there's no guarantee you'll live to see me graduate either." But, of course, he said nothing, and continued down the hall to the conference room.

Nick Givens had been walking a few steps behind Billy and Dr. Ryder. To this day, Billy doesn't know if Nick heard the exchange, but for the ensuing four years, Billy and Dr. Ryder never again worked on the same service or the same call night.

CHAPTER TEN

I'M QUITTING

TOWARD THE END OF MY INTERNSHIP YEAR, I rotated through orthopedic surgery (ortho). After general surgery (GS), it was the busiest service in the hospital. Many of the ortho patients came through the GS admitting area, but just as many, or more, came directly from the ER. The barrage of people with broken bones or extremity soft tissue problems (infections, lacerations) often left the doctors with huge backups of work each day. As with GS, the real problem was finding time and personnel to operate on everyone who needed it.

Being a GS intern on the orthopedic service gave me added responsibility that I didn't expect. While rotating through the GS services, it was drilled into us to take care of absolutely everything we could, including high blood pressure, electrolyte abnormalities, failing kidneys, infection, and respiratory failure. In contrast, the ortho residents didn't want to take care of medical problems, so they usually called medicine consults for all non-orthopedic issues. But when they had GS interns, they knew they could just ask us to manage the medical problems, since it was way more efficient than waiting for a medicine resident to show up.

On any day or night, I would get the following: "Hey, Harch, this lady has low potassium. Can you fix that up before morning so we can take her to surgery?" Or, "Hey, Harch, this guy has low urine output. Can you figure out why and straighten it out so we can operate?" It wasn't that they didn't have the smarts to do it themselves; they just didn't want to bother. And the less frequently one treats a problem, the less skillful one becomes.

In addition to being the jack-of-all-trades on ortho, I was trying to learn something about the specialty while doing my share of the physical work. On busy days, it was impossible to keep up with that work.

One night, we got bombed. The admitting ward, 3300, was full to the gills, and patient gurneys spilled out of the exam rooms into the hallway. People were moaning because of their fractures. Some hadn't been evaluated yet or given pain medicine. Others were splinted and awaiting surgery.

We were working on a young guy who'd been run over by a car. He had a broken leg (below the knee) on one side and a broken femur (above the knee) on the other side. Both

181

upper extremities were broken as well. We were trying to put all four fractures in traction until we could get him stable enough (and could get time enough) to repair the mess. He was in a huge traction bed. It had overhead metal bars on which to attach pulleys and ropes for the complex array of traction devices. Four of us were crawling all over this bed attaching things, like monkeys in an exhibit at the zoo.

This same patient had sustained an injury to one eye. All patients with multiple trauma had to go through a GS evaluation before being sent to a specialty service, and he had, but the GS team must have overlooked (no pun intended) his eye injury. I noticed it when he arrived on ortho, and we decided to call ophthalmology for a consult. Uh-oh, I cringed, another ophthalmology consult.

At about 2 a.m., we were still working on the patient.

"Fred, pull harder on that hook and set the weight," said the resident.

"Ahhhhhhhh!" yelled the patient.

"Harch, get the nurse to give him some more pain medicine."

"Gary, let off the arm traction a little and hang another two pounds on the left leg."

"Someone needs to add another pulley up top."

"Ahhhhhhhh!"

In the middle of this chaos, the elevator doors opened and a doctor shuffled slowly over to where we were working. He had his head down and his eyes half-open. He looked like he'd been asleep until five minutes ago. I noticed him in my peripheral vision, but everyone else had their backs to him or were focused on their work. The doctor stood there for about 30 seconds.

In a faint, nasal voice, the waiting doctor said, "Um, you guys…"

No one looked up. I was holding some ropes and weights, watching things unfold, happy that I wasn't in charge.

"Um, you guys," he repeated, slightly louder.

Everyone stopped and looked at him.

"Are you the ophthalmology consultant?" asked the ortho resident, yanking on some traction.

"Yes…"

"Well, this is your guy. You can take a look at him while we work."

There was a pause. He looked at us and we at him.

"Um…well…I have a really bad headache," the ophthalmology resident whined. "Do you mind if I do the consult in the morning?"

My resident looked at him in disbelief, then looked at the rest of us, who were hanging from metal bars or holding various equipment.

"Just get the fuck outta here!" yelled the ortho resident. And the ophthalmology resident shuffled back to the elevator, a little more quickly this time, and disappeared.

"Can you believe that shit?" asked my resident. "I'll bet he's been asleep all night, then when you need him, he's got a goddamn headache. What a fuckin' wimp." We all agreed and went back to work.

Saturday morning rolled around again, which meant sitting through another M and M Conference. It was still difficult to watch, but we were gradually getting desensitized. We recognized it was part of the game, and the resident in the hot seat just had to endure the incoming fire.

Several junior residents were on the docket to present cases one after the other, and each got a moderate whipping. Then it was Scott Seibert's turn up front. He was a second-year resident with whom I'd shared call on a few occasions. He wasn't the smartest or most confident guy amongst us, but he was solid and a nice person. He had two cases to defend.

"Dr. Seibert, would you present the missed common bile duct stone?" asked Dr. O'Donnelly.

"Yes, sir," replied Scott. He described a gallbladder removal in which a gallstone had been overlooked on an X-Ray and left in the patient, requiring a second operation. This wasn't a very serious screw-up compared to some complications.

"Let's see the films," said Dr. O'Donnelly.

About half the doctors in the room (perhaps 15) got up and looked at the films, which were displayed on a light box to our left.

"Do you think it's there on the third cholangiogram, and possibly the fourth?" asked Dr. Everett, in a low voice, querying the resident next to him.

Then, Dr. Rollins declared, loudly, "I think it's pretty clear the stone is visible on two cholangiograms."

"In retrospect, I think you're right, sir," said Scott.

"Did you even look at the films?" asked Rollins. The disparaging little curly-headed bastard was at it again.

"Yes, sir."

"No, I mean did you really stop and look at them carefully, or did you just hurry on to the next case?"

"We did look…carefully…but somehow missed it."

"Why do you think we require that you do these X-Rays?" asked Rollins. "To waste time? Or money? Or for fun?"

"No sir," said Scott. "I realize it's important to be thorough."

"Maybe you should tell that to the patient next time you see her," added Rollins.

There was silence after that comment. Scott was squirming and didn't know what to say. His face was red. He'd sustained a significant shark bite and was bleeding.

"The point, ladies and gentlemen," interjected Dr. O'Donnelly, "is that we have a solemn responsibility to our patients to slow down a little and examine the details of each and every case. These patients have put their lives in our hands. We can't be planning the next operation before we're done with the one we've started. If you spend time taking cholangiograms, review them carefully. Then look at them a second time. Call your senior resident to read them with you if you're uncertain."

The room was silent. No one wanted to jump in the water.

"Alright," said Dr. O'Donnelly, "let's move on to the next case, which I think is also yours, Dr. Seibert. This is a take-back for bleeding after a gunshot to the abdomen. Go ahead."

"Yes, sir," said Scott. He explained how they fixed the damage from the bullet but had to take the patient back to the OR to stop ongoing bleeding seven hours later.

"How do you think this happened?" asked Dr. O'Donnelly.

"I guess we missed the bleeder when we resected the small bowel. It looked dry when we finished."

"When you clamped the vessels, did you take big bites with your clamps?" asked Dr. Ryder, the same guy who had made the callous remark to Billy about his father two months ago.

"I don't think so," said Scott.

"Well, that's how this usually happens," said Ryder, gruffly. "When you gather a big wad of fat and vessels, and attempt to tie them all together, one vessel can slip out of the ties and bleed."

"We tried to tie the vessels separately," said Scott.

"But did you allot a segment of time at the end to see if you had all the bleeding controlled?" asked Ryder.

"Yes, sir...I thought we...checked carefully." Scott looked distressed.

"Not carefully enough, evidently," said Ryder.

Scott stood there fidgeting. He was thrashing around in the water, all alone, his bleeding more severe than that of the patient he was presenting.

"Dr. Seibert," chimed in Dr. Rollins, "you seem to specialize in taking patients back to surgery for complications." There was another awkward silence after this affront. "Do you think this case also demonstrates being in too much of a hurry?"

Scott stared at Dr. Rollins but didn't respond. Scott's senior resident could have jumped in to save the hemorrhaging swimmer, but all the residents knew it wasn't acceptable to make excuses for the juniors, who were expected to stand on their own two feet. But some of us in the room looked at Ryder and Rollins with loathing; it was hard to believe their intent was teaching.

"Let's look for the lesson in this," said Dr. O'Donnelly. "Technique is critical for much of what we do. Whether we're dividing and ligating vessels or closing the midline fascia, we have to pay close attention to every step. Precise technical skills are essential to good outcomes. Dr. Seibert, that will be all. You can take your seat."

When the conference ended and we filed out, I couldn't find Seibert. I did, however, run into him the following morning in the hallway. He looked glum.

"Hi, Scott," I said. "Sorry you got such a butt-fucking yesterday."

"Yeah...I've been thinking about it all night and this morning," he said. "I didn't sleep much. I'm going in to see Dr. O'Donnelly this afternoon. I'm quitting the residency."

"What?" I shouted. "Don't do that. That's nuts. Everybody gets grilled in M and M."

"No…my mind's made up. I'm quitting."

"Why? You've put in so much work. Don't let those pricks get to you."

"I don't want three more years of what happened yesterday. I'm not having any fun. I need to get myself into a program where they don't treat you like shit."

"What are you gonna do?"

"I'm thinking about urology. I like the specialty, and I think I'd like the lifestyle better."

"I hate to see you make such a dramatic change based on what happened yesterday. I get how you're feeling, but I hope you think about it real hard before you do something irreversible."

"I've already thought about it hard. I've been thinking about it for months."

Scott did go in to see the chief later that day. And he did quit, effective six weeks later. And he did secure a spot in the urology program. I don't know if it made him any happier, but the whole experience made me uneasy about my future.

One evening, I was sitting at the nursing station on ortho writing some progress notes. A middle-aged male nurse with a very heavy East Indian accent was talking on the phone. He was a charge nurse, whose job it was to stamp out fires all over the hospital. These nurses knew about all the bad cases and all the dirt at LA County.

When he put the phone down, he said, "Hello, Dr. Harch." Apparently, he also knew who I was. This surprised me because there were more than 600 doctors in the hospital.

"Hi, Mr...Patel," I said, looking at his name tag.

"It's nice to meet you," he said. "The nurses are saying nice things about you." I was hoping he meant Darla and Tiffany.

"They say you are gracious and hardworking." Not really the nice things I was hoping for.

"Good to meet you," I said. "What's going on tonight in the hospital?"

"Oh, Dr. Harch, since you've asked, I'll tell you. You know, the most horrible things happen to people, and they come here. Tonight, a man, a very big man...you know, about six-foot, four-inches tall, about 240 pounds, broke into a home to burglarize it. But the family was home, so he shot the husband and tied the children up next to the bed and raped the wife—right in front of the children."

"That's a terrible story, Mr. Patel."

"Oh, that's not the end of it. As this man was leaving the house, the wife retrieved a gun and shot him. He's being operated on by your residents right now."

"I'm not inclined to root for his survival, Mr. Patel."

"No, me either."

"I better get back to my notes. There's plenty of crazy stuff to deal with right here on ortho."

"Indeed. Speaking of crazy things, did you hear what happened yesterday?"

"Um..."

189

"Well, a young schizophrenic man, just recovering from slitting his wrists, got instructions from his 'Supreme Commander' to cut off his penis. This he did, severing about half of it, which he placed in his rectum."

"That's pretty sick," I said. Why was Mr. Patel telling me all this morbid stuff, unsolicited, with such enthusiasm? "What happened to him?" I asked.

"Oh, they retrieved the penis from his rectum, but decided not to sew it back on. Now he must live with no penis!" said Mr. Patel, grinning broadly.

"Thanks for those uplifting stories, Mr. Patel, but I gotta get back to work. You can tell me some more stories on another night."

"Very well, Dr. Harch. It was a pleasure meeting you." He walked away jauntily, as if he'd just made the world a better place.

There was a light at the end of the tunnel. I had a little over a month remaining in my internship. I was tired all the time, but I was learning to take care of gravely ill people. Nick Givens had guided me through about six central line placements. He said that if I chose the patients carefully, I could now place these lines myself. I did just that on a heroin abuser who'd been shot in the arm and had no places to put IVs. But when I advanced that long, sharp needle into his chest, I didn't immediately get blood, and I was worried that I might have punctured his lung. I ordered a stat chest X-Ray to check for such a problem.

After the film was taken, the X-Ray technician told me it would be ready in about 10 minutes. After 15 minutes, I headed down to check the film.

I had been to X-Ray hundreds of times over the prior 11 months to request films. Some were critical; some were not. Some were available; some were not. Some clerks helped you; some did not. If you couldn't find what you wanted, you might have to beg or come back later.

I entered the room where we requested the films. There was an opening in the far wall, about eight feet wide and three feet high, just above a counter. On the other side of the counter stood a clerk, leaning on one elbow reading a magazine.

"Hey, how're you doin'?" I asked.

He looked up indifferently and muttered, "Okay."

"I'm after the portable chest that was just done on 3300. Patient name is Phillips."

"You need to fill out the form."

"Sure." I took the form, filled in the required information, and handed it to him, smiling.

"Hang on," he said. He disappeared around the corner and out of my view for perhaps three seconds, then reappeared and said, "Nope, it's not here." He handed me the request form, gave me a smug look, and went back to his magazine.

"It was shot about 15 minutes ago, and the tech said he was coming straight here to develop it. I'm pretty sure it's back there somewhere."

He didn't bother to go look again. Instead, he looked straight into my eyes and stated, more emphatically, "I said it's not there. You'll have to come back later."

"Look," I said. "I just put a central line in this guy, and I'm worried about a possible pneumo. I really need to see that film."

"I said…it's not…here."

I glared at him. I knew he hadn't checked for the film. He knew that I knew he hadn't checked. It was a standoff. He sensed my anger, but the look on his face said, "This is my little kingdom, and I'm in control. You can go to hell if you don't like it, doctor."

For a few seconds, I didn't say or do anything. Eleven months of simmering frustration now came to a full boil. I put both hands on the edge of the counter, then slowly bent both knees and lowered myself until I disappeared from his view, except for my fingers. He leaned forward a bit, trying to see what I was doing down there on the other side of the counter. Then, in an instant, I jumped up on the counter, crouching to avoid hitting my head. Completely startled, he fell backward, banging into the wall behind him and landing on the floor. His eyes were momentarily wide with fear. I suppose he thought I was going to punch him. Instead, I jumped off the counter and onto the floor, stepped over him, rounded the corner, and looked on the desk. There, in plain view, right on top of all the other X-Rays, was a film labelled Phillips. It took me less than two seconds to find it. I grabbed it and rounded the corner again. By this time, the clerk was back on his feet and had moved about six feet away, still facing me.

"Thanks for nuthin', asshole," I said flatly. I hopped back over the counter and left with the film. Fortunately, the central line looked good: there was no pneumothorax.

I wondered whether I'd get accused of battery or some other trumped-up offense, but to my surprise, I heard nothing about this event. Two days later, however, I had to return to the scene of the trespass to get another film. Expecting a hostile reception, I entered the same room to discover that a large, thick Plexiglas window had already been installed above the counter to prevent any future acrobatic theft of X-Rays. I'm certain this was the fastest infrastructure change ever made at LA County-USC Medical Center.

CHAPTER ELEVEN

"I CHOSE THE SWALLOWIN'"

ENDING INTERNSHIP AT LA COUNTY was like being released from the torture chamber of a prison, but having to stay on the prison grounds. The work would be more gratifying and intellectually demanding, but the hours would be just as long. I watched the poor saps arrive to fill our shoes as menial laborers, knowing I could focus on consulting, operating, and managing surgical patients.

On this, my first rotation as a second-year resident, I had the good fortune to be matched with Nick Givens. I'd be helping him with complicated elective and trauma cases. The cases I'd do as primary surgeon would be simpler, like appendectomies, until I gained additional knowledge and technical skill.

My beeper went off at 3:15 p.m. on one of our call days. I called the number, and it was Nick.

"Hey, meet me in the ER as soon as you can. They're bringing in a lady from an MVA [motor vehicle accident] who sounds pretty bad."

When I hit the ER, Nick was waiting. The paramedics were just rolling in with a young woman on a stretcher who appeared to be badly injured.

"This lady was in an MVA on the freeway and fell out of her car," said one of the paramedics. "Then a pickup truck ran her over." Our patient had tire marks across her abdomen, which was now swelling up. Nick asked me to place a chest tube (another procedure!), and we went straight to the operating room. There were massive injuries, and after five hours of surgery, our patient barely survived. She now looked like the Pillsbury Doughboy (or perhaps Doughgirl). I counted the number of tubes, drains, catheters, and IVs sticking out of her: 22 in all.

Back on 9200, there was a new consult for a guy on the jail ward who had ingested some rigid metal wires and had a tender belly. I put my initials next to the entry in the book and hurried up to the thirteenth floor.

"I'm here to see the guy who swallowed the wires," I declared.

"Oh, yeah, he's down the hall in room four," said the deputy. Up to this point, I had visited the jail ward only a few times, and on each occasion, the patients were in a holding area near the entry desk. I hadn't been into any inmate rooms, which I expected to be single rooms.

"This guy was brought over from the county jail," added the deputy. "The idiot was just released from this hospital about a month ago for the same damn thing."

I looked at the X-Rays: there were three long, thin objects lying horizontally in the patient's upper abdomen, about the thickness of sturdy wire. As I looked more carefully, I thought I could see some free air in the abdomen, indicating perforated bowel.

I dug through the chart for a few minutes. Sure enough, he had been admitted five weeks ago after swallowing a piece of coat hanger. He had required surgery to remove it from his stomach and had been discharged four weeks ago.

"Okay, where's his room?" I asked the deputy.

"Follow me," he said.

We walked down the hallway until the deputy stopped at a door. He drew his keys and unlocked the door, pushing it open widely.

"He's there on the right, bed two." I walked in, and the deputy closed the door behind me, saying, "Knock loudly on the door when you're finished." Then he locked the door.

I thought, "What the hell?" as I heard the dead bolt click and the deputy's footsteps fade away. I looked around the room. There were six convicts arrayed around the room in beds, none of them handcuffed or restrained in any way. They were lying sideways on one elbow, or leaned back with arms behind their heads, watching me. Most of them had no shirt on; they were wearing only hospital-issued loose pants with drawstrings. One guy had a huge tattoo of a skull on his chest and snakes on his arms. Another had tattoos covering most of his body. Two had shaved heads. None of them said a word. My next thought was, "I'm about to get beaten up and butt-raped, and by the time they find me, I'll be the next admission to 9200, if I'm still alive."

I decided to act as I did when I had to walk between the meth addicts outside the back door of the hospital last year: try to show no fear and push forward.

"Mr. Brunner?" I asked, looking at the guy in bed two. I walked over to him.

"Yeah, I'm Brunner," he said. I pulled the curtains around the bed for a little visual privacy, which made me feel so much safer. The other five guys lay in their beds listening.

"I'm Dr. Harch, one of the general surgeons here. They've asked me to see you because of the wires in your stomach."

"Okay."

"How did they get in there?"

"I swallowed them."

"When was that?

"Yesterday."

"Weren't you here a month ago for the same thing?"

"Yeah, but I only swallowed one last time. I swallowed three this time."

"Why do you keep swallowing these things?"

"It wasn't my fault; they made me do it."

"What do you mean?" I asked. "Who made you do it?"

"Doc, I'm one of the tattoo guys at the jail. We get hold of old coat hangers, bend 'em till they break, then sharpen 'em on the floor. We use 'em as needles to put tattoos on each other. But we ain't supposed to be usin' 'em. So, when I got caught, the guards said I had a choice: swallow 'em, get 'em shoved up my ass, or get an ass-whuppin'."

"Not very good choices," I admitted.

"No, cuz I already had a bad ass-whuppin' by those guys and didn't want another."

"I had a ass-whuppin' by 'em, too," chimed in one of the other inmates, loudly. "No fuckin' fun."

"And I didn't want 'em shoved up my ass," continued Brunner, ignoring the eavesdropper, "so I chose the swallowin'."

"I get it," I said. "I think I would choose the swallowin' too. Are you having any pain in your belly?"

"Yeah, right here," he said, pointing to a spot on the right side, about three inches below his ribs. I finished taking his history, and proceeded to his physical exam. He had a recently healed vertical midline incision on his abdomen. When I pushed gently on the spot he identified, he winced and jumped.

"Ooh, shit, Doc. That hurts."

"Sorry, man. I needed to find that out. Look, I'm pretty sure one of those tattooing wires has perforated your intestines. I'm afraid you'll have to go back to the operating room for us to remove the wires and sew up the hole."

"Okay, whatever. I kinda' knew this might happen, especially when it started hurtin'.""

I pulled the curtains back and looked at the other inmates. They stared back, several nodding their heads signifying their agreement, or approval, or I'm not sure what. They didn't seem the least interested in bothering me. I knocked on the door loudly and waited. After about a minute, the deputy unlocked the door and let me out. So, I reasoned, these guys would have about a minute with me before I got help. If I could call for help, that is.

What I didn't comprehend was that these jailbirds consider a trip to the hospital to be a vacation from the monotony and violence of prison. A medical problem was literally a "get out of jail free card." Maybe shoving six-inch pieces of coat hanger down your gizzard was a reasonable gamble, even if it meant surgery. They didn't want to mess it up by assaulting a doctor who had the power to prolong their vacation.

There was another reason why these guys didn't cause trouble on the jail ward of LA County-USC Medical Center. I would discover that unsettling truth on a future visit.

I went back to the consult book. There was a 44-year-old rule-out appy in the ER. Despite being repeatedly admonished by senior staff that a patient wasn't an appy or a gallbladder or a colon, we still used this shorthand to describe our patients. It was just quicker and easier. I headed downstairs.

I entered one of the ER examining rooms and asked, "Dennis Gerber?"

"That's me," replied a rough-looking, middle-aged guy with a beard and moustache. He was thick and muscular, and clearly in pain. After doing a history and physical exam, I recommended removing his appendix.

"One more thing," I said. "You mentioned you had a couple beers yesterday. Did you have any today?"

"No. I felt too sick."

"How many do you usually have each day?"

"I won't lie to you, Doc. I put away two six-packs each night after work. I'm a welder. I work hard and I drink hard. On the weekends, I drink beer and whiskey."

"Just to let you know," I said, "we'll have to watch you for alcohol withdrawal while you're in the hospital. You're gonna need an operation to remove this sick appendix, and that means no beer for a couple days. And you've already skipped today."

"Oh, don't worry. I'm fine without the booze."

Nick and I took Mr. Brunner to the OR and removed the wires, which had indeed perforated his bowel. I got to do the entire case. When we finished, I went directly to another room and removed Mr. Gerber's appendix. I was elated. This is what I came to LAC-USC to do: move from room to room doing surgery while someone else did all the grunt work!

The morning after a busy call day is important for several reasons. First, it's an opportunity to assess the chaotic battlefield you'd occupied the prior 24 hours: pick up the wounded, clear the bodies, collect the weapons, and see how many soldiers are fit to continue. Second, you can estimate what the new day will look like. Are there more operations to do? Is anyone seriously sick or dying?

We started in the ICU. We now had a name for our Jane Doe who'd fallen out of the car and gotten run over: Lena Vasquez. She looked terrible, but at least she was alive. Mr. Brunner, the needle-swallower, was recovering nicely, with a deputy sitting at his bedside. When we arrived at Mr. Gerber's bed, he was sweating, tremulous, and had a slightly wild look in his eye.

"Good morning, Mr. Gerber," I said.

"I'm not going!" shouted Mr. Gerber.

"Going where?" I asked.

"Where they're taking me," he replied, looking around the room suspiciously.

Nick was stroking his chin. "Let me see those vital signs." We handed him the sheets. "Hmmmm... heart rate about 120. Blood pressure up." He leaned toward me and whispered, "Is he a drinker?"

"Yeah, about two six-packs a day," I said. "None for about 36 hours now. I wrote for Librium for withdrawal."

"Hey, I know what you guys are planning, and I don't want any of it," accused Mr. Gerber.

"No one's planning anything," I reassured him. "We're just trying to get you better from your operation."

"What operation?" asked Mr. Gerber.

"The one to remove your sick appendix," I replied. Mr. Gerber said nothing, his eyes scanning the room.

"The problem with writing for Librium on the ward," said Nick, "is that the nurses are too busy to give it as frequently as it's needed. Then these guys get too far along in their withdrawal, and you can't catch up. That's why we use alcohol drips."

I was aware of this treatment. Ethyl alcohol (the pure form of what's found in most adult beverages) was mixed in IV fluids and poured straight into the patient's vein. It prevented withdrawal and could be slowly tapered down and stopped when the patient was stable. It was slow detoxification. But I didn't like it philosophically because it was treating an addiction with exactly the same drug that caused the addiction. In retrospect, my stance was a naïve and pointless objection to a very effective therapy.

"My suggestion," said Nick, "is to get the nurse to give him a stat dose of Librium to calm him down, and order an alcohol drip. You can catch up with us on rounds later." Nick walked off with the team.

I hurried to the nurses' station. There was only one nurse in sight. "Hey, Becky, could you do a big favor for me right now?"

"Sure. What do you need?"

"It's Mr. Gerber in bed five. He's going into withdrawal, and we need some Librium right now. Can you give him 50 mg IV? Then we need to start an alcohol drip. I'll write for both if you can get a dose in him now."

"Sure thing. I'll get right on it."

I sat down to write the orders. The Librium order was easy and quick. The alcohol order was more complicated, since I had used it only once or twice before, and reluctantly. I decided to call the pharmacy to double check the total dose of alcohol and the fluid in which to carry it. While I was speaking to the pharmacist, I heard a commotion down the hall. There was a loud male voice, then a high-pitched female voice which I recognized as Becky's. I dropped the phone and sprinted toward the voices. I saw Mr. Gerber run out of the room, tear off his hospital gown, and disappear, completely naked, into the stairway at the far end of the hallway. I ran into the room to check on Becky, who was holding Mr. Gerber's IV pole. There was a Foley catheter on the floor surrounded by some splatters of blood.

"He ripped out his IV and Foley," explained Becky, "and shoved me aside."

"Go call security and I'll try to catch him in the stairwell," I said. I ran down the hall and entered the stairwell. I assumed he went down, so I followed, taking two stairs at a time. I started imagining an NFL-style tackle of a naked, delirious, 40-year-old guy who was twice as strong as me, in a poorly lit stairwell. What the hell would I do then? After descending about two floors, I heard a door close far down the stairwell, and knew my chances of catching him were slim, especially because I would have no idea where he exited. I ran back up the stairs and onto the ward. Becky was on the phone with security.

"Yes," said Becky, "I don't think he'll be hard to find. He's naked and confused, and maybe violent. He could be anywhere. Try not to hurt him." She hung up the phone. "I'm sorry about this, Dr. Harch, but he just freaked out when I walked in with the Librium. Ripped everything out, pushed me out of the way, and ran. There wasn't anything I could do."

"I know," I said. "I hadn't seen him since surgery and didn't realize that he was already withdrawing."

"We didn't realize it either, or we'd have given him the Librium earlier."

"Let's just hope we can find him before he gets hurt...or hurts somebody else."

A few minutes later, the phone rang and Becky picked it up. "Yeah...yeah...good. Hold on. Dr. Harch, they got him. You talk to them."

"Dr. Harch," said a voice on the other end of the line, "this is officer Nance. We caught him running out the back door. It took four of us to subdue him. He's incredibly strong."

"Can you bring him up to the ICU on the ninth floor? I'll arrange for a bed and we'll get him sedated."

"No problem. See you in about five minutes."

After several minutes, there were loud voices in the hallway and the door opened. Three officers had poor Mr. Gerber in four-point hard restraints and were wrestling with him to keep his gurney from overturning. He was a little bruised and scraped up, but otherwise intact. I was worried about the sutures I'd placed a few hours ago and whether the escape and recapture had loosened any of them.

"I demand my fucking rights!" shouted Mr. Gerber. "I don't want you experimenting on me!" He tried to hit one of the officers, but the leather restraints prevented him from connecting. We needed to get an IV in him, but this seemed impossible.

"Cathy," I said to the nurse, "let's draw up 100 mg of Librium and give it IM [intramuscularly]. If we can knock him down a little, maybe we'll be able to start an IV and give him the alcohol drip."

"What are you talking about, you fuckhead?" screamed Mr. Gerber. "Let…me…go!"

We held him down and administered the sedative in his thigh. After more yelling and flailing around, he calmed down a bit and we started the IV. Soon the soothing alcohol was flowing into his system, and he became a docile little lamb. I turned to see Nick standing behind me.

"Exciting morning, huh?" asked Nick.

"Yeah, no kidding," I replied.

"Any new insights?"

"I better jump on these drinkers a little sooner. And I guess the alcohol drip is the best way to go."

"It's primitive, but it works every time. Sometimes it's just easier to go with tried and true. Then you just taper them down over a day or two. If you don't treat them early, some go into DTs and seize. Occasionally they die."

205

Mr. Gerber got better very quickly. We tapered and discontinued his alcohol drip, moved him out of the ICU, and advanced his diet. He went home in fewer than 72 hours.

Lena Vasquez, who we discovered had a husband and 7-year-old daughter, had been deteriorating for the past few days. She required a return to the OR, where multiple abscesses were found and drained. But she continued to decline, and she died about a week later. I never met her husband or daughter.

I was kind of depressed about losing Mrs. Vasquez and the effect her death must have had on her family. I called Lori.

"Hey, can I come over tonight?" I asked.

"What's your sleep-meter like?" she demanded.

"Uh…not too much the last few days. But I feel fine."

"The last time you drove over here, you fell asleep five times on the freeway and once at a stoplight." I wished I hadn't told her.

"I'll be alright."

"I'll drive over to the dorm."

"No. This place is too dangerous for you. I'll come there."

"I insist. You can meet me in the parking lot. I'll bring food."

I wondered how this relationship was possibly surviving. I was available once or twice a week, and was exhausted most of the time. Some of her friends didn't believe I existed. And the end of my training was years away. Surely she could find someone better.

Fortunately, the rest of Lori's life was full. She loved her work. She had lots of friends. She took dance classes frequently (mostly ballet), and spent time reading. Her freedom and independence were the keys to our part-time, but enduring relationship.

CHAPTER TWELVE

"TORE MY HEART OUT, BROTHER"

THERE ARE MANY REASONS I FIND IT HARD to believe in God, one of them being my experience on the pediatric surgery service. Patching up drunks and gangbangers is one thing; taking care of innocent, sick, traumatized babies and kids is quite another.

Adjacent to the 2,000-bed main hospital were two other medical facilities: the Women's Hospital and the Pediatrics Hospital, each with about 250-300 beds. Early in my second year of residency, I was assigned to cover the neonatal and pediatric services, respectively, in those two buildings, along with a fourth-year general surgery resident, Matt Reynolds. Matt was easy going, and I looked forward to working with him.

On the first day, Matt and I made rounds in the Pediatrics Hospital. Kids were crying in nearly every room. The din was unbearable. Were they in pain? Were they here without their parents?

"How do you stand this all day long?" I asked.

"After a few days, you won't even hear it," he said. "But what's worse is having to go over to the Women's Hospital each day to round on the FLKs."

"FLKs? What's that?"

"Funny-looking kids."

"What do you mean?"

"Oh, my God, you won't believe what's over there in the neonatal intensive care unit. Super-sick premies. Kids with weird genetic abnormalities. Right now, there's a really rare case of trisomy 13; the kid has only one eye in the middle of his forehead."

"No…you're kidding, right?"

"I shit you not. His nose looks like a little potato. Mouth is a little slit. All sorts of other abnormalities. He's not expected to live more than a few days."

"Are we gonna see that kid today?"

"Well, we don't have a good reason to see him. And the nurses don't want people just gawking at this baby; they're real protective. But we'll be right there seeing other kids, so we can maybe take a quick look."

"I didn't know anything like that even existed."

"Me either, until I saw him yesterday."

We crossed the parking lot, entered the Women's Hospital, and took the elevator to the Neonatal Intensive Care Unit (NICU). It was quiet and the lights were dimmed. The small ventilators were swishing, and monitors beeped in low tones. There were about 20 incubators, mostly occupied by tiny babies, all various shades of pink despite their various ethnicities. One nurse, hovering over an incubator, looked in our direction and glared, as if to say, "Intruders."

One of the pediatricians asked us to consult on a three-day-old baby, delivered three weeks premature to a heroin-addicted mother. She thought the baby might have an abdominal problem.

The tiny infant in the incubator was thin and very fragile looking. Her skin was translucent, revealing minute, branching veins everywhere. Her feet were blue. Her abdomen was swollen, unlike the rest of her shrunken body. She looked like a baby bird. Her eyes were shut and her hands were closed in tight little balls—balls about the size of marbles.

Matt put gloves on and gently examined the baby's abdomen. The baby drew her arms and legs up weakly, like a helpless, injured animal.

"This baby may have necrotizing enterocolitis," said Matt. "We'll have to get the chief of pediatric surgery in here to see her."

As we moved around the NICU visiting a few other babies, Matt subtly tilted his head and gestured with his eyes toward an incubator along the wall. I managed to wander over in that direction to get a glimpse of the trisomy 13 baby. Its face looked nonhuman…a little slit of an eye in the middle of its forehead…an odd-looking round nose that looked like it might fall off…and a mouth that was way too small for any baby. A nurse at an adjacent incubator saw me loitering there and scowled at me. I moved on.

The sight of this baby scared me. The parents carried it to term with high hopes, only to discover something they could never imagine. I knew this was a rare problem, but there were so many things that could go wrong with any baby that I feared having kids.

About five days later, after finishing my work at the Pediatrics Hospital, I walked up the hill to help cover call for the Thursday Service. When the elevator doors opened on the ninth floor, I was surprised to see the hallway was filled with gurneys—and it was only 6:30 p.m.

I was about to get started when the phone rang. The clerk picked it up and said, "Mmm-hmmm…mmm-hmmm. Right away." She put the phone down. "One a' you-all needs to go down to the ER and see a guy from a MVA with a buncha broken stuff."

"I got it," I said, and headed down.

Luis was 18 years old. He had been driving his car at about 70 miles an hour when he lost control and crashed into a cement abutment. The car was totaled. Luis had several broken bones, but didn't appear to have other major injuries, despite the magnitude of his traumatic event. I

211

wrote admitting orders, asked for more X-Rays, and called an ortho consult.

Later, Phil Conway and I were trying to organize the colossal mess on 9200. When we reached Luis's bed, the intern produced all the X-Rays that had been done. Yes, broken arm…broken leg. Then we looked at the chest X-Ray I'd reviewed more than two hours ago.

"Hey, Harch, did you see this chest X-Ray earlier?" asked Phil.

"Yeah, I thought it looked okay."

"What about this aortic arch? Don't you think it looks a little fuzzy, and maybe a little wide?"

I looked more carefully than when I was in a hurry in the ER. I got a hollow feeling in my gut.

"Yeah…shit…it does look a little abnormal." I looked at Phil. "He needs an angiogram ASAP, doesn't he?"

"It may be nothing, but we can't be sure," said Phil. He was worried about Luis having a ruptured aorta, one of the most feared injuries a car accident victim can sustain. The partially torn aorta can contain pressurized blood only so long; when it completely bursts, the ball game is over. I ran down to X-Ray to schedule an aortic angiogram. The X-Ray technician wasn't at the scheduling desk, so I walked into a back room and found him sitting in a chair, leaned over with his head on a counter, sleeping.

"Excuse me," I said.

"What?" he mumbled, without lifting his head.

"I need an emergency aortic angiogram," I blurted out.

"Come back later. I'm trying to get some sleep," he mumbled again.

"No, I'm not coming back later. I got a guy with a possible ruptured aorta, and you need to get up and get the goddamn study going now," I insisted.

"Alright, alright," he replied, slowly raising his head with an irritated look on his face. "You don't have to be such an asshole about it."

When I returned to 9200, Luis was resting comfortably in his bed; as comfortable as a guy could be with two broken bones. I was reassured by how stable he appeared.

When X-Ray called for Luis, I grabbed his chart and explained our plan to him.

"We're worried about the big blood vessel in your chest," I said. "We have to make sure it didn't get torn in the accident. If there's no tear, you can get your bones fixed and you'll be okay."

"What if there's a tear?" he asked.

"Then you'll need a pretty big surgery to fix it."

"Could I die?"

"Well…I think you're gonna be alright," I said, hoping to convince him and me. I didn't want to answer the question directly, since I'd missed the abnormality on chest X-Ray initially. It's really a bit shameful how much a doctor can know in situations like this and feel unable (or unwilling) to share it with the patient. Besides, what was the use of scaring him unnecessarily?

We wheeled into the angiogram suite. The staff radiologist, Sam Finney, was there with his residents and staff. They moved Luis onto the procedure gurney. I handed the chest X-Ray to Sam.

"I have to tell you that I didn't see anything on my first look at this film," I confessed.

"Hmmm…" said Sam. "I can see how you might miss this. But I have to agree that the mediastinum is a little abnormal. If I had to guess, I'd say it's gonna be negative. But I'm not sure." As Sam got started, I stood behind the protective viewing window so I wouldn't absorb any X-Rays. I could see Luis's face. "Everything okay, Luis?" I asked.

"Yeah," he said. His monitor showed about 80 heartbeats a minute.

"Blood pressure's 110 over 72," said the nurse.

Dr. Finney took the first X-Ray of the aorta. It was hard to make out details on the blurry fluoroscopy screen.

"What do you see?" I asked.

"Uh…doesn't look exactly right," he responded. "I think I need a shot of dye."

He squeezed the syringe, and we could see a flash of dye hit the aorta.

"What was that?" he asked, looking at the screen with alarm.

Just then, Luis's heart rate hit about 150, then precipitously dropped to 40. I looked at him, and he was unconscious, his head tilted to one side. One arm flopped off the table. I rushed out from behind the window.

"What happened?" I shouted.

"He may have ruptured," said Sam.

I looked at the monitor. Luis's heart rate was now about 10 per minute. I rammed my hand into his left groin and could find no pulse.

"Luis!" I yelled. No response. I checked for a carotid pulse. There was nothing. I ripped the drapes off his chest and started CPR.

"Get a crash cart!" I said. "Get me some epinephrine!" I looked at the heart monitor. It was already flatline, in less than 90 seconds. I'd seen a lot of people die, but I'd never seen a young person go from awake to having no electrical cardiac activity so quickly. I continued to do chest compressions.

"John," said Sam. "I think you should stop CPR. He's already emptied his entire blood volume into his left chest. There's no saving him."

I stepped back. I couldn't speak. Luis was greyish-white and just…gone. Gone in seconds. I looked around the room. Everyone just stood there, looking back at me.

"There's nothing you can do about this sort of thing," said Sam. "When the aorta pops, it's over. It's terrible. I'm sorry."

But I felt I could have done something, like recognizing the problem four hours ago and pushing for an immediate angiogram. I checked Luis's carotids again. Absolutely nothing. He was stone dead. I felt guilty…and inadequate. How could I possibly know enough about this job to avoid killing people on any day?

"Can I…help you…do anything?" I asked the nurse.

"No, I can handle it," she said. "You better talk to Dr. Conway and look for the family."

Back on 9200, I asked the clerk if any family members had shown up to visit Luis.

"No. No one yet," she said.

"Well, he just died in angio," I said. The clerk was stunned. "He ruptured his aorta. Can you try to find some family? It's best if I talk to them."

"Yeah, I'll look for them," she said.

"And where's Dr. Conway?" I asked.

"In the OR."

"Okay. Thanks."

I went up to the fifteenth floor, where Phil was exploring a gunshot to the abdomen who arrived while I was on the way to X-Ray.

"Phil," I said, despondently. He looked up. "The guy with the abnormal mediastinum just ruptured his aorta in angio and died." He was quiet. He could see that I was distraught, even though most of my face was covered by a mask.

He looked back down into the belly of his patient so he could continue to work. "I know you think it's your fault because of the delay. But if you'd seen it immediately, and called for an angio, it still would have been hours...and hours more to get a cardiac team in. Then a surgery with a very high mortality. And maybe the catheter ruptured the aorta."

"Yeah, but..." I started to say.

"We need to get everyone together in the next few days and go over the chest X-Ray signs of traumatic aortic injury. You're not the first one to miss this sort of thing."

"I gotta go look for the family," I said. I turned and left the OR.

I couldn't find any family, which, I'm ashamed to say, was a relief. Many of our patients were gang members or drug dealers or drug-takers or not living with a family. Sometimes it took days to locate a family, if we found them at all. I don't know who lost Luis that night, but I knew that I lost Luis. And I lost some of my confidence as well.

"You're not just tired," said Lori, as we sat down to eat dinner at her apartment. "You look stressed out."

"Well...I sort of killed a guy the other night."

"What are you talking about?"

I related the story about Luis. "And I was just standing over this dead kid, thinking it might have come out differently if I'd been smarter...better...something."

"Wait...you don't really think you killed a guy who ran his car into a cement wall at 70 miles an hour, do you?"

"Well, kind of. I mean, I contributed."

"C'mon. You just started your second year. You think you're supposed to know everything already?"

I sat quietly, thinking. "I need to know some things...already."

"Jesus, John. This is a twisted way to think. And they've got you thinking this way. You can't be expected to save everybody's ass every day. And under the conditions you work in? It's sick. It isn't healthy."

I was quiet again. "Yeah…I guess you're right."

I needed her perspective—badly.

A few nights later, I was back on general surgery call, this time with Billy. He was the junior resident on the Saturday Service. Most Saturdays were a test of your ability to keep pace with relentless human illness, depravity, and suffering.

"Hey, Billy," I said as I stepped onto 9200. He was writing some orders. "What are you up to?"

"Oh, my brother," he said. "It's good to see you. We're not too far behind, yet."

"What can I do?"

"I got a guy with a stab wound to the forearm who just arrived. He needs a workup."

I grabbed the chart on Jimmy Ray Richards. He was sitting upright in bed, naked from the waist up.

"Hi, Mr. Richards," I said to a guy a little older than me. "I'm Dr. Harch."

"Oh, no need to call me Mr. anything," he said. "My name's Jimmy Ray. That's what everyone calls me. Nice to meet you, doc." He stuck out his right hand and I shook it.

"So, what happened to you tonight?" I asked.

"I got stabbed in the arm over here," he said, pointing to his left forearm.

"Do you know who stabbed you?" I asked, breaking my rule.

"Oh, yeah," he said. "It was my wife."

I looked at the bandage on his forearm and I noticed another laceration, only partially healed, further up on his arm. Now it seemed this line of questioning was worth the extra time.

"What about this laceration?"

"My wife stabbed me there two weeks ago," he said unemotionally, as if he were giving his food order at the drive-up window.

"How about this scar on your abdomen?"

"My wife stabbed me in the belly a year ago."

"And this scar on your chest?"

"Wife got me in the heart at the same time as the belly." This sequence of replies was too much to ignore, even for a seasoned, second-year surgery resident like me.

"This marriage of yours...sounds kind of dangerous to your health," I suggested.

"I guess you could say that," he said. "But my wife is actually a very nice person...things just get kinda crazy around our place when we drink."

"I guess so," I agreed.

Billy and his senior resident got called to the ER for a 34-year-old man named Kit, who was wanted for murder. He got in a gunfight with police, shot one officer, and then escaped the scene in a car with his girlfriend in the passenger seat. The ensuing car chase reached 90 miles per hour, ending in a collision with a tree. The girlfriend was killed immediately, and Kit got very smashed up. Billy and his team took Kit to the OR to fix his injuries, then put him in the

ICU. Billy phoned to ask if I'd come babysit Kit, due to his very tenuous state and need for frequent adjustments to his ventilator and medications.

When I arrived in the ICU, I looked carefully at Kit. He was badly swollen, covered with lacerations, and he had tubes and hoses coming out of everywhere. Broken arms and legs were in splints. He was attached to a ventilator. A beefy, angry-looking cop sat at his bedside, since Kit was officially under arrest.

"He looks like shit," I said to Billy.

"He is shit," interjected the officer.

Billy gave the cop a dismissive look, turned to me, and said, "I'll give you an idea how hard this guy hit the tree," said Billy. "We dug some of his teeth out of his knee."

"Now that's a deceleration injury," I said, raising Kit's upper lip to see bare, bloody gums where teeth should have been.

"I gotta go," said Billy. "Do your best to keep him alive." The cop sneered. Billy ran out the door.

"Why are you guys putting so much effort into saving this scumball?" asked the police officer.

"Well, it's…" I started to respond.

"Why don't you just turn off some of these medicines and let the bastard die?" he snarled.

"Look," I said. "I don't know the whole story here. My job is to treat injured people to the best of my ability. The rest of it is up to you guys and the courts."

"If it was up to me, I'd pull his breathing tube out or just shoot him right now."

"We both know you can't do that, and you know I can't do anything to hurt him either, no matter what we think of him. So you might as well just guard him, and I'll do my job."

The nurse had been busy with medicines, IV machines, and vital signs. But she'd heard the entire conversation. She looked at the cop and said, "We've got enough to do around here. We don't need to be judge and jury too."

The cop sat there with his arms folded, looking resentful, but didn't bother us any further.

Down in the ER, Billy had received a mother and her two-year-old baby from the scene of another high-speed wreck. The ER docs were working on the baby, who had no blood pressure and no pulse. Mom had multiple broken bones, a head injury, a distended belly, and low blood pressure. As Billy and his senior resident rolled the mother out of the ER and straight to surgery, the ER docs were doing CPR on the baby.

Back in the ICU, I was losing my battle too. Kit's blood pressure continued to fall while I turned up his medications. His heart was giving out after all the blood loss, extensive surgery, and massive transfusion. Despite all my efforts, Kit slowly circled the drain and died.

"Turn off the monitor," I said. "We're done." I looked at the cop, who'd been watching carefully. He now had a satisfied look on his face.

As I walked toward 9200, I couldn't help thinking that the cop was right. This guy was wanted for murder; it's likely he did murder someone. He shoots a cop and endangers the public with the shootout. Then he drives away at 90 mph, further endangering the police and the public. I didn't feel bad about seeing him die. He was a scumbag. A real low-life. Then I stopped myself.

This isn't my job, to make these judgments, I thought. If I'm going to survive around here for four more years, I need to push this stuff out of my head, or it will drive me crazy. I just have to focus on being a surgeon, the best one I can.

Up in the OR, Billy and his team were working on the baby's mother, who had numerous injuries, including a ruptured liver. They did everything possible to save her, but she bled to death on the table. They were also informed that the baby had died in the ER.

Back on 9200, the clerk told me that Kit's wife, brother, and kids were outside the ICU waiting for information about Kit.

"His wife?" I asked, incredulously, recalling that Kit's girlfriend had died in the crash earlier today.

"Yes, his wife."

As I walked down the hall to meet Kit's family, I wished like hell I could avoid this discussion. I wasn't involved in the surgeries, didn't have much detail to give them, and hadn't met any member of this family during the evening. There had been no opportunity to prepare them for what was coming.

I hoped someone had broken the news to them, or at least informed them of how badly he was injured.

I could see a group of five people in the hallway waiting outside the ICU: a rough-looking woman in her early thirties, a late-twenties guy covered in tattoos, and some kids ranging from about 10 to 15.

The woman rushed up to me, grabbed my arm and asked, "Are you the surgeon?"

"I'm one of the surgeons," I said.

"How's Kit?" she asked, with big, pleading eyes. It was clear that no one had given her the news.

"You know that he got in a high-speed wreck tonight, right?" I asked.

"Yes," she said. Now she had a hold of my shirt sleeve.

"Well, he was very badly injured, and required major surgery…"

"But how is he now?" she pleaded.

"We brought him to the ICU in really bad shape…put him on a ventilator and gave him medicines to keep him alive…" They were all holding their breaths. "But he was too badly hurt…" I couldn't prolong the inevitable anymore. "He didn't make it. I'm sorry."

"No!" she screamed, and it echoed down the hallway. "It can't be! Why couldn't you save him?"

"We tried," I said. I wanted to say, "He was running from the cops at 90 miles an hour and hit a tree. His girlfriend got killed. His girlfriend, lady! We dug his teeth out of his knee." But I allowed myself to say only, "I'm sorry. Everyone did everything they could."

The kids were crying. She buried her face in the chest of the young man and sobbed.

"Kit's my brother," said the young man. "This is bullshit."

"I'm sorry. I wish I could give you better news."

"I want to see him," demanded the woman.

"Just a minute," I said. I went into the ICU. Fortunately, they hadn't bagged Kit up yet. The nurses said the two adults could come in.

My beeper went off. I was needed on the admitting ward. I opened the door to the ICU and motioned for the wife and brother to enter. After they passed me, I walked down the hall and could hear wailing behind me.

I finished the consults and helped Billy with pass-on rounds. We headed down to the cafeteria shortly afterwards.

"I heard you had to talk to Kit's family," said Billy.

"Yeah," I said.

"How bad was it?"

"Pretty bad."

"Thanks. It was a shitty thing to dump on you."

"I don't think you had much choice. I heard you lost the mom of the baby who died."

"Yeah, I'll have to give you the whole rundown on the case later. Really amazing learning case, despite the tragedy."

"So, a dead mom and baby?"

"Yeah, and they sent me, the most junior member of the operating team, to give the news to the family, right after they heard about the baby."

"No!"

"Yes."

"And how bad was that?"

"Tore my heart out, brother."

CHAPTER THIRTEEN

PENIS IN HIS POCKET

TOM HUNT WAS PARTWAY THROUGH his two-year fellowship in cardiac surgery. He was the interface between the attendings and the rest of us grunts down the ladder. That's how he saw it. He was impatient, condescending, and in charge of the chest surgery team.

Fortunately, his arrogance was offset by my flippant senior general surgery resident, Jacob Neuman. Neum, as we called him, was a short, comical Jewish guy with a big, bushy mustache. He spoke in short, staccato bursts of words. He reminded me of Groucho Marx. The rest of the team was comprised of me, two interns, and two medical students. This entourage made rounds every morning and evening. There was teaching, banter, and the excitement of being on a cardiac service. We generated a mountain of scut work each day, but Neum and I got to go to the OR on many days to participate in some fantastic cases.

"This is Isolde Corrales," said Tom on rounds my first day, gesturing to an attractive early middle-aged woman. "Hello, Isolde."

"Hello…all you good-looking…gentlemen," she replied, short of breath and with a heavy, Hispanic accent.

"Hello," we all chimed in together.

Neum leaned over and whispered to me, "She couldn't be talking to me."

"Isolde is a 35-year-old lady…" said Tom.

"Oh…so nice to be called…a lady," said Isolde, speaking between breaths.

"…from Argentina," continued Tom, a little annoyed at the interruption, "who has symptomatic mitral stenosis. She's scheduled for mitral valve replacement in a few days."

"Yes…I'm looking forward…to it," she said. "But…I'm scared."

"Me too," whispered Neum.

"Don't be scared," said Tom. "Surgery's going to go well, and you'll be able to breathe again."

"I'm holding you…to that," said Isolde. "I got lots of things…to do in my life."

Tom put his stethoscope on Isolde's upper back. "She's still wet. Give her 20 mg of Lasix IV now, and increase her PO dose to TID. Get a new chest X-Ray in the morning."

"Shall I put on…makeup…before…the new X-Ray?" she asked.

"Couldn't hoit," said Neum.

"If you wish, if you wish," said Tom, ignoring Neum and not even getting Isolde's joke. We moved to the next room.

"This is Mr. Treadwell," said Tom, waving to him. "He's now six days status post CABG, three days out of ICU. Chest tubes are out. How are you today?"

Mr. Treadwell was about 60 years old, moderately overweight, and he didn't look very happy. "OK, I guess," he replied.

"Temps?" asked Tom.

"99.4, 100.2, 99.8," said one intern.

"Chest X-Ray today?" asked Tom.

The intern produced it and handed it over.

"Hmmmm," said Tom, holding it up to the overhead fluorescent lights. "This fluffiness in the right lower lobe looks a little worse. How's the coughing going?"

"It hurts to cough," said Mr. Treadwell.

Tom scowled at the intern, as if to say, "Well, what have you done about this?"

"We've been working at it pretty hard," said the intern, "but he just can't cough up anything significant."

"Have you been up walking?" asked Tom.

"A little," said Mr. Treadwell.

"Mobilization has been difficult, to say the least," said the intern.

Tom turned to Neum and said, "Let's put in a cough tube. Otherwise he's gonna get a bad pneumonia and go downhill. And put him back on antibiotics." Tom walked out of the room.

When rounds ended, I pulled Neum aside. "What's a cough tube?" I asked.

"Well," said Neum, "you're not going to believe this, but when some of these post-ops won't cough and they're getting pneumonia…" he twisted the end of his mustache and narrowed his eyes, adding a German accent, "we have ways to make them cough, guaranteed. We insert a feeding tube through their cricothyroid membrane, sew it in place, and squirt saline in there three times a day."

"You're fuckin' kiddin' me," I said.

"No, I don't kid. I only joke. Didn't you know that LA County is, in reality, the new Auschwitz? Let's get the stuff together, and I'll show you how to put it in. Bring the interns. Go to the ICU and get Valium and lidocaine. I'll go tell him what we're gonna do."

I walked into the chest ICU. The nurse had her back to me and turned around when she heard me walk in. She was absolutely beautiful: 5-feet, 8-inches tall, blond, trim, about my age, wearing white nursey nylons with a seam down the back. I almost lost it.

"Can I help you?" she asked politely, looking at me with a pair of penetrating blue eyes.

229

"Hell, yes," I thought. But I said, "Uh…yes…I…I'm Dr. Harch, the new second-year resident on the service. Dr. Neuman and I need to do a procedure on a ward patient, and I'd like to get some Valium and lidocaine."

"Sure," she said sweetly, sensing my nervousness and trying to be nice. This exchange was nothing like speaking to Darla or Tiffany downstairs. She opened the medicine cabinet, selected the medications, and handed them to me.

"Thanks…Alexandra," I said, looking at her nametag.

"Alex," she said. "Who's the patient?"

"Mr. Treadwell. Thanks again." I left the ICU, worried that I might drool on myself if I stayed any longer.

Looking back, it is embarrassing to admit that we placed cough tubes in our patients. It would be considered barbarism today. At least we gave Mr. Treadwell a dose of Valium to make him sleepy, compliant, and to eradicate his memory of the procedure. When the Valium had taken effect, we injected some lidocaine just below his Adam's apple and inserted a tube directly into his trachea. Mr. Treadwell coughed hard, even though he was sedated. He immediately brought up a glob of green-tinged sputum. We sewed the tube in place and applied a bandage.

"Nicely done, Dr. Goebbels," said Neum. Mr. Treadwell coughed intermittently.

"That was pretty simple," I said.

"You guys," said Neum, looking toward the interns, "need to squirt some sterile saline down this tube a couple times a day, until he starts coughing on his own, which I predict will be damn soon. I'll do the first irrigation when he's awake, so it won't scare the hell out of you."

"I'll return the leftover Valium to ICU," I volunteered. When I entered the ICU, another nurse had returned from her break, so making small talk with Alex wouldn't be easy.

"Hey, Alex," I said. "Here's the leftover Valium." I handed it to her.

"Thanks," she said. "Most doctors just throw it away, then I have to chart that they used it all, which doesn't match with their procedure record."

"Well, we used 5 milligrams, so everything should agree." We chatted for a few minutes, then I had to go. "See you later," I said.

"Okay," she said.

About an hour later, Neum, the interns, and I returned to Mr. Treadwell's bedside.

"Mr. Treadwell," said Neum, "I'm gonna inject some fluid into your trachea to make you cough. You're not gonna like me one bit when I do it, and I apologize now, but we need to do this to keep you from getting pneumonia, which could seriously impact your recovery." Mr. Treadwell didn't say anything; he just watched Neum.

Neum drew up some saline into a syringe and injected it into the tube. Mr. Treadwell instantaneously took in a huge breath and coughed hard, his eyes bulging out. He let out a scream because of the pain in his chest incision, and coughed hard several more times. We could all hear the congestion coming loose deep in his chest, and he brought up blobs of thick, green sputum, which the interns scooped up in a specimen cup.

"Green is the color of success," said Neum.

"Damn!" wailed Mr. Treadwell, between coughs. He continued to cough, each time bringing up less and less sputum. Finally, he calmed down and the coughs slowed. Tears streamed down his flushed face. "That hurt like hell, Doc."

"Sorry 'bout that," said Neum. "Let's get those loogies to the lab, boys."

Late that afternoon, we were joined on rounds by one of the attending cardiac surgeons, Dr. Walton Bain. He had a practice at one of the nearby private hospitals, but also did cases a few days a month at LA County. He was mid-fifties, brusque, and overconfident, but entertaining in an odd way. He had a square jaw and bold, good looks.

"Hello, boys," he said with a gravelly voice and a slight southern twang. "Ready to make quick rounds with me? I still have rounds to do at Good Sam and I don't want to be late for dinner—my wife'll tan my hide."

"Let's go," said Tom.

Dr. Bain swaggered into a room with four patients and stopped at the bedside of Ethel Majors, an older white lady. "Hello, honey," said Dr. Bain.

"Hello, Doctor," said Ethel.

"Mrs. Majors is a 78-year-old woman," said Tom to the team, "who has been having increasing angina for the last six months. Her angiogram showed triple-vessel disease, and she's scheduled for a CABG tomorrow morning. Her estimated..."

"Oh, enough of that crap," interrupted Dr. Bain. "Do you have any questions for me, dear?" Tom looked wounded after being shut down that way.

"No, I think I'm ready."

"OK," said Dr. Bain. "You guys... get all the usual pre-op stuff together."

"I'll finish the consent," said Tom.

"Fine, fine," said Bain. "See you in the morning."

As we walked out of the room, I was right next to Dr. Bain. He turned his head in my direction and I said, "She looks great for a 78-year-old with coronary disease, don't you think?" Seventy-eight was ancient for anyone at LA County Hospital.

Dr. Bain paused, looked at me like I had a lot to learn, and said, "Oh, don't you worry, sonny boy. When I get done with her tomorrow, she'll look every damn minute of her 78 years, and more."

Early the next morning, Mrs. Majors was lying on the operating table as preparations were underway all around her. Tom was barking orders to anyone and everyone. Mrs. Majors slowly drifted off to sleep, and Dr. Bain sauntered in.

There is a subtle balancing act which occurs in any teaching hospital. The attending surgeon, whose name and reputation go on the record, supervises the entire process. The rest of the team, whose senior member (in this case, Tom) is trying to gain operative experience, does all the menial preoperative work and all the post-op care. The payback for that senior team member is to perform the bulk of the operation. Some attendings are comfortable with this arrangement, while others have difficulty trusting a subordinate or relinquishing the scalpel and scissors. One never knows what will happen in the OR until it's time to put knife to skin.

"Let's go, Tom," said Dr. Bain. He gave Tom access to the right side of the table. Tom made a big incision from the base of the neck to the abdomen, and cut through the bony sternum with an electric saw.

A rib spreader was inserted, and when it was cranked open, the heart could be seen, beating in all its glory, with the lungs expanding and contracting on either side as the ventilator oscillated. This was big, ass-kicking surgery, and we were excited to see the anatomy. Neum and I harvested a vein to use for the bypass, and Tom was given the freedom to complete the entire case.

"Not bad, Tom," said Dr. Bain, as he ripped off his gown and gloves. "Let's go talk to the family and get some coffee. Will you guys close the skin?"

"Sure thing," said Neum.

"Oh, one more thing," said Tom. "Meet us at 1 for the pulmonary conference." He and Bain sauntered out. Neum and I finished the closure, applied bandages, then accompanied Mrs. Majors to the ICU. Alexandra wasn't there, dammit.

"What happens at pulmonary conference, Neum?" I asked.

"Oh, the pulmonologists and cardiologists present their patients to us for our opinion. They think we're cowboys who want to operate on everyone, which is true, of course, so they try to protect the patients. Even if a patient obviously needs surgery, there's an under-the-radar battle to get to that conclusion."

At 12:50, we walked down to the conference room and sat in the back. A few minutes later, Dr. Bain and Tom entered and sat in the front row. About 20 pulmonary and cardiology residents and attendings filtered in and occupied the other seats.

"Thank you for coming today," said one of the pulmonary attendings. "Let's get started. Dr. Reich, will you present the first case?"

A resident took the podium. He presented the case of a 53-year-old smoker with a lung mass whose biopsies had been negative. A discussion ensued about whether the mass was cancer or not. Some recommended further testing; some wanted another biopsy.

Finally, the head pulmonologist said, "Dr. Bain, what do you think?" There was an uncomfortable pause.

"Well…" said Dr. Bain, with his drawl, "there's no way to rule out cancer no matter how many tests you do." He paused again. "And if that sumbitch was in my chest, I'd want it cut the hell out." He folded his arms on his chest and said nothing more.

"You tell 'em, John Wayne," whispered Neum.

There was some murmuring, and a few more opinions were floated, but the conversation waned. Everyone realized that Bain was basically right, even though they didn't want to admit it.

"We'll get the patient in for a surgical consult," conceded the pulmonary attending.

The second case was that of a 72-year-old man with a complicated heart problem. As the discussion veered toward asking if he might be a surgical candidate, some of the doctors debated whether an abnormal EKG might exclude him from surgery. Someone passed the EKG along the front row, and the question was posed, "Dr. Bain, what do you think of this EKG?"

There was another long pause.

"Well...askin' me to analyze this EKG..." said Bain slowly, "is like tryin' to teach a pig to whistle. It's a wasta yer time, and it annoys the pig." He handed the EKG to his right, folded his arms again, and looked straight ahead. I could almost hear people cringing. Neum pinched my arm hard under the desk as we tried not to laugh out loud.

Neum's, Tom's, and my beepers all went off together. One of the cardiologists had an emergency coronary angiogram to do. This circumstance required the cardiac team to set up the OR in preparation for a bypass in case anything went awry with the angiogram. Tom ordered us to get everything ready and went to get a late lunch.

By about 4 p.m., all our ward work was done, and we were assembled in the OR. Sterile trays of surgical instruments sat on shiny steel tables so they could be opened at a moment's notice. The heart-lung machine was outfitted with tubing and ready to go, with the perfusionist (technician) sitting next to it. The blood bank had units available for surgery. The scrub nurse gathered supplies while the circulating nurse filled out paperwork. With a half-dozen workaholics trapped in one room and nothing immediate to do, the banter began.

"What a pathetic life we lead," said Neum. "Here we are stuck at work again while the rest of the world is out there getting ready to head home, have dinner, and boff each other."

"My life isn't pathetic," said Tom. "I do everything I want, including that."

"Oh, please," said Neum. "You haven't had four daylight hours outside this place for months."

"I do my best work at night," said Tom. "I was the most eligible bachelor in my general surgery program before I came here."

The perfusionist snorted. Tom was standing in the middle of the room, leaning on the operating table. He was packed into surgical scrubs that were too small for his 40-pounds-overweight body. Two rolls of fat sat contentedly just above the tie strings on his pants, and the fabric was gathered too tightly around a smallish-looking bundle at his crotch.

"Dr. Casanova," goaded the perfusionist. "Who are you bedding these days?"

"Well, none of your business," said Tom, "but I can assure you that I'm quite busy in that department."

This was so preposterous that I had to suppress my laughter once again. But at my junior level, on a foreign service, with a fellow I didn't know, I wasn't about to join in the repartee.

"What's your plan when you get out of this hellhole?" asked Neum.

"I'll be a full-fledged cardiac surgeon," said Tom. "That'll give me lots of options and a big salary, unlike you guys who will only have a general surgery background."

"Can we wash your cars to make a little extra income?" asked Neum.

"Sure," said Tom. "I'll have Mercedes and Porsches."

"They won't let you through the gates of his community to wash the cars," said the perfusionist.

"And it'll be a good thing," said Tom, who didn't seem to notice or care that he was insulting nearly everyone in the room, and that everyone thought he was an ass. The conversation continued for quite a while across a range of topics, but always coming back to Tom. My thoughts wandered.

"Let's call the cath lab to see what's happening," said Neum. We got them on the line, and they reported that the angiogram was finished and there were no problems. This meant we were free.

"Let's get all this stuff put away," said Tom.

"Hey," said Neum. "We do have a slush machine here, full of beautiful, finely ground ice…"

"Yeah…" said Tom.

"And it's the end of the day," said Neum, smiling. "Most of our work is done…"

"Yeah…" said Tom again, smiling back at Neum about some inside joke.

"I hate to waste all that perfect ice," said Neum.

"Let's have a margarita party," said Tom.

I looked from Tom to Neum, then to the perfusionist, then to the nurses. Was this a prank on me?

Neum walked into an adjacent storage room and retrieved a bottle of margarita mix and a bottle of tequila that was nearly empty.

"Shit," said Neum. "Not much left over from the last party." He scooped up some ice in a steel irrigation pitcher, poured in the mix and the remaining tequila, and started handing it out in small cups. We all drank some.

"Hey, we need more tequila," said Neum. "C'mon, Harch, let's go."

"Where?" I asked.

"Across the street to the liquor store." Everybody burped up a dollar or two and we dashed out of the OR.

We took the elevator down to the basement and headed into the attending doctors' parking garage (larger, closer, and safer than the one we used). This led us down a long ramp and into the street. It was getting dark. We walked to the end of the block, turned left, and went about a hundred yards, stopping at a lighted crosswalk.

"Hey, man," said a derelict, appearing out of the darkness and surprising the shit out of me. "Do you guys have a couple bucks so I can get a bottle?"

"No, dude," said Neum. "We're in a hurry to get our own bottle."

The light changed, and we ran across the street to the liquor store. Just to the right of the doorway was another bum, lying on his side, shaking or seizing. He had a large pee-spot soaking his pants. There was foam coming out of his mouth.

"Shouldn't we do something for this guy?" I asked.

"Fuck, no!" said Neum. "We'll find three more just like him if we look very far. We're not even supposed to be here. We gotta just get our bottle and get the hell outta here. We'll call the ER and report a man down when we get back." We selected a bottle of tequila, paid for it, and hurried back to the OR. I called the ER to make the report, and we made more margaritas.

Late that evening, I was completing some chart work when I looked up and saw none other than Mr. Patel.

"Oh, hello, my good Dr. Harch," he said with his heavy East Indian accent. "How are you tonight?"

"I'm fine," I said. "How are you?"

"Very well, thank you."

As late as it was, I couldn't help myself. "What's the latest news around here?"

"Oh, you'll never believe it," he began.

"Try me," I replied.

"Well, last week, a 30-year-old man got high on PCP and stabbed his wife."

"That doesn't seem very unusual around here."

"You're right, but that's not all. The man disemboweled his baby."

"That's a bad story, even for you, Mr. Patel."

"Yes, it is. But the wife was brought in and survived after some surgery. Baby, however, lost most of her intestines and died."

"That's unfortunate."

"There's more. From another hospital across town."

"You mean you're collecting stories from other hospitals now?"

"Well, sometimes I talk to the police, and they tell me these things. Or nurses I know at other hospitals tell me."

"What did they tell you?"

"There is a young man who cut off his penis a year ago."

"Another penis story," I observed.

"Yes, and when he arrived at the hospital, he had the penis in his pocket."

"Nice."

"The doctors were able to sew it back on."

"That's good."

"Yes, but two days ago, he cut off his penis again."

"A really determined guy."

"Yes, but when they admitted him to the hospital, he said, 'Ha, ha...I fooled you this time...I flushed it down the toilet!" He gave me the big grin that followed all his grisly stories.

"You've certainly made my day brighter, Mr. Patel. Thank you."

Two days later, Isolde Corrales was taken to surgery. Although valve replacements can be tricky, and many things can go wrong, her surgery went well. She recovered quickly in ICU and was transferred to the floor. On her fifth day post-op, we stopped at her bedside.

"How are you today, Mrs. Corrales?" asked Tom.

"I'm a little nauseated," she said, now no longer short of breath.

"She's not eating much," reported one of the interns.

Neum sat on the edge of her bed and began palpating her abdomen. "Her lower belly's a little distended," he said. "And I think her uterus might be a little enlarged."

Tom was stroking his chin. "Mrs. Corrales, do you think you might be pregnant?"

She pondered the question for a moment. "Well, I'm not sure," she said, raising her eyebrows and focusing on Tom. "When I was asleep in that operating room, just exactly what did you boys do?"

The entire group erupted in laughter. As we exited her room, Neum whispered to me, "That was funny, but tell the intern to get a pregnancy test anyway, OK?"

CHAPTER FOURTEEN

"ANY OTHER QUESTIONS?"

APPROACHED MY STINT ON VASCULAR surgery with trepidation; my nemesis, Dr. Rollins, was the chief of the service. No matter how hard you prepared, you couldn't be ready for the incessant interrogating by Rollins. He would find what you didn't know and turn his laser focus on it. This was made easy by the fact that vascular surgery was a niche subspecialty of general surgery that required a more detailed physical exam and a knowledge of rare diseases.

"Mr. Forrest is a 49-year-old man," I said, standing in front of Dr. Rollins, "who developed a cold, painful foot two days ago." This was my ninth patient presentation on afternoon rounds. Rollins had chewed on me with every case. I defended myself adequately for a junior resident, even though I hadn't excelled.

I reviewed the possible causes for Mr. Forrest's complaints, including chronic atherosclerosis (fatty plaque in the artery), a diseased aorta, or a clot loosened from the heart and sent floating down to plug the leg artery.

"What else?" asked Rollins.

"Um…" He had me.

"I don't suppose you've heard of hypercoagulability."

"Yes, sir. I know it can afflict cancer patients."

"That's not what we're talking about here," he said, irritably. "What are the other causes of hypercoagulability?"

"I…I don't know, sir." This was esoteric enough that I hadn't come across it in my reading.

"Well, if you took your education as seriously as your desire to do another surgery, perhaps you'd know about this subject," he said.

"I'll read up on it, sir."

"Yes," said Rollins. "I expect that the next time we meet, you'll know something, anything, about hypercoagulable states." It was the end of rounds, so Dr. Rollins walked away without another word.

It was close to dinner time and I was starving. I headed down to the cafeteria and ran into Skip.

"Harch, you fool. Get over here," he said.

"You're a sight for sore eyes," I said. "I just came from vascular rounds with Rollins."

"Oh, you poor bastard. You probably need some Preparation H for your asshole."

"Yeah, it's burning."

"What did he get you on?"

"Well, lots of things, but hypercoagulable states was the big thing."

"I don't know shit about that. Glad it was you. You know, I hate that little prick. Every time he chops one of us down, he thinks he grows an inch. I'd like to strangle him with a dirty jockstrap."

"I'd love to see that. Hey, what are you up to tonight?"

"Cleaning up after call last night. I'm almost done."

"Get anything interesting?"

"Nah. Just the usual...fat gallbladders, people stabbed and shot by the Dudes, and a guy with a Red Delicious apple stuck up his butt."

When we finished eating, my beeper went off. It was 9200 calling; workups were piling up.

"Hey Skip," I said, getting up to go. "One more thing. Have you met that nurse up in the chest ICU named Alex?"

"Oh, yeah. She's finer than frog's hair. If I had the chance, I'd be up that like a rat up a drainpipe...but, of course, she wouldn't be interested in a prematurely balding, pointy-nosed lecher like me."

"You have such a way with words, Skip. Is she dating anyone?"

"Hell if I know. Did you and Lori break up?"

"I gotta go. See you later."

My first patient on 9200 was Miguel Padilla. He was 35 years old, and sent up from the ER for stab wounds.

"Hi, Mr. Padilla," I said. "How are you tonight?"

"Not so good," he replied.

"What happened to you?"

"Well, I guess I was in the wrong neighborhood. Some guys from another gang got pissed that I was there. They pushed me out of my wheelchair, beat me up, and stabbed me with an ice pick."

"Your wheelchair! Why are you in a wheelchair?"

"I had polio as a child, and I'm paraplegic. I'm also a heroin addict." Now that I looked at him more closely, I could see that he was quite short, fat, and was covered with tattoos. Several of the tattoos contained gang-related symbols. I was trying to imagine how he participated in gang activities from his wheelchair.

When I got around to examining him, I found 12 small holes scattered all over his body where the ice pick penetrated. The injuries could be serious if intestines, arteries, urinary tract, or brain had been hit (one of the holes was on his scalp). In this situation, he was lucky to be fat, since it provided some protection from superficial stabs. Finding no serious injuries on exam, I ordered a raft of X-Rays and tests, then dictated an admission note.

The chief resident on call with me that night was Reggie Carter, the only black upper-level general surgery resident in the program. He was a big, muscular guy, but soft-spoken and calm. Everyone liked him.

The phone rang. The clerk said, "Doctors, they're bringing in a 23-year-old male shot multiple times. CPR in progress."

"Call the OR and tell them we might be coming their way," said Reggie.

On the way downstairs, Reggie said to me, in a very matter-of-fact way, "I don't know how much more of this I can take. It's been nearly five years of nonstop carnage." This comment was hard to comprehend, because for me it was all rather exciting. If the violence had to happen, I wanted to see it.

"You're in the home stretch," I said. "You just have to make it a few more months."

"Yeah, but how many more young bodies do I have to send to the morgue?"

We walked into C-booth, but the patient hadn't arrived yet.

"Have any details?" Reggie asked the chief ER resident.

"Young, Hispanic guy shot execution style," he responded. "At least one gunshot wound to the head, one or two to the neck, two to the chest."

The doors to the loading dock flew open, and a big group of paramedics and cops rushed in with a guy on a gurney. They were pushing on his chest. Blood was everywhere.

247

"No blood pressure, but he's still got EKG activity," said one paramedic.

Reggie looked at the guy. There was a bullet hole in his forehead, and one near his left temple. Blood oozed out of both. He had one bullet hole in his neck with some active bleeding. His shirt had been cut off to reveal a bullet hole over his sternum and one in the center of his right chest near the nipple.

"He doesn't have much of a chance with these injuries," said Reggie with resignation, "but he's still alive and we have to give it a go. Get me a thoracotomy tray."

Reggie opened the guy's left chest quickly. The heart was, in fact, beating, but there was no blood pressure. Reggie clamped the aorta, and we were able to palpate a slight pulse in his neck. A lot of blood was coming from the heart, which had a hole in the right ventricle.

Reggie put a lap pad over the heart and applied pressure. The bleeding slowed.

"We can't repair this kind of damage here," said Reggie. "Stab wounds, maybe. Not gunshots. Let's try to get him up to the OR where we can enlarge this incision and have a chance to fix him."

We rushed upstairs and put on gowns without scrubbing. Reggie extended the incision across the sternum and over to the right chest. Blood now poured out of the heart. Reggie sutured the hole in the ventricle, but the bleeding continued from the back of the heart.

"The problem with gunshots to the heart is that there's always a hole in the back of the heart as well," said Reggie. "It's nearly impossible to fix before the patient exsanguinates."

Reggie was right, of course. In addition, the patient was bleeding from his head wounds and the neck wound. When we lifted the heart to get a look at the back of it, we saw a huge hole in the back of the right atrium, extending to the left atrium. All the patient's remaining blood (which wasn't much at this point), poured out. The heart contractions slowed and stopped.

Reggie looked across the table at me and said, "We're done here. Nothing more we can do." Reggie and I returned to 9200 in silence.

"Dr. Carter," asked the clerk, "can you speak to the family of your John Doe?"

"Yes," said Reggie. "Where are they?"

"Right over there by the elevator. They're Spanish speaking, and we have an interpreter."

Reggie and I, with a fair amount of blood on our greens, walked over to the distraught family, whose eyes were wide with trepidation.

"I'm Dr. Carter," said Reggie. The interpreter translated. "Tell them their son got shot…and we're sorry, but he died."

The interpreter translated only what Reggie said.

The blood drained from their faces, and they looked down at the floor. The loss was so sudden, so devastating, and so complete that they couldn't even cry. They looked at Reggie again. He shrugged his shoulders!

"Any other questions?" Reggie asked.

"*Hay preguntas?*" asked the interpreter.

The family members shook their heads slowly.

"Okay," said Reggie, and he turned around and went back to work.

I was dumbfounded. In an instant, I realized that making the cut here wasn't the challenge. Surviving the horrible conditions and long hours didn't seem so daunting. The real question was whether I'd have any empathy or compassion left after five soul-crushing years in this place.

"Let's go sit down in a private place so we can talk about what happened," I said to the interpreter. She translated, and we walked down the hall with the family.

In October of 1983, Lori and I were spending a rare, quiet Sunday afternoon together. Our casual conversation dwindled a little and then it was quiet.

"We need to talk about something," she said. This is a sentence that has always alarmed me when delivered from the lips of a girlfriend.

"Okay," I said cautiously.

"We've been dating for almost three years."

"Yeah…" I said, checking the dates in my head.

"And I know we've both been avoiding commitment, deliberately, and by agreement."

"Yeah."

"But, I want to have kids sometime…soon…maybe two. The time to do that is before the age of 35. But before I do that, I want to be married. And I think you'd make a great husband and a great dad. And this is all weird for me, but that's how I've been feeling lately."

"Oh…" I said, now more alarmed than ever.

"How do you feel about that?" she continued.

"Well, I have to admit that I'm a little shocked. I thought you didn't believe in marriage."

"I thought so, too. That was before I fell in love with you."

My mind was racing. Different thoughts and responses were swirling around. She was watching me carefully.

"I love you, too, Lori, but…I just don't think I'm ready. I've got three more years of this shit ahead of me, and…" My voice trailed off as I imagined the finality of marriage.

"I think the prospect of never having sex with anyone else but me scares the shit out of you." She set her jaw and waited for my response.

"No…that's not it. It's just that…" I stopped to think. I'd taken every hard course my high school had to offer. I crammed everything I could into four years of college while working two jobs during summer breaks. Med school was largely the same. Now I was racing through residency, putting in 15-20 hour days, sometimes longer. I felt I hadn't had time to live life. And, to be totally honest with myself, perhaps she was correct. After all, I was ogling every nice-looking woman in the hospital. And Alex, in the chest ICU…

"I just don't think I'm ready," I said.

"Then, if we're not moving forward, I think we should date other people."

251

This sounded ominous, and the possibility of losing Lori scared me, but deep inside I think some freedom is what I really wanted.

"Okay," I agreed.

"But before we sleep with anyone else, we should let each other know."

I nodded my head.

CHAPTER FIFTEEN

ALEXANDRA

RETURNING TO THE ALTERNATIVE REALITY of the burn ward meant two things to me: another month of hell, and probably the last time I'd have to work there.

"We've got a number of big burns on this service," said Mark Pearson, the outgoing resident. "And Zelinsky is preparing to torture each one to the very end. Get ready for a nasty month."

Just what I didn't want to hear. The very next day, we spent seven punishing hours in the OR excising and grafting a guy with an 80% burn (removing the burned skin and applying skin grafts). I had to battle with the insufferable Mrs. Santino.

"Could I get some more 4-0 nylon for these grafts?" I asked her.

"You are using too much suture," she said, in her halting, heavy accent.

"I'm instrument tying all the way down to the needle to make it go as far as I can," I said with exasperation.

"Still, you are using too much," she insisted.

I was dying to get up in her face and whisper, "Like a fucking bowling ball." But I held my tongue. Despite (or maybe because of) the long surgery, our patient died 48 hours later. We completed two more extensive surgeries that week and admitted some new burn patients.

The cases were piling up, and I had to do something to stop the madness. I decided to try a new approach on Tuesday afternoon, when the burn team was assembled to plan our upcoming surgeries.

"Good afternoon," I said. "The first case is Mr. Collins, who sustained a 56% burn in a house fire three days ago. His burns are mainly on his arms, back, and chest. I propose taking him to the OR tomorrow and…" I laid out a detailed plan to cut off the burned skin and graft him all in one day. Dr. Zelinsky nodded, added a few suggestions, and was satisfied.

"The second case is Mr. Watts, who has a 78% burn from an enclosed-space gas explosion. He's burned most everywhere, with areas of intact skin on his lower back, buttocks, and thighs. I suggest we take him to the OR two days from now and…" I gave a very complicated plan to fix him up all in one fell swoop. My intern looked at me like I was bonkers. This proposal would demand dozens of hours of work by him (and me). Dr. Zelinsky started to raise a few questions about the wisdom of trying to accomplish so much in one day.

"The third case is Mr. Lewis, who has a 90% burn from a gasoline explosion/suicide attempt. I know he's pretty sick, but I think we could get him stabilized in a few days and get him to the OR for a near-total excision." By now, Zelinsky thought I had no judgment, was crazy, or just wanted to get lots of cases under my belt (or perhaps all three). My intern was planning to kill me.

"Hold on, Dr. Harch," said Zelinsky. "I'm not sure these last two patients could withstand so much surgery. We have to be a little more cautious and methodical."

"Hallelujah!" I thought. "The power of reverse psychology!"

We did reduce the pace of our operating. Mr. Lewis was so sick that he was dead by the next morning.

I was still spending long hours on the burn ward. Lori and I continued to see each other, but less frequently. Given our agreement, I started dropping by the chest surgery ICU more often to flirt with Alex. I just couldn't help myself. I finally asked her out, but our schedules were so busy that all we could do was meet for a drink. The short evening was a little awkward, but enjoyable, so we planned a second date.

One morning, my beeper went off and the display told me to call Billy.

"Hey, what's up, man?" I asked.

"Can you get free on Saturday afternoon? We can get a game at a park on Fourth and Vermont. It's serious basketball. Percy can come, and I just met a brother who's the deputy district attorney for the city; he's a player."

"I'll try. I need it."

On Saturday, I went through some gyrations, but got free. We picked up Percy and headed out. Andy, the attorney, would meet us there.

"Billy, who is that babe you were talkin' to in the hallway?" asked Percy in the car. "She's fine."

"That's Tia. She's a friend." Billy was very reserved about any woman he knew or dated.

"Well if you aren't gonna hit on her, you gotta introduce me."

"What are you talkin' about, you fool? You got a live-in lady."

"I just want to get to know her...you know."

"Yeah," said Billy, rolling his eyes. "I know."

We arrived at the park. It was a seedy place. There was a full-length, aging, asphalt basketball court, with no nets on the hoops. A game was in process, and lots of guys were milling around on the grass. Some weren't dressed in basketball clothes, and they looked high on something. The game, however, was for real: fast play, occasional slam dunks, lots of yelling and arguing. I was the only white guy in the entire park. Andy joined us after about 10 minutes. He was slender and just over 6 feet. I was worried about our ability to compete with the athletes around us.

Billy approached a player on the sideline. "Hey, man, who's got next?" he asked.

"I do, with my boys," he said.

"And after that?" asked Billy.

"I think Bobby," pointing to a guy spinning a ball on his finger.

"Anyone else?"

"I think that's it, man."

We waited about 10 minutes for the game to end. The next team stepped up, shot some practice baskets, and soon the game was underway. After another 20 minutes, that game ended. The third team walked on. We were next in line.

Percy came over to me and said, "Hey, that dude over there just asked if I wanted to buy some heroin."

"Well, don't," I advised.

The game lasted 25 minutes and nearly ended in a fight. We walked onto the court and started shooting around, anticipating our game. Just then, some guy came running over from the other side of the park and yelled, "I got next!"

"No," said Billy. "We been waitin' an hour here for this game."

"I said it's my game!" the guy yelled.

"No fuckin' way!" shouted Percy, getting right up in the guy's face. "Where the hell were you an hour ago?"

"Right over there, nigger," he said. The two started pushing and shoving, and we jumped in to separate them. I worried about how many friends this guy had in the crowd, and if anyone had a weapon. After more arguing and lots of opinions from other bystanders, we relented and waited another game. We picked up our fifth player from the waiters and now had a full team. When the game ended, the interloper had lost. As he walked off the court, he said, "Your sorry-ass little group ain't gonna last five minutes in this kinda game anyway. And what's that skinny white boy doin' here in our park?"

"Back off, motherfucker," threatened Percy. The shoving nearly started again. There's no doubt in my mind that we never would have gotten in a game that day if Billy and Percy hadn't pushed things to the limit.

I assessed our competition. One guy was 6-5 and brawny; two leapers, about 6-2; and two shorter guys, one quick and the other lazy but a good shooter. They looked at us with amusement. To anyone watching (and to us, as well), the circumstances didn't appear encouraging.

They had the first possession, having won the prior game. Their lazy guard brought the ball up the court. Billy got in his face, immediately stole the ball, and scored a layup. On the second trip up the floor, they tossed it into the big guy, who put a spin move on Andy and went up for a shot. Andy jumped up like he was on a trampoline and swatted the ball out of bounds. Everyone on the sidelines hooted and howled. A couple guys shouted, "Take that!" and "Get that shit outta here!" and "Where'd that come from?"

They tossed it into the big guy again, he went up, and Andy stuffed him, badly. Percy grabbed the rebound, tossed it to Billy on the run, and we had a second layup. Billy stole the ball again, we passed it around, and I hit a 20-footer. It was 6-0. People gathered around the court to watch, wondering who we were. The other team scored a hoop, then Andy threw down a monster dunk, which elicited more hoots and hollers. When I hit my second outside shot, a guy yelled, "It's Larry Bird! Larry Bird!" I just grinned. We won the game by 10.

In the second game, two big guys tried to body Andy out of the middle, but Percy got in there and threw some big elbows, taking the pressure off Andy. We won that game, then the third and fourth games. The locals put together a stacked team and finally beat us. We discussed waiting around for another shot at regaining the court, but it was so crowded that it wasn't worth the wait. And we didn't want another confrontation. We departed feeling satisfied, suspecting we could return with a lot less resistance.

Miraculously, Alex and I found an evening that was open for both of us. We went to dinner and walked around town, and our conversation was more comfortable. When it got late, we ended up at her apartment. Conversation led to kissing, and soon we were in bed. But it required more coaxing from me than I had hoped. I left long before morning, juggling feelings of guilt and disappointment. I couldn't shake the sense that I'd done a disservice to Alex, Lori, and probably myself. Within a week, I was seeing Lori again.

"We need to talk," she said. It was that portentous phrase again, but I needed to talk as well. The outcome of the date with Alex was weighing on my mind.

"I've been seeing this guy...a DJ," she said, "and we're starting to get serious. And the next step is to start sleeping with him." I was surprised, but I shouldn't have been.

"Wait a minute," I said. "I have a confession to make. I've been out twice with this ICU nurse..."

"Did you sleep with her?"

"I did."

"I thought we agreed to tell one another before we did that." She was disappointed, but not angry, at least not outwardly.

"I know, I know...but one thing led to another...and it just happened. I'm sorry. But it made me realize what a great thing we have. And it made me realize that I don't want to lose you."

"You sure about that? Because this guy I'm seeing, he's a good person. I don't want to let him go if you're gonna look around some more."

"I'm sure." I took her hand. "I love you." This was a big declaration for me. "Can you forgive me?"

She looked at me while she thought about it. "Yes. I love you, too." We kissed, which I thought would be the end of things for the evening. In fact, I expected it would be a while before she forgave me and would feel like being intimate. But we continued, and had sex right there on the couch.

"Wow...that was great," I said.

"Well, it was makeup sex. Makeup sex is always great."

I let out a big sigh. "I guess we should get married."

"Jeez," she said. "That was a fuckin' romantic proposal."

CHAPTER SIXTEEN

A GUTSY GROUP

I WAS ELATED TO BE OFF THE BURN WARD, but had to step right into the busiest and wildest of the services, the Saturday Service. I told Lori that I might not see her much—or much of her—for an entire month. My senior resident was Marc Feinberg, whose reputation as the meanest resident in the program had only grown.

On the first day, the team gathered at 7 a.m.: Feinberg, two interns, four medical students, and me. After brief introductions, Feinberg took control.

"This is the last day we'll start so late," he said. "We'll start rounds at 6:30 on non-call days; 6 a.m. on call days. I expect you to see your patients prior to rounds. Any critical labs must be drawn before rounds, so they can be cooking in the lab. It doesn't matter how you split up the work, so long as it's done when I need it." He was all business. He wasn't watching any faces for reactions; he didn't care what anyone thought. The interns appeared sadly resigned to their fate. I expected the students to look scared and worried, but they were calm—even eager. Hmmm…

We started in the ICU. Our patient was a 42-year-old man who got run over by a bus while intoxicated. He had injuries to nearly every part of his body.

"Get CBC, blood cultures, SMAC panel, and new chest X-Ray," said Feinberg. "Change all his dressings. Put in a central line if needed. Roll him and check for bedsores."

This went on for an hour as we visited all 16 patients on the service. The students were taking notes, asking questions, and were marvelously engaged.

"Harch, get these guys organized," said Feinberg. "We got a gallbladder to do this morning. Meet me in the OR in an hour. And I want everyone in the clinic at 1." He marched off.

I decided that "good cop/bad cop" was my best bet with this service.

"Okay, we have a hard month ahead," I said to the group, "but we're all in this together. We can be miserable, or try to have a little fun." The students nodded their heads enthusiastically; the interns just listened. "You two," I said to the interns, "split up the patients and get going on this mountain of scut. I'll send these students to help you in a minute." The interns hustled off.

I looked at the students. They were all smiling.

"What's with you guys?" I asked. "You should be scared stiff."

"No," said one of them. "We're excited!"

"Excited?" I said incredulously. "You've been assigned to the meanest resident, and the stupidest junior resident," I said, pointing a finger at my chest. "And you do know that we're gonna get killed every time we're on call, right? I mean absolutely slaughtered."

"We didn't get assigned to this service," explained a second student. "We asked to be on the Saturday Service. We're friends, we love surgery, and we wanna see all the action."

"You're shittin' me!" I smiled. This was a gutsy group. Spending a month with them could be a kick, even if there was suffering ahead. "Okay, give me your names again."

"Ralph."

"Kate."

"Chris."

"Laura."

"Alright, Ralph, Kate, Chris, and Laura. I'll try to keep you out of trouble. Ask when you don't know and I'll try to answer. Each of you take four patients to learn about, and go help those interns."

At 9 o'clock, I met Feinberg at the scrub sink. "How's it goin'?" I asked.

"Okay," he said flatly, not even looking my way. I had to do something to loosen him up if we were going to spend a month together.

263

"Hey, Marc," I said, "What's red and has seven dents in it?" He shook his head and shrugged his shoulders.

"Snow White's cherry," I said. He smiled. I was encouraged.

"Okay…an older Swedish couple, Olle and Elsa, are talking. Olle says, 'Elsa, if I die, will you remarry?' She says, 'Yeah, probably.' 'Well, will you let your new husband wear my clothes?' 'Yeah, probably.' 'Drive my pickup?' 'Yeah, probably.' 'Well, Elsa, will you let him use my golf clubs?' 'No, Olle…he's left-handed.'" Marc chuckled. We walked into the OR and started gowning up.

"An elderly Jewish couple are in bed at 3 a.m. Saul goes to the toilet, pees, and leaves the lid up. Pearl goes into the bathroom, sits down in the dark, and gets stuck. A plumber is called, but when Saul lets him in, he remembers that Pearl is naked. He rushes over and puts his yarmulke on her crotch. The plumber looks the situation over and says, 'Saul, I think I can save your wife, but I think the rabbi's gone.'" Now Marc was laughing.

The case went well. Marc let me do some major parts of it. I told jokes at every opportunity.

Three days later, our call day came up. We "pre-rounded" at about 5:30, did rounds with Marc at 6, and met for pass-ons at 7. The admitting area was a mess, full of partially worked-up patients. The team split up to start the scut work.

Marc and I got our first case. Sydney was a street person who either never had much of a brain or had destroyed it with drugs. He was jaundiced, had a fever, and was found to have gallstones in his main bile duct. This was enough of an emergency to earn him a surgery that day.

Midday, I was asked to see a 25-year-old Mexican guy who was in the U.S. only two days and now had increasing abdominal pain, vomiting, and distension. When he couldn't stand it any longer, he came to the ER. An X-Ray showed numerous ovoid densities throughout his intestines, resulting in a bowel obstruction. This guy was a "mule." He had pure cocaine wrapped in condoms or plastic bags, which he'd swallowed in Mexico before crossing the border. He'd hoped to poop the bags out and collect his fee, until things got plugged up. Cops and DEA agents—alerted by doctors after the telltale X-Rays—were already swarming around the ER. We had to get him to the OR before one of the bags broke open and killed him.

The DEA agents came to the OR to watch us remove the drug bags, counting how many were on the X-Rays and how many we removed. Each bag could be worth tens of thousands of dollars, and strangely, a bag or two sometimes went missing when the doctors removed them…thus, the counting and documenting. The students loved seeing the whole process. Law enforcement personnel made me promise to testify in court if needed.

Around 6:30 p.m., we got a frantic call from an area of the ER that took care of low acuity complaints, such as coughs, flu, and urinary infections. I collared Ralph and Kate and rushed downstairs.

In the waiting area, a group of nurses and doctors were huddled over a young Hispanic guy on the floor. They were kneeling in his blood, and someone was applying pressure to his neck.

"What happened?" I asked.

A bystander blurted out, "He stabbed hisself in the neck. I seen him do it."

"I guess this guy's been waiting six hours to be seen for a sore throat," said a nurse. "He got tired of waiting, so he pulled a knife out of his pocket and stabbed himself in the neck."

"I think he just got moved to the front of the line," said Ralph.

I leaned in to check his neck. "Come off the pressure," I said to the nurse holding gauze on the wound. She slowly pulled her hand away. Blood started pulsating out of the wound, shooting about two feet. She rammed her hand back on his neck.

"Kate, call 9200 and have them send Dr. Feinberg to the OR," I said. I picked up the phone and called the fifteenth floor. "I have a red blanket...stab wound to the neck with arterial bleeding." Addressing the group around me, I said, "Get an IV in him and send off a type and cross."

We went directly to the OR. Marc and I explored the guy's neck and fixed a laceration in his carotid artery. Kate and Ralph got to scrub; they loved every minute of it.

"Great case, Marc," I said. "This dude would have bled to death, and we fixed him, just like that."

"Yeah, fun, huh?" said Marc. "See one, do one…"

"Teach one," I added.

When we got back to 9200, Jose, our intern, was admitting a Mr. Pruitt, who'd been seen by Marc as a consult earlier. He had a huge dildo stuck in his rectum and couldn't get it out. We put him up in stirrups in the admitting room. Marc got a vaginal speculum and looked in the guy's rectum. He grabbed the lower end of the rubber dildo with a sharp, toothed instrument and pulled. The dildo was too big to easily come back across the anal sphincter.

"Jose," said Marc. "Put pressure on Mr. Pruitt's abdomen and try to push this thing out." Jose got up on a stool and started pushing. The patient started groaning. Marc leaned back and pulled. Jose pushed some more. The patient groaned loudly. Marc pulled. Jose pushed. Push, groan, pull. We all watched. Other patients in the room were enjoying the entertainment, even though the curtains were pulled.

"Oh, God, doc!" exclaimed Mr. Pruitt. Suddenly, the resistance gave way with a sound like the release of a big suction cup. Marc Feinberg flew backward and landed on his butt about eight feet away from the gurney, with a huge, green dildo on the floor between his legs.

"Ohhhhhhhhhhhh, Jeeeeeesus, Dr. Feinberg," Mr. Pruitt sighed in relief. "Thanks. If I ever have a baby, I'm gonna name it after you." We all focused on the dildo; it was about 12 inches long and five inches in diameter. We sent Mr. Pruitt to the ward; the dildo went to pathology.

It took a while to recover our composure after that, but we had to keep working.

On Sunday morning, we began the long process of cleaning up. We were bone weary, but I thought we could still have some fun. I suggested to the students that every time Marc gave them an order, they should reply, "Sir, yes sir," as in boot camp. The first time they tried it, Marc cracked up. It went on all morning, as the scut list grew.

At one point, we stopped at the bed of Ruby, a 72-year-old black woman who had gastric ulcers. Marc sat on her bed and pulled her bedsheet down and her gown up to expose her abdomen, which he proceeded to examine. Ruby pulled the bedsheet down to her knees, exposing her crotch area. Marc pulled it back up. About 20 seconds later, she pulled it back down again.

"Now, Ruby," said Marc. "I'm trying to keep you modest. You wouldn't want the team to get the wrong idea, would you?"

"Are you kidding?" responded Ruby. "Rape would be fun at my age!" Amidst the laughter, Marc said he'd come back later to discuss his surgical plans for her.

Shortly thereafter, we reached Sydney's bed. He was the dull street person who had his gallbladder removed the day before, and we had placed a T-tube, or drain, in his main bile duct. Post-op, we carefully instructed him to leave all his drains alone, and we taped the hell out of them. Now we could see a big bile stain on his sheet. Jose pulled the sheet back to reveal that Sydney had ripped out his T-tube, his gallbladder drain, and his IV. He was working on his Foley catheter.

An exhausted Dr. Feinberg looked at Sydney and declared, "Sydney, you stupid piece of shit…you've pulled out your T-tube and now you have to go back to the OR." Sydney stared back at us with no apparent comprehension, and said nothing. Mark left the room without another word.

On Monday, we heard that our Journal Club for Tuesday afternoon (typically a didactic meeting to discuss journal articles about diseases) would instead be a special conference. Oddly, they assigned no reading. I ran into Skip in the hallway.

"Hey, Skip, what's this conference about?"

"Hell if I know, white boy," he said. "Something's up, though. I can feel it."

The conference, unlike the usual Journal Club, was to be held in the large lecture hall used for Grand Rounds. We were instructed to sit in a group down in front on the right. Nearly all the general surgery residents and interns were there, except those on call.

"Dr. Pearson," said Dr. O'Donnelly, "will you come up and present a few of your patients?" Mark Pearson was in my year and was the guy who passed the burn service on to me five weeks ago. He seemed to get his work done, but wasn't around much after hours or on weekends.

"Tell us about Mary Maguire," instructed Dr. O'Donnelly.

Pearson started presenting the case. They grilled him on the history, physical exam, labs, X-Rays, and hospital course.

He was missing a lot of facts. He guessed on some of the lab results. They sent interns out occasionally to retrieve test results that were in question. Many of the paper results didn't match the details Pearson provided. As the interrogation progressed, the rest of us slowly sank down into our seats and covered our faces. We were trying to become invisible, lest someone ask one of us to step up and present our patients.

They moved to the second and third and fourth cases. Rollins was especially brutal. It was painful to watch. Pearson was flailing around in the water, bleeding badly. An organized attack was clearly under way.

"Thank you, Dr. Pearson," said Dr. O'Donnelly. "Everyone is released to return to their services."

In the hallway, there was a lot of murmuring.

"What the hell was that about?" I asked Billy and Skip.

"That was a raping," said Skip.

"He's been dumping his work on his interns lately," said Billy. "One of 'em mentioned it to me recently."

The following day, Mark Pearson was gone. He just evaporated. They shuffled us around to cover his service, and we never saw him again. The rumor was that he'd been leaving the hospital early, work incomplete, and partying all over town.

The conference had been a clear warning: do your work, no matter how hard it is or how long it takes, or you'll be out. You are expendable. This message was disconcerting. The directors of the residency had such high standards that they were willing to release someone who wasn't fulfilling their expectations after nearly two years of their time and his invested. Who might be next?

It was a grinding month, made better by the energetic students and an evolving friendship with Marc Feinberg. He remained uncompromising about patient care, but warmed up to me and the rest of the team. One morning after we'd been on call, I made a ridiculous suggestion for our increasingly sassy students.

"Hey, when we finish getting all the scut assigned for the morning, the four of you should stand side by side and, in unison, smack your heels together, extend your right arm, and say, 'Heil Feinberg!' But don't do it in front of the patients." They embraced the idea enthusiastically.

When the moment came, they were all lined up and delivered the gesture. Marc Feinberg thought it was hilarious. The irony of giving a Nazi salute to a Jewish commander wasn't lost on him. The students looked for any opportunity to repeat it.

Finally, the crowning event happened a few days before we left the service. One of the big, shared ward rooms had two ladies in adjacent beds. One had just had her gallbladder removed three hours earlier. The other was scheduled to have her gallbladder out in the morning. The whole team entered the room.

"Well, Lucy, are you ready to have your gallbladder out tomorrow morning?" asked Marc.

"I think so," said Lucy.

"Any questions?" asked Marc.

"No."

We all walked to the next bed. The post-op patient was lying face-up, trying to cope with her severe pain. Gallbladder surgery in those days required a large incision through lots of muscle in the abdominal wall.

Marc put one foot up on the raised side rail of the bed, and rested his elbow on his knee.

"How are you, Mrs. Winston?" he asked.

"I'm really in a lot of pain," she replied.

"We'll get you some more medicine in a minute." He turned to Jose. "How are her vital signs?"

"Blood pressure and pulse are okay," said Jose. "Temps…"

Suddenly, the side rail release gave way, and the side rail swung down under the bed, removing the support for Marc's entire body weight. Because he was leaning forward, he had no choice but to fall forward. Instinctively, he put his hands out and landed squarely on Mrs. Winston's fresh incision.

Mrs. Winston let out a shriek. Marc removed himself from on top of her and stood up, shocked. I had to run to the doorway with my mouth covered to keep from exploding with laughter (not that this was necessarily funny, but Feinberg was always so efficient and businesslike that the scene was absurd and, therefore, funny to me). The students and interns were horrified.

"Oh, my God, I'm sorry, Mrs. Winston," said Marc. The patient was crying. "I'm sorry. The rails just gave way."

Then, in a little, faint voice from the next bed we heard Lucy ask, "Can I cancel my surgery, doctors?"

CHAPTER SEVENTEEN

SILLY AMERICANS

MY SECOND YEAR WAS WINDING down. I had a rotation or two to go, and the in-service exam was looming. Things were settled with Lori, and we were making wedding plans. As a bonus, I'd arranged to have my vacation month as the last rotation of the year.

I was describing these details to my oldest brother, Joe, on the phone. We had lived together in west Los Angeles for my final three years of medical school at UCLA. He was trained as an accountant but had transitioned to investment banking.

"John," he said, "I've been traveling all over the world the past two years doing bond deals. I've got a zillion airline miles that I'll never use. Why don't you take a big slug of miles and take Lori anywhere American Airlines flies?"

"Really? Are you serious?"

"Yes. It won't cost me anything."

"If you're sure, I'll take you up on it."

"Yeah, find out everywhere American goes and pick the coolest place."

Lori and I checked the American Airlines routes and a world map. We chose Fiji for our premature honeymoon: far away, tropical, exotic.

Back at the hospital, the weirdness continued. Craig Kelly had a consult for me.

"The ER has a nutcase who thought he was covered with bugs," he said. "He lit his bed on fire and jumped out a second-story window."

"Name?" I asked.

"I don't know. But he'll be easy to find. Young, black, Spanish-speaking. That means he's a Marielito."

"A what?"

"You know. One of the lunatics Castro sent us from his prisons a couple years ago. We're seeing them more and more."

In the late 1970s, Cuba had a serious economic downturn, and Cubans were trying to leave the country. Citizens started invading the embassies in Havana, seeking passports to South American countries. At one point, 10,000 asylum seekers had penetrated the walls of the Peruvian embassy and were squatting on grounds the size of a football field. Safety, food, and sanitation were dire concerns. To end the crisis, Castro announced that anyone who wished could leave the country, and a fleet of decrepit boats was assembled in Mariel Harbor. From April 1980 to October 1980, about 125,000 Cubans departed the harbor and made it to U.S. shores. Later it was discovered that approximately 3,000 of them had been released from Cuban prisons and mental health institutions. Lots of them joined gangs in America and were frequently the perpetrators and victims of serious trauma.

Fredo was out of control. He talked incessantly while he swatted at imaginary bugs. His back was broken (without paralysis), and he had a fractured femur, meaning he couldn't get up and run away. He had minor burns on his hands. His chest and arms were covered with thick scars. Later I discovered that some of these guys practiced religious rituals involving body scarring. I had to exclude chest and intra-abdominal injuries from his fall, and could expect to transfer him to ortho later.

That afternoon, I was called to the jail ward for a guy who was running from police after an assault. As he climbed over a wrought-iron fence, he punctured his thigh on a sharp metal rod. The jail ward doctors wanted us to rule out a vascular injury (damage to blood vessels).

When I walked into the admitting area on the jail ward, a wrestling match was already underway. The officers had removed the patient's handcuffs so the nurse could place an IV.

"Let me go!" yelled the patient. "I don't want an IV!" He tried to wrench free of the officers' restraining hands. I walked to the bedside to get a better look at him. One arm broke free, and he swung it in my direction. I leaned back a little, and the punch missed my face but glanced off my shoulder.

"Hey, no hitting!" yelled an officer, sternly. I started examining the thigh wound while the nurse continued working on the IV placement. The patient's arm got loose again and this time his punch caught the nurse on the side of her face. She reached up and put her hand on her face, stepping back.

"Everyone out of the room!" yelled an officer. Apparently, aggression would be tolerated only up to a point; that point was reached when a nurse was smacked. The medical staff started leaving, but I continued looking at his wound.

"I said, everyone out," repeated the officer, more sternly. I dutifully complied. The door shut behind me, leaving three officers with the patient. Standing in the hallway, all of us could hear the ensuing fight. Yelling, scuffling, muffled screams, metal instrument stands hitting the floor, a gurney slamming against the wall. It went on for a while. And then...

"Ahhhhh! You're breaking my arm." We could hear it clearly. "You're breaking my fucking arm!" Then it was quiet. The door opened.

"Okay," said one officer. "You can come back in."

When we entered, the guy lay on the gurney with hard restraints on his ankles and steel handcuffs connecting his wrists to the side rails. He was a mess: cuts on his face and arms, bruises everywhere, and an obviously broken arm. He was whimpering. Now I had a full trauma workup to do. I examined him, ordered a bunch of X-Rays, and called ortho for the arm. Later that day, we took him to the OR and removed his ruptured spleen. The ortho guys had to fix his arm. He ended up with a 10-day hospital stay. Now I understood why the jailbirds didn't dare assault me when I visited their communal rooms.

Billy's father was deteriorating, and his mom called and asked him to come home. Knowing the circumstances, Dr. O'Donnelly shuffled the residents around to cover Billy, who was rotating on pediatric surgery.

Billy did make it home in time to join the bedside vigil for several days until his father passed away. The funeral was held two days later, and within a couple of days, Billy was back amongst us, working his ass off. He didn't say much, but I knew he was really suffering.

Concern about the in-service exam was intensifying. About 25 of us gathered in a room to have our academic competence measured. The American Board of Surgery sent a monitor to ensure there was no cheating, either by the doctors or the residency program. Some of the topics were familiar, others were about tumors or diseases I'd never heard of. They curved the results to allow for the level of the test-takers, and I passed with a margin of safety. I was now free to take my fiancée to Fiji.

The flight from Los Angeles International Airport to Fiji was long: six hours to Hawaii, a three-hour stopover, and six hours to the island of Viti Levu. When they unloaded our bags onto the tarmac, I became apprehensive about a decision I'd made. I liked to smoke pot occasionally; it jacked me up to about twice my usual energy level and I liked the high. But my schedule rarely allowed me to use it, so vacation was my chance. I watched from the arrival area as the police walked their drug-sniffing dogs around the array of suitcases on the tarmac. I had wrapped a small amount of pot and a little pipe in a plastic bag, re-wrapped it five more times in plastic bags, inserted it into a sock, and placed it inside a shoe. The dogs reached our suitcases. I held my breath, trying to look relaxed, but my heart was pounding like a jackhammer. The dogs sniffed around and walked on. I casually adjusted my sunglasses and let out a long, slow breath. Who knows what would have happened if we'd been caught? Or rather, if I'd been caught?

A large, catamaran ferry took us to Castaway Island, about 30 minutes from Viti Levu. We were greeted by a mid-dle-aged Fijian woman who walked us to our thatched hut. On the way, I whispered something to Lori and disappeared. The woman noticed me walking off and asked, "Where is your husband going?"

"Oh, he wants to make sure our luggage gets off the water taxi."

She continued shuffling along in her flip-flops, in no hurry at all, shaking her head, and said in a singsong voice, "Silly Americans...worried about luggage..."

I confirmed that our luggage had been offloaded, and then found our hut, which was quaint and comfortable. We were jet lagged, but couldn't pass up a chance for an af-ternoon tryst. Afterward, as we lay naked sleeping on the bed, we were awakened by two maids just as they finished dropping off towels; they had snuck in while we were asleep and now slipped out the door giggling quietly, covering their mouths. We realized it was time to decelerate and stop worrying about anything on this remote, South Sea island.

The place was idyllic. We ate fresh fruit, vegetables, and fish, all grown or caught on site. We lounged, sunned, and enjoyed each other. There was no intrigue about our relationship or our future. It was marvelous.

On our third day there, I decided to try windsurfing. I'd been watching others for two days and figured I could do it without any lessons. After all, I had played football, basketball, tennis, Ping-Pong, handball, volleyball, baseball, and spent summers body-surfing. How hard could it be?

I rented the board and sail, and headed into the surf. It took me multiple tries, but I finally got upright and was riding along the water outside the waves for short distances. Lori watched for a while from the beach, then got bored and went back to her book. The wind started to pick up, and it became harder and harder to stand and keep the sail in check. I kept falling into the water, and each time it was more difficult to get back upright. After about 45 minutes, I looked toward the beach. It was no longer there! I was so far out in the ocean that Castaway Island was a little dot on the horizon. In fact, I was now closer to an adjacent island, which seemed deserted. I saw a guy in a tiny sailboat and waved to get his attention. He zipped by, and I didn't know if he'd seen me. There was no one else in sight.

Back on the beach, Lori looked up to discover that I wasn't visible. She stood up and scanned the ocean. No sign of me anywhere. Alarmed, she went to the rental shop and alerted them that her "husband" was missing.

By now, the wind had really whipped up. The waves were so high that I couldn't see the island at all now. I was getting cold. I began to envision a bad end to our early honeymoon.

In about 20 minutes, I heard an engine. A 20-foot skiff was approaching. I knelt on the board and waved my arms wildly. They pulled alongside and scooped me up. They were very kind, but I could imagine their conversation later: "We had to save another stupid American from the ocean today."

The last few days of our vacation were spent on the main island, in a big hotel with lots of amenities. In front of the hotel was a lagoon, with a bridge leading out to a restaurant on a little island. On our last night in Fiji, we enjoyed a late dinner there and were headed back to the hotel. The sun was setting and the moon could be seen low in the sky. It was a spectacular tropical evening. Halfway along the bridge, I stopped and got down on one knee.

"Lori, I didn't do it right the first time. I want to correct that now. I love you, and I want to spend the rest of my life with you. Will you marry me?"

"Absolutely…now stand up and kiss me."

CHAPTER EIGHTEEN

TOO MUCH PRESSURE?

RETURNING TO THE DREARY HALLS OF LA County-USC after 28 glorious days off was almost unbearable. The third year meant more independence, but I was too junior to run a major service. Still, the daily banquet of wild cases challenged my abilities and offered needed operating experience.

The nurses had put an attractive, 28-year-old woman into the female room on 9200 for evaluation of abdominal pain. My intern, Aaron Zimmerman, entered the room and completed his exam. The patient stated she needed to urinate, so Aaron got a plastic urinal from the cabinet. As he walked back to the bed, a nurse stopped him and said, "Doctor, you don't give a woman a urinal to void in."

From behind the curtain, in a deep, husky voice, the patient chimed in, "He knows what he's doin', darlin.'"

Aaron was a fantastic intern. He was quiet, unassuming, and diligent. He arrived early each morning and completed his work efficiently. He could draw blood from or get an IV into anyone. You could depend on him unconditionally.

About midday, we got a stat call from the sixth floor. The details weren't initially available to us, but it was later revealed that a 21-year-old woman had been admitted after an overdose/suicide attempt. She was only partially conscious at first, but after waking up, was placed in a bed on a medicine ward. Shortly thereafter, a nurse witnessed her trying to strangle herself with the bedsheets. She was placed in hard restraints and a psych consult was called. The psych resident spent some time interviewing her, after which the resident put a note in the chart stating that the patient was no longer a threat to herself, and recommended removing the hard restraints. The resident was gone no more than a few minutes when the patient, still in hard restraints, scooted her bed over to the window (by jerking her body sideways, violently and repeatedly), leaned over, and broke the window with her head. With even more effort, she reached one arm out far enough to grab a shard of glass and slit her own throat.

Aaron and I raced down the stairs and arrived on a scene of pandemonium. There was blood everywhere. Three nurses and one medicine resident were trying to stop the bleeding from the patient's neck, but applying pressure caused the patient to have trouble breathing. Each time the patient inhaled, blood and air entered her trachea, causing her to cough, and blood would be sprayed around the room.

"Get us a crash cart," I shouted. "We need to control her airway. And we need a working IV."

"I'll handle the IV," said Aaron calmly. "Just focus on her airway." He popped a new IV in her in seconds. We sedated her, paralyzed her, and I inserted an endotracheal tube down her throat and into the injured trachea. With the tube in place, we could control the bleeding from her neck without compressing her airway.

"Aaron," I said, "call the OR and get us a room. Get hold of Dr. Neuman…we'll need help. And call the blood bank… tell them to be ready with some O-negative blood. I'll stay here and control the bleeding and the airway. Got all that?"

"Yeah," he said. "And we need RT, too, right?"

"Good thinking," I responded, pleased that he thought of calling respiratory therapy. Off he went.

When Neum, Aaron, and I got the patient in the OR, we discovered that she had nearly cut her trachea in half and lacerated one jugular vein, but spared her carotid arteries. We repaired everything and tucked her into the ICU, making sure her restraints were very secure.

"Hey, Aaron," I said, "thanks for all your help in that fire drill."

"No problem. That's what I'm here for."

"You're pretty cool and composed for a brand-new intern. And how did you get so good at IVs already?"

"Oh, I've had a lot of practice...as a med student."

"Amazing. Anyway, good to have you on the team."

"Thanks. Nice to be here."

A few days later, the residents were asked to attend another "special conference" in place of Journal Club. Each of us worried that we might be the one to get grilled. Soon we were assembled, and there was perfect silence.

"Dr. Lyle, would you come forward and present a few of your patients?" asked Dr. O'Donnelly. Dennis Lyle was a nice enough guy, but was known amongst us as a corner cutter. Coincidentally, he was on the same service with Mark Pearson when Mark was dismissed from the residency the prior year.

The conference was a replay of Mark's harrowing interrogation: uncertainty about details, confusion, stammering, guessing on lab results. The staff doctors were aggressive and persistent, and it didn't take long. Their prey was taken down in short order. We were released to return to our services.

Guess what happened to Dennis? In the first month of his fourth year of a five-year residency, he was dismissed. It was another unambiguous message to all who remained.

Lori and her mother, Pat, were making wedding plans. We'd already set the date, which had to be during my vacation month next year. But where would we get married? How many guests? How many bridesmaids? What color would the dresses be? Who would be the maid of honor? What color flowers, and what type? I didn't give a damn about any of it, except for a few details.

"What's your feeling about where the ceremony takes place?" asked Lori.

"Not a church," I said. "Can we get away with that, with all three parents being Catholic?"

"It's our wedding."

"Yeah, but you said your dad's paying for it. And I don't want to piss everyone off."

"I don't wanna step foot in a church, either, no matter who gets pissed off. I jettisoned Catholic dogma long ago. My parents know it, and they'll be fine with our decision."

"Well, good. Another thing we agree on."

"What about the ceremony? Who are we gonna get to do it?"

"I have no idea. But I don't want any mention of God in it. Who would do it under those constraints?"

"The only one I can think of is my brother-in-law, Larry. He might do it the way we want." Larry was a Methodist minister. He lived in Pennsylvania with Lori's sister. "I'll ask him. And we can write the vows and all that ourselves."

"I think it should be a short ceremony," I said. "Very short...as in, 'Do you want her, and do you want him? Okay, done.'"

"Well, we might have to have a few more lines than that."

"Fine. You're the editor. But really, I just have one significant request."

"What's that?"

"A hosted bar. I don't want anyone at our wedding having to pull money out of their pocket to get a drink. And I'm happy to pay for it."

"Honestly, I don't think my dad will have any problem with that, and you won't have to pay."

"Well, just so we're clear: I'm willing to pay for it. All the rest of it, you and your mom can decide."

Billy was rotating through the Sunday Service two months later. He had Aaron Zimmerman as his intern. Billy stopped me in the hallway one day.

"Have you had Aaron on your service yet?" he asked.

"Yeah, in July, on the Wednesday Service," I said.

"Have you ever had a better intern?"

"No. He's the best. Comes early, stays late, gets everything done quickly. Very knowledgeable. But keeps to himself."

"Yeah, that's exactly my experience, too. He'll be a great resident and surgeon."

A week later, Billy was about to start rounds, but Aaron was nowhere in sight. Billy beeped him. No answer. He beeped again. Still no answer. He called Aaron's dorm room, with no response. He checked the ICU and the wards. No Aaron. Now he was worried.

Billy called Dr. O'Donnelly, who obtained the master key to the dorm and hurried over there with Nick Givens, both with rising apprehension. When they opened the locked dorm room, Aaron was facedown on his bed, motionless.

They rushed in and turned him over, but recognized he'd been dead for hours. They were devastated.

Nick opened the top drawer of the bureau next to Aaron's bed. It was stuffed with vials and packages of prescription drugs, needles, and syringes. The second drawer had boxes of pills. The third drawer was full of various street drugs. The trash can next to the bed had discarded needles and syringes, and vials of drugs that appeared to have come from the operating room.

The ICU nurses reported that they had awakened Aaron several times throughout the night with questions. It was deduced that after each call, he likely took a larger dose of drugs to get back to sleep. The last dose, or the combination of drugs, must have been too much.

With some further detective work, it was discovered that Aaron had grappled with a serious drug problem since high school. He'd managed to excel in college, gain admission to medical school and subsequently our surgical residency, all while consuming a cornucopia of drugs. His ability to perform at such a high level was astonishing. How could we have missed it?

Other clues began to surface. No one ever made much of the fact that Aaron always wore long-sleeve T-shirts under his surgical greens, even on hot days. Now we understood that Aaron was covering up needle tracks on his forearms. Billy and I asked the anesthesia residents, off the record, if they ever saw Aaron stealing drugs in the OR.

"Don't repeat this, but Aaron was always hanging around the drug carts after surgery," said one anesthesia resident. "We suspected that he might be stealing the leftovers."

"Why didn't you say something?" we asked.

"I dunno. Didn't want to get mixed up in it." The other possible reason is that some of the anesthesia residents had their own troubles with abuse of easily available narcotics. This is a constant danger in the specialty of anesthesia, where drug abuse ends many a career.

Aaron's death hit the residency directors and the residents hard. Everyone silently implicated the pressure, the hours, the criticism in conferences; but no one discussed it openly. It seemed that our senior staff went easier on us for a few months, but the workload didn't change; there was no mechanism to achieve that. In fact, we had lost an intern and a fourth-year resident in a matter of two months, following the loss of Scott Siebert and Mark Pearson the prior year. We did add a resident to my year (to replace Pearson), but we remained seriously shorthanded on many of the services.

Aaron's parents scheduled his memorial the following Saturday. Dr. O'Donnelly strongly urged everyone to attend, even though our weekend free time was extremely precious. Two entire rows of the memorial hall were filled with young residents and senior doctors in coats and ties, much in the way police officers show up en masse to honor a fallen comrade. Aaron's brother spoke for some time, tearfully describing what a loved and accomplished brother Aaron had been. It was tough to endure.

Next, Aaron's mother stepped to the microphone. She reviewed Aaron's life and how he had enriched her existence in so many ways. Partway through her comments, she completely lost her composure and began sobbing uncontrollably. With a voice distorted to a high pitch because of the intermingled crying, she begged to know how this could have happened. No one knew if she was asking God, her family, or the gathering of doctors. She seemed to imply that someone was responsible. We sat there stone faced as tears streamed down our faces. None of us looked at the others. It was agonizing.

CHAPTER NINETEEN

OPERATION COVER-UP

THE PALL OF AARON ZIMMERMAN'S death hung over us for some time. But the grueling schedule provided an enveloping numbness that eventually allowed us to stumble forward as if Aaron had never existed.

"Dr. Harch, could you call the ER?" asked the clerk. "They're sending up a stab wound who may need some extra attention."

I rang the ER. "Dr. Harch, from surgery admitting. You got somethin' for me?"

"Hold for Dr. Lee."

"Hey, John," said Ken Lee. "I'm sending up a 23-year-old black guy who smoked PCP and stabbed his mother and father a couple hours ago, then stabbed himself in the upper abdomen. Problem is, the guy's skinny and he already got out of hard restraints once. He ran out the ER doors, and the cops recaptured him in the parking lot. He's tied up better now, and I'd like to send him up."

"Okay," I said. "The jail ward might be a better place for him, Ken, but since he probably needs to go to surgery, you might as well send him here."

A few minutes later, the guy rolled out of the elevator accompanied by a cop. He was about 5-feet, 7-inches tall, 135 pounds, wild eyed, and tightly strapped down with hard leather restraints.

"You'll pay with everlasting damnation in hell!" he shouted. "I command you to release me! I am the devil! I am Superman!"

"Put Superman in the middle bed in the male room so we can see him from the hallway," I whispered to the nurse. The nurse and cop rolled the bed into our communal room, which had patients in all five of the other beds. Those patients watched nervously as the entourage rolled in.

The cop pulled me aside. "Jamal here stabbed his parents this morning. His dad is dead. Mom was at Harbor General having surgery last I heard, but she's in bad shape. We finally got him tied up real good."

I looked at Jamal. I was grateful that the ER personnel had gotten an IV, Foley catheter, and NG tube in him. It must have been a real battle. He was naked except for a white sheet tossed over him.

"Hi, Jamal," I said.

"We all come from the heavenly sperm bank," he stated. "We are God subjects with no fear. You shall pass through the eye of a needle."

"Jamal, do you have any medical problems?" I asked.

"You are not the peacemaker, and you have no right to question me," he responded.

I began my exam, looking for injuries to his head, neck, and chest. I listened to his lungs and heart. He watched me very carefully but was quiet. I pulled the sheet down to his waist. There was a one-inch gash in the skin of his upper abdomen, with a small wad of yellow omentum (fatty tissue that covers the intestines) hanging out of it.

"Let me see your back," I said softly.

He surprised me by rolling up as much as he could, given the restraints; no visible injuries. I checked his arms and legs. I did check his genitals, but decided not to attempt a rectal exam. This I thought I could justify, under the circumstances.

"Do you have any allergies to medicines?" I asked.

He glowered at me for about five, long, uncomfortable seconds. "No."

"Jamal," I said, "the tissue hanging out of this wound suggests that you have a good chance of intestinal injury. We need to take you to surgery and fix whatever's damaged. Do you understand that?"

"Kings direct warriors," he said, with a cold, unemotional stare, "which are four thousand strong. I deny anyone's existence…here or anywhere."

"I'll come back later and talk with you some more," I said, as I walked away to write orders and dictate a note.

"I hear your thoughts!" he yelled. "You are not supreme! Give me back my mind, which you stole!" The cop just watched. The other patients were scared.

I added Jamal to our operative list for the day. Since he was frankly psychotic, there was no way to consent him for surgery. Two doctors would have to sign the consent form saying that he lacked the capacity for decision making but required emergency surgery. Physically getting him to the operating room might be problematic; we'd sedate him if necessary.

I was dictating Jamal's note when I heard an alarmed shout from the male room. I ran to the doorway. Jamal had gotten out of his hard restraints again and was standing in the middle of the room naked. He'd ripped out his NG tube and thrown it on the floor. He had separated his IV tubing from the IV catheter in his arm and blood was running down his forearm onto the floor. His Foley catheter was hanging out of his penis and had been disconnected from the tubing and collection bag. Urine dripped onto the floor.

I looked around the room. The cop was nowhere to be seen! The other patients were petrified.

"Jamal, I need you to get back in bed," I said, calmly but firmly.

"I have plans," he said.

"Yeah, but you're injured and you need surgery."

"My job isn't complete. I need to kill my grandparents and stab the cobra in my stomach."

"Jamal…I want you to get back in bed."

"No. I'm leaving for Long Beach." The other patients waited anxiously to see what would happen. There was absolute silence for a few moments. It seemed like a standoff at high noon in a western movie. A nurse stood in the hallway behind me watching. I heard the clerk calling security.

Time seemed to slow way down while I sized up Jamal. He was smaller than me, but crazier (I was pretty sure). He was skinny, but sinewy and likely strong. He was on PCP and had already killed one person that day, perhaps two. I had innocent, sick, and injured people all around me, and medical staff out in the hallway. Could I risk going on the floor with this guy? Would he bite me? Gouge my eyes? And where the hell were the police?

Then I thought, "Subduing this guy is not my job. It's just too risky. And stupid. If he wants to leave, he's risking his life, not mine or anyone else's. I don't think there's a chance in hell he'll make it to Long Beach." I stepped away from the doorway and swept my arm toward the hall, inviting him to leave. He took several steps, ripped the sheet off some poor guy waiting to have his appendix taken out, and walked into the hallway. He wrapped the sheet around himself, got in the elevator, and disappeared.

I ran to the phone and got security on the line. "You better catch this guy," I said. "He's on his way to kill his grandparents. And why the hell did the cop guarding him leave? He'd already wiggled out of his restraints once today." I was really pissed off.

I figured that Jamal would be seen walking or running around the first floor, naked except for a sheet, and would be returned to us in minutes. Instead, he somehow found a hospital gown, made it to the parking lot, and hotwired a car. He drove to Long Beach to search for his grandparents. Friends in the neighborhood saw him walking around in a hospital gown and called the police. He was arrested again and brought back to us several hours later.

"You cannot leave him here without an officer at his bedside every second," I said angrily, to the newest cop. "You guys put all of us in danger earlier today. What if he'd reached into one of these drawers and pulled out a scalpel?"

"Yeah...sorry...I don't know what happened," the cop replied.

We did get Jamal to the OR later that night. He had no significant injuries in his abdomen. We took the appendix out of the guy whose bedsheet was stolen by Jamal. There was no sleep that night.

Midmorning, I was sitting in a big, soft easy chair in the residents' library, trying to recover from the long night. Skip was on the couch nearby, also recovering from his night on call. I had just finished telling him about Jamal.

"Have you ever noticed," began Skip, "that on mornings after being up all night working…you get a big woody that won't go away?"

"Yeah…you're right. I got one right now."

"I call it a 'post-call boner,'" he said.

"A PCB?"

"Yes. A toxic PCB, because it won't go away."

We were pleased with this newly created descriptor. There was a lot of discussion in the news about toxic PCBs, or polychlorinated biphenyls, which were chemicals used as lubricants and coolants. These substances were released into the environment accidentally and intentionally, and were thought to cause a wide variety of medical problems and possibly cancer. Now we had our own version of the toxic PCB.

"Getting rid of a toxic, post-call boner is easier than cleaning up a chemical PCB," asserted Skip.

"I agree," I said, "but it requires leaving the hospital, which we can't do right now."

"Where are High and Low Gomco when you need 'em?"

"They've never helped me," I said, looking at the ceiling.

"Me either," he said, staring out the window. "But this one's too toxic to leave the resident's library right now. These greens are just too thin to conceal anything."

"We have two choices," I said.

"Take things into our own hands?" he asked.

"That's one solution…but I'd rather wait until I have some help. Besides, I've got to get back to work right now."

"So, what's option two?" he asked.

"Operation Cover-Up." I tossed Skip a white hospital coat. I grabbed one, put it on, and we walked out to finish our day.

"Onward!" he said, pointing down the hallway.

That afternoon, I ran into Billy.

"I heard you had a standoff with a murderer last night," he said.

"Nah…it amounted to nothin'," I said. "But the cops hung us out to dry. Left this nut case unguarded. Someone's gonna get hurt around here, sooner or later."

"Yeah, we need more security, for sure. Hey, can you play this weekend? We'll go down to Fourth and Vermont."

"Maybe. But do you really want to take this skinny white boy back there?" I smiled.

"Hell, yeah. Fuck them if they don't like it. We'll play team ball and kick their asses again."

"Let me work on getting free…"

Just then, Mr. Patel rounded the corner.

"Oh, no," whispered Billy. "This guy gives me the creeps."

"I love him," I whispered back.

"Oh, hello, Drs. Harch and Goodwin," he said.

"Hello," we both said. Then I just had to add, "What's going on around here today?" Billy furrowed his brow at me.

"Oh, you know, crazy, crazy things," said Mr. Patel.

"Will you tell us?" I asked in a low voice, leaning toward him.

"Dr. Harch, you will like this one," he said. "A man and a woman in their late 60s were admitted to the jail ward in custody with facial bruising and lacerations. The couple tells the doctors that a man broke into their home, tied the old man up at gunpoint, and raped the wife. Police tell the doctors that this older couple went cruising late at night, pulled up to a bus stop, and abducted a young man at gunpoint. They took him to their home and tried to force him to have sex with the old woman as the old man watched. The young man scuffled with them, took the gun away, and called the police." He smiled broadly.

"I gotta go," said Billy. "Let me know about this weekend." He walked away.

I was about to squeeze another story out of Mr. Patel when my beeper went off.

"Sorry, Mr. Patel, I gotta run, too. Save up some juicy stories for later."

I left the hospital that evening to go to Lori's apartment. As I entered the freeway, I opened my console and pulled out something that Lori had given me. It was a little, battery-powered device that fit over my ear. Any time I fell asleep while driving, an annoying alarm would sound as my head tilted forward, blasting me back into the world of awareness. It was extremely effective; on this particular trip, it awakened me 22 times. Lori was amazing at solving problems like this. I couldn't wait to ask if she knew anything about toxic PCBs.

"I need to ask you a question," said Lori.

Uh-oh, I thought. This sounds like trouble. She saw the look on my face.

"Don't worry. It's nothing serious." She pulled out a brochure. "I need to know what you want to wear for the wedding."

We started to flip through the photos of different jacket/pants combinations.

"That one right there. I like the tails. It's cool."

"You can't wear tails. Tails are formal, for evening. This is a late-morning wedding."

I raised my eyebrows. "Oh, really?" We looked at a few more examples. "How about that one? I like the colors and the style."

"No, that's a tuxedo. You want a morning coat."

"Lori...why don't you just show me what I'm gonna wear at this wedding?"

"I think you'd look nice in this morning coat right here."

"That's fine. But why did you even ask me?"

"I just wanted you to feel like you're participating in the decisions."

"Stop worrying about that. Just make the decisions and don't ask me anymore."

That Saturday, Billie and I left the hospital and met Andy at Percy's apartment. The four of us piled into one car for the drive to the basketball court. There was lots of banter, mostly about women and sex, but also about drinking, pot, and cocaine. The testosterone was flowing in anticipation of the battle we knew we'd have with the locals at Fourth and Vermont.

We had to wait the usual two or three games, but Percy and Andy took on a nasty, confrontational attitude about the queue, and no one dared to cut ahead of us. As our game time neared, we had to pick up a fifth player. Out of the crowd milling around, one guy approached and asked if he could join us. Not knowing any of the other players, we couldn't really turn him down, so we agreed. Then we took a closer look at him. He was about 6-feet, 2-inches tall, and 200 pounds. His shirt and shorts were tattered. On his feet were purple, suede tennis shoes that were untied and loose. I could never understand why some players didn't tie their shoes. Sometimes they'd run right out of them when the game got going.

We were worried about our decision to add this guy to our team; the competition was fierce that day, so we'd need all five guys to play well to win. Our fears were magnified when the last game ended and our new guy walked onto the court to warm up with us. He was pigeon-toed and looked slow, and he had sort of a big ass. He immediately dribbled the ball off his foot and out of bounds. We looked at each other with utter disappointment. But then, he retrieved the ball, walked back onto the court, and stood right in front of the basket. Suddenly, he jumped straight up from a two-footed stance—in his loose, purple suede shoes—turned in midair, and did a reverse slam dunk that rocked the backboard.

"Fuck, yeah!" yelled Percy.

"That's what we're lookin' for!" shouted Andy. "What's your name, my man?"

"Davis," he replied, in a very soft voice.

"Well, Davis," said Andy, "let's kick some fuckin' ass and keep this court all day long."

And that's exactly what happened. Just like the last time we visited, but Davis made it even easier. He and Andy swatted balls left and right, and scored inside. Billie got steals and turned them into layups. We hit midrange and outside jumpers. Playing as a team, we were untouchable. We held the court for two hours and departed when we were tired, not because anyone beat us.

The ride back to Percy's place was a sweaty, stinky, raucous, joyful trip.

CHAPTER TWENTY

MRS. DR. HARCH

OUR WEDDING WAS JUST A COUPLE months away, and we had some major decisions to make. Lori still had her one-bedroom apartment, and I stayed there when I wasn't too tired to drive. I was still paying rent on my cramped little dorm room because of the convenience and safety it offered during and after call nights.

We wanted to find a two-bedroom house to rent so we could have visitors, and because there might someday be…a little one, or little ones. But we couldn't justify paying rent on the dorm room and a house, so we agreed that the dorm would have to go soon after the wedding.

Finding a decent house to rent in the Los Angeles area, near enough to LA County-USC that I could respond to emergencies promptly, was difficult. There weren't many "safe" neighborhoods in the area and, for some reason, Lori was running into invisible roadblocks with landlords. Was it because we weren't married yet? Not "established"? Too young? We were 29 years old and both employed!

Lori had made several calls from work to inquire about rentals. Sitting near her, and overhearing these unsuccessful calls, was her art director, Nathaniel Hawthorne Billingsly II. He was the eccentric offspring of an East Coast, blue-blood family. We thought he might be holding down his job for fun, not because he needed the money.

"Lori," said Nathaniel, "you're going about this the wrong way."

"Oh? Well, Nathaniel, do tell me. How exactly does one go about securing a rental in the greater Los Angeles area?"

"On the next call, introduce yourself as Mrs. Dr. Harch. That'll do the trick."

"That's fucking preposterous, Nathaniel."

"No, it's not. Just try it."

"Mrs. Dr. Harch? There's no such thing in the English language as 'Mrs. Dr. Anyone.' I'd feel stupid saying that."

"Trust me. Do it."

Now Lori was annoyed. "Okay. I have another listing right here. Let's call right now and we'll try your silly idea." She dialed the number.

"Hello," said a business-like, female voice, "can I help you?"

"Hello," said Lori, "This is Mrs. Dr. Harch, and I'm calling regarding your listing for a two-bedroom house in Glendale."

"Oh, yes. Can I get your information?"

Lori viewed the rental later that day (a cute little home on a quiet street), and we signed a lease two days later.

Meanwhile, Billy was ready to dump his dorm room as well, and was having difficulty finding an apartment. His problem, however, was slightly different. He'd found several adequate places, but when he arrived to view the rentals, suddenly they weren't available any longer. He was frustrated, and very pressed for time.

One weekend, Billy's mom was visiting from Washington, D.C. When Billy's father died (15 months previously), she had decided to become a real estate agent. This was after raising six kids, mostly by herself, since her husband had been at the hospital most of the time, working. Billy had identified a desirable one-bedroom apartment in the Glendale area, not far from the home we'd just rented. He'd spoken to the owner/manager/real estate agent handling the rental process, who said the apartment was still available. Immediately after the conversation, Billy and his mother headed over to see the property.

Billy and his mom, Evelyn, got out of their car and walked over to meet the owner. Evelyn was an attractive woman who had an elegant bearing about her. When they introduced themselves, the owner, a middle-aged Iranian man, began to stammer about how someone had called in the last 20 minutes and was also interested.

"It's very nice to meet you," said Evelyn.

"Yes, thank you," said the owner, nervously. He walked them through the apartment, adding that it wasn't quite ready yet because of this and that.

"Are you a member of the National Association of Realtors?" asked Evelyn, casually.

"Uh...yes, I am," said the owner.

"So am I," said Evelyn, "and we'd be happy to take this apartment." She looked directly at him and said nothing more. Fifteen minutes later, they were signing papers.

The reality of working in a multicultural, inner-city hospital every day created a bond that allowed Billy and me to comfortably talk—and even joke—about racism and its many ugly dimensions.

In a later conversation, Billy, who was (and still is) a very modest guy, stated matter-of-factly, "You know, John, isn't it ironic that I attended an Ivy League college, graduated near the top of my med school class, was president of my med school class our final year, was completing my third year of surgical residency, and could fix someone who'd been stabbed in the heart, but I couldn't rent a one-bedroom apartment in Los Angeles without my mom subtly threatening legal action against the owner?"

It was also ironic that Billy developed a friendship with the owner over the next two years, and it became routine for the man to unabashedly seek Billy's free opinions for his family's medical issues.

While Lori and her mom finalized all the excruciating details required for the perfect wedding day, my job was to get my closest buddies from college and med school to show up. Five of my fraternity "brothers," all of them as financially strapped as I was, had made the decision and sacrifice to fly in for the event. Six of my best med school friends also made it.

The venue Lori and I picked for the wedding (yes, she consulted me and considered my opinion, I think) was a "romantic hotel" in Manhattan Beach, California, named Barnaby's. The lobby, the rooms, and the courtyard had a charming, Victorian character; it was beautiful.

With everyone flying and driving in on a tight schedule, there were no plans for a formal bachelor party. After the rehearsal dinner, Lori planned to get a good night's sleep, and I decided to have a get-together right in my hotel room. I didn't want to spend the night in a crowded, noisy bar trying to catch up with so many important friends.

I was nervous as I pulled up in front of the hotel. When the valets offered to take my bags, I asked them to also transport two boxes from my trunk containing beer, wine, hard liquor, and mixers. I slipped the guy 20 bucks and he didn't bat an eye.

As you might imagine, the party got a little out of hand. I kept trying to shush the noise down so the guests in adjacent rooms could sleep, but somewhere around 1:30 a.m., the hotel manager called, and I sent most of the group packing.

Several who could keep their voices down remained, and we drank until about 3 a.m. One or two (I can't quite remember) ended up crashing right in my room.

Seeing no sign of me by midmorning, an unsurprised Lori knocked on my door. I shuffled slowly to the door and opened it a crack. I must have looked like hell.

"John, we've got pictures in about 30 minutes," she said. "And this room, it's a total disaster."

Just then, my college roommate stumbled out of the bathroom in his underwear, very hungover.

"Hi, BR. You obviously never made it to your hotel last night," she said, rolling her eyes.

"No…I didn't," he said, as he slumped in a chair and put his throbbing head in his hands.

"John, get in the shower and get your tux on. Things are about to start."

I wanted to say, "I thought it was a morning coat," but for my own well-being, kept my mouth shut.

Despite feeling miserable, BR and I cleaned up the room. I shaved, showered, and got dressed. I took a couple Advils and headed out to pose and smile, all the while suppressing the pounding in my head.

The wedding ceremony was indeed short—so short that one guest arrived four minutes late and missed it entirely. Brother-in-law Pastor Larry did, after all, insert one or two God references into the heavily edited service, but we just smiled and ignored it. Soon the party was underway.

Skip, Billy, Nick Givens, and Dr. O'Donnelly were all in attendance.

I'd chosen my older brother, Paul, to be my best man. When it came time for the wedding toasts, Paul took the mic. He had on a tux…er, morning coat, along with white, high-top tennis shoes and some ridiculous sunglasses with pinwheels sticking up off them. He gave a toast that, among other embarrassing things, implied that Lori was promiscuous and I was wimpy and stupid. Lori's parents were a little uncomfortable (which always happened when Paul spoke publicly), but everyone laughed like hell.

After the partying was over, and we said our good-byes to so many family and friends, we drove to a hotel in the hills of Los Angeles. I carried Lori across the threshold, and we collapsed on the bed and fell asleep.

The following day, we flew to Hawaii for a six-day honeymoon. While on Maui, we made the nearly four-hour drive to Hana to see the Seven Sacred Pools. I saw a guy dive off the rocks into the second pool and decided to do the same. Lori watched me climb about 20 feet up the rocks and prepare to dive in. I looked down, measured the dive, and jumped. While in the air, I realized I hadn't seen a rock shelf sticking out into the water. Petrified, I attempted to alter my trajectory—and missed the rock shelf by inches. This was one of the stupidest things I've ever done, although the list is long. I shudder to think how it might have ended just four days after getting married, and just two days after Lori stopped taking her birth control pills.

CHAPTER TWENTY-ONE

"THERE'S A MURDERER IN THERE!"

WHILE ROTATING THROUGH THE TUMOR Service, I was asked to see a young guy on the jail ward with a "tumor on his arm." After passing through jail ward security, I sat down with his chart.

Chris was 21 years old, and was diagnosed with a sarcoma, an aggressive type of cancer, on his right arm a few inches below his shoulder level. It was removed surgically, and then he was lost to follow-up. He got himself into trouble and eventually landed in prison. The chart didn't state why he was incarcerated, but the most likely explanation was drugs. The medical personnel at the prison noticed a problem on his arm and had him shipped over to the jail ward for evaluation.

I was ushered down the hallway and into a room with six prisoners. I was now an experienced jail ward consultant, so my anxiety level was much lower, but I remained vigilant. The deputy locked the door behind me, and I looked around the room. The only guy that seemed to fit the profile of my patient was on my left, relaxing in bed quietly, with a sheet pulled up to his neck. It looked like he had stuffed his pillow under the sheet to lean on. The other prisoners milled around or sat on their beds.

"Chris?" I asked, looking at him.

"Yeah, I'm Chris," he said, in a timid little voice. He was thin and looked like he was 17 years old. I wondered how he survived in a prison environment.

"I'm Dr. Harch. They've asked me to look at your arm."

"Okay," was his simple response, as I pulled the curtain around his bed.

"Have you noticed that your arm is different from the way it was after your surgery?" I asked.

"Yeah, I guess so."

"How long has it been that you've noticed a change?"

"I don't know."

"Days, weeks, months? What do you think?"

"Uh…a while. I'm not sure." I was getting nowhere. Chris was so detached that I wondered if the prison staff were mistaken and maybe he didn't have a problem after all.

"Are you having pain?"

"No."

"Lost any weight?"

"I don't think so."

"Weakness or numbness in your hand?"

"Nah."

"Well, let's have a look," I said, becoming impatient and a little annoyed at his seeming disinterest. He watched me as I pulled the sheet down, exposing his right arm and shoulder. I nearly gasped out loud. The "pillow" I thought I saw under the sheet was, in fact, a gigantic tumor. It started just below the curve of his shoulder, ballooned out to about the size of a basketball, and tapered down again at the elbow. It was pushing up against his chest wall, and must have weighed 20 or 30 pounds. The thing looked nefarious. I tried to conceal my shock. I couldn't imagine how he could even walk around, given its size. How the hell did he keep up with daily life in this condition, especially in prison?

I needed to get an idea of how fast this tumor was growing, so I tried one more time. "Chris, how long has it taken to get this large?"

"Well…maybe six months." If true, that would be a frightening growth rate.

I examined his neck: scattered hard lymph nodes. Under his arm were multiple large, hard nodes. The tumor itself was fixed to his humerus, the large bone between elbow and shoulder. These were all bad signs for Chris. It was likely that any surgery to remove it would require amputating his arm and shoulder, and then he wouldn't be cured because of the nodal spread.

Here I was again, standing at a bedside staring down at someone with a fatal disease who either didn't know it or was in complete denial. I felt powerless to solve any of his problems, medical or social. He was a casualty of the system, like a flood victim being carried off by a rain-swollen river. And I was on the shoreline, watching helplessly.

"Chris," I said, "you know this is…a pretty serious problem, right?"

He looked away, toward the window. "Yeah…I guess so."

"You're gonna need something done with this…either surgery or…maybe radiation. Maybe chemotherapy."

He turned his gaze from the window back to me, but seemed to be looking beyond me…or through me. The seconds ticked by. "Whatever you think," he said passively. None of the other inmates said anything, but I knew they were listening.

"Well, I think you need treatment of some kind, and fairly soon. Let me talk it over with some other doctors, and we'll come back and discuss it with you."

"Fine," said Chris. I lingered a little longer, waiting for any questions or comments from him. I wished I could read his thoughts. He said nothing further.

I covered him up again. "See you soon," I said. I banged on the door and got let out by the deputy.

Later that day, I presented Chris's case to my senior resident and the attending staff, who were so fascinated that they went upstairs to see Chris themselves. They were as amazed as I was. They also concluded that the cancer was too advanced to offer surgery, and Chris was referred for radiation and chemotherapy. I never saw Chris again, and I'm sure his survival was short. I hoped the courts released him for his final days.

About three months after our wedding, Lori and I were sitting at the table after a late dinner.

"Doctor," she said, "I need your opinion on a medical matter."

"Okay," I said, confused about her odd introduction to whatever was going to follow.

"Well, do you have any idea what might cause a girl to miss a period?"

"No...really? Are you kidding?"

"Not kidding."

I jumped up and hugged her. In truth, I wasn't as excited as she was, given that I had two more difficult years ahead. But I knew she was ready and would make a fantastic mom. And really, it was exciting, even though the responsibility of having a child seemed overwhelming.

"You gonna get a pregnancy test?"

"Yeah, tomorrow."

"Any need to study for it tonight?"

One evening, I was the backup call resident for one of the trauma services. The ER reported that there had been a drive-by shooting, thought to be drug- or gang-related. Three victims were coming in, all with gunshots to the torso. Could we send several residents down to help? Marc Feinberg and I headed down.

"Hey, Marc," I said in the elevator. "Zed and Zeke are talking. Zed says, 'Zeke, if I sneak into your house and make love to your wife, and she has a baby, does that make us kinfolk?' And Zeke says, 'No, Zed, but it would make us even.'" The elevator doors opened and we jogged to the ER. I was asked to see a guy who'd taken a bullet in his left flank (left lower back).

"How you doin', man?" I asked.

"Not too good, doc," he said. "I can't feel anything or move anything below my waist."

We got some quick X-Rays. The bullet was on the right side of his abdomen, and there was shattered bone in his spine. The bullet had traversed from left to right, through his spinal column, and he'd obviously sustained a spinal cord injury. When we inserted a Foley catheter, there was bright red blood in his urine. His kidney was hit as well.

"Can you move your toes?" I asked him.

"Well, doc, I've never been able to move my toes much, since I had polio. I've been in a wheelchair since childhood." Now I looked at him more closely, with a rising sense of astonishment.

"Are you the same guy I admitted about 18 months ago after some gang dudes stabbed you and shoved you out of your wheelchair?"

"Yeah, that was me, Miguel Padilla."

"Holy shit!" I said. "So you had a little motor and sensory ability before tonight, but now it's gone?"

"Yeah."

"It looks like your left kidney was hit as well."

"That's bad, doc. My right kidney hardly works at all because of stones and infection."

When I got things sorted out, Miguel had indeed lost the remaining small amount of spinal cord function not stolen by the poliovirus. His right kidney was already nearly useless, and the bullet had destroyed two-thirds of his good, left kidney. There was a high probability he'd need dialysis in the future.

"Miguel, I know this isn't really my business, but I gotta ask you," I said. "You've been nearly killed twice, that I know of. Now you're in much worse shape than before. Is this gang thing really worth it to you?"

He thought about it for a while. "Doc, I know this is hard for you to understand. But I got nuthin.' No job, no girl…not much family…" He lowered his voice. "I'm a paralyzed little fat guy in a wheelchair. Pushin' drugs is the only way I can survive. So I stick with it. It's my only safety net. And the gang…they're my family."

I was quiet for a few seconds. "I get it, Miguel. I get it."

Friday mornings meant compulsory attendance at Grand Rounds, which were teaching sessions focused on a specific topic. A resident would be chosen to present a case (in front of a large audience) to a senior faculty member, who would then question the resident about his or her knowledge of the disease or injury. It was an anxiety-provoking experience that we all had to endure. If chosen, one had to spend hours, even days, preparing for the questions.

Today's faculty member was the much-feared Morris Rosenberg, the former chief of surgery (preceding Dr. O'Donnelly). He was especially demanding and demeaning. We were all happy he'd relinquished the reins of the program before our arrival. The victim being served up for dismemberment that day was Paul Takata, now a fifth-year resident. Most of us sat in the back rows, in the shadows, as far from the infested water as possible. Interns, residents, and faculty from other specialties filled many of the other seats in the auditorium.

The case was that of a Hispanic farm worker found to have a rare tumor called a pheochromocytoma. The physiology, diagnosis, and treatment of the disease is very complicated, so Paul had a big challenge.

Paul was doing well. He answered most of Rosenberg's questions adequately, even admirably. Then Rosenberg got more and more detailed in his questioning.

"Exactly what dosage of that medication would you use to prevent a life-threatening episode of hypertension in the operating room?" asked Rosenberg.

After a few seconds, Paul replied, "I don't know, sir."

Rosenberg stopped, looked out at two hundred doctors in the audience, and said, "You remember Juan Corona, who killed 25 migrant farm workers a few years ago? I don't know what the big deal was about that, since our residents here kill that many every week."

There were a few snickers, probably from faculty members, but the rest of us just sat there in stunned silence, not believing that he'd said that in a public, educational meeting. We had disliked Rosenberg before; now we hated the son of a bitch. I wanted to yell out, "Fuck you, Rosenberg! You're a sick bastard! Hasn't anyone learned anything from Aaron Zimmerman's death?"

Paul remained calm and said nothing. He didn't appear to be bleeding. The fact that Paul didn't dignify such an outrageous comment with a response now made Rosenberg look foolish.

Dr. O'Donnelly stood up and said, "Let's conclude with a summary of the physiologic aspects of pheochromocytoma." He was clearly embarrassed by Rosenberg's behavior, but couldn't admonish him. Rosenberg was, in fact, senior to him in this highly hierarchical surgical world.

As we walked out of the conference, Skip said, "Wouldn't you like to grab Rosenberg by the balls and squeeze until he stops breathing?"

"I'd like to put electrodes on his tongue and apply a little current," I said.

"That was the worst breach of respect for another professional I've ever seen," said Billy. "I hope I can contain myself if that ever happens to me."

Skip was on trauma call one afternoon when a consult came in for a female in the ER with multiple stab wounds. When Skip arrived at C-booth, the ER doctor was in a discussion with a police officer.

"Hey, Dr. Cline," said the ER doc, "your patient, LeeAnn Dawson, is over there in bed two. She's 30 years old and has a couple small stab wounds to the abdomen and one to the left chest, with a small pneumo. Her vitals are stable, her belly's soft, and I got a junior resident working on a chest tube right now."

"Good work," said Skip, "I'll take her off your hands. I bet she was walking her grandmother across the street when she was stabbed by some dude for no apparent reason."

"Well, not quite," said the ER doc. "I'll let officer Vega give you the rest of the story."

"LeeAnn was released from prison yesterday," said the cop, "after serving four years for shooting her former girlfriend. Today, she went over to the same girlfriend's house for a visit. While LeeAnn was reclining on a couch, her girlfriend stabbed her several times."

"Welcome home, honey," said Skip.

"Anyway," continued the cop, "even though she's fresh out of prison, it appears she's the victim this time. But you might want to keep an eye on her. She does have one felony assault on her record."

"Can we get an officer to watch her while she's here?" asked Skip.

"Nope. She's not under arrest or under suspicion for any crime. Besides, we don't have the personnel for it right now."

"Great," muttered Skip. "We'll just do what we always do."

"What's that?" asked the cop.

"Take care of these dirtballs and pretend it's safer inside the hospital than outside."

Skip wrote orders to get LeeAnn upstairs. Before leaving the ER, he evaluated a 72-year-old Hispanic guy who'd gotten drunk and fallen down a stairway. When he looked more closely at the guy's chart, he noticed that his first name—no kidding—was Inebrio.

LeeAnn remained stable on 9200 and was transferred to Skip's ward (9800) for observation and management of her chest tube. Around 10 p.m., 9200 got a frantic call from the nursing station on 9800.

"You guys need to get over here immediately!" shouted a nurse. "There's been a stabbing in room two."

Skip and several members of his team raced down the hall and around the corner.

"A stabbing…on our own fuckin' ward," panted Skip, between breaths. "What next?"

There were four nurses around a bed, two of them applying pressure to wounds. The bed was stained with blood. The patient was LeeAnn Dawson.

"A few minutes ago," said one nurse, "a woman dressed as a nurse ran out of this room yelling, 'There's a murderer in there! There's a murderer in there!' But she wasn't someone any of us recognized. We've called security."

LeeAnn had stab wounds to her chest and abdomen, and her pressure was falling.

"Call the OR and tell them we're coming up from our own goddamn ward with multiple stab wounds," said Skip.

Skip and his team managed to keep LeeAnn alive long enough to repair stab wounds to her heart, belly, and arms. She was moved to the ICU around 4 a.m., in critical condition.

In the morning, I walked into the cafeteria to see a blood-covered, tired-looking Skip sitting at a table with one of the cardiology attendings we knew.

"Skip," I said, "you look like you got ridden hard and put away bloody."

Skip retold the previous night's story, adding that it was LeeAnn's girlfriend who dressed up as a nurse and came to the ward to finish her off. The nurses found a 10-inch butcher knife discarded in a corner of the room. The girlfriend was apprehended before she could leave the hospital grounds and was now in custody.

"Now that's a great one to add to my journal," I declared. I whipped out a 3x5 card and began writing.

"What are you doing?" asked the cardiologist.

"I'm keeping a record of all the weirdest things I see here at LA County," I said.

"I can give you one almost as good, if you want it," he said.

"Hell, yeah," I said. "Go ahead."

"I was moonlighting in the ER one night at Charity Hospital in New Orleans near the end of my residency. It was a bit of a slow night. Suddenly, we heard a *pop, pop, pop-pop* outside the ER. Then it was quiet. We opened the sliding doors and cautiously looked right, then left. We couldn't see anything, except a pickup truck parked at the end of the loading dock. Then we heard some groaning, and found a white guy about 50 years old lying at one end of the loading dock. He was bleeding from a gunshot. As we scooped him up, he asked if we'd go get his son from the other end of the loading dock."

"No shit," said Skip.

"Yeah, it turns out this guy had gotten into an argument with his son. It got so bad that they grabbed their guns, got in the pickup truck together, and drove the 23 miles to the hospital in complete silence to settle things outside the ER doors."

"Awesome," said Skip.

"Yeah, and when we got both of them onto gurneys in the ER, the father asked, 'Hey, how's my boy? Shot up pretty good, huh?' And the son asked, 'How's my pap? Is he gonna make it?'"

"That's just fantastic," I said. "Can I use it if I ever write a book?"

"You bet," said the cardiologist. "I got some more, too. Charity Hospital is a pretty wild place, just like here."

On Tuesday, January 28, 1986, at 8:30 in the morning, Billy and Craig Kelly (the biggest jerk in our program) were sitting in the resident's library with Brad Elliott, a third-year resident. Brad was preparing for his Grand Rounds presentation on Friday, and he was nervous. The topic was adrenal neoplasms, rare tumors that few of us knew anything about.

"Learn as much as you can about these tumors," said Billy, "and then just do your best. Admit what you don't know and move on."

"Just pray you don't have to present to Rosenberg," said Craig, "because he'll ream you a new asshole, no matter how hard you study."

All three residents turned to the television, which was broadcasting the impending launch of the *Challenger* space shuttle. At 8:39 a.m., the shuttle blasted off, and the three doctors watched in silence. About a minute later, the shuttle exploded in midair and pieces spiraled downward into the ocean.

"Oh, my God!" exclaimed Billy.

"Jesus!" said Brad. "With the size of that explosion, they must have all died instantly!"

Craig fixed his eyes on Brad, and said, "Unlike the slow, painful death you're about to experience this Friday in Grand Rounds."

CHAPTER TWENTY-TWO

WILD RIDE

I T WAS A TYPICAL SATURDAY NIGHT: 8 P.M.
and no dinner break. Outside, it had been a beautiful day.
I thought of sunbathers at the beach, 30 minutes away by
freeway yet impossibly distant from my confined existence.
I knew that girls in short shorts and halter tops were skating
along boardwalks while people in bathing suits spiked vol-
leyballs and shouted challenges through the net. But inside
the hospital was a totally different world.

The phone rang. One of the nurses answered it. She
stated, without emotion, "Doctor, you have a stab wound
to the precordium coming in with hypotension."

"Great," I thought. "I'm hours behind in my work. And
I still have two new patients waiting for me."

This call, however, trumped all other demands for my attention. The precordium is the area of the left chest immediately in front of the heart, and hypotension simply means the patient's blood pressure is low, probably dangerously so. This combination of words delivered in the same sentence portended a high probability of life-threatening injury.

"Jim!" I yelled to my junior resident. "Let's go. We have a stab to the precordium who sounds bad." I rushed over to the elevator and anxiously poked the down button hard, several times in succession, as if the elevator would realize the urgency and find a way to arrive more quickly. Jim and one of the medical students jumped in the elevator with me for the trip to the first floor.

The elevator doors opened and we ran down the long hallway. Just before we got to the double, sliding doors of the ER, I slowed up and stopped Jim and the medical student.

"Hold it. I don't like to rush in there looking frantic. We want to enter totally relaxed, like we've seen all this before. If we're not composed, no one else will be." I hoped I could maintain this pretense even if all hell broke loose and I didn't know what to do. With two more steps, the doors sprang open, and we marched in.

When we entered C-booth the tension in the air was tangible. My patient was lying on a gurney, surrounded by a horde of nurses and emergency room doctors.

Ronny was a 25-year-old male. His body was completely still and his eyes were staring vacantly at the ceiling. His mouth hung open. One arm dangled off the gurney. He was in magnificent shape: six-pack abs and bulging biceps. A perfect specimen except for a three-quarter-inch gash on his left chest. Bad location, I thought.

A nurse looked up and said, "Doctor, he has no blood pressure and no detectable pulse." The EKG screen, however, showed cardiac activity—he was still alive. I thrust my right hand into his groin to check for a femoral pulse, often the easiest pulsation to detect when the blood pressure is low, and felt nothing.

The nurses and other medical personnel paused, waiting for my direction. "Get me a thoracotomy tray, gloves, and Betadine," I ordered. "Get another IV line in him. Call for some O-negative blood. And let the OR know we might need a room, if we're real lucky. Splash some Betadine on his chest." Jim and I donned sterile gloves but didn't wait for gowns. It seemed to take forever to tear open the tray and reveal its array of glistening steel instruments. I grabbed a scalpel.

So far, our unconscious victim had received no anesthetics or pain relievers at all. I set the knife on his skin and made one huge, continuous slice from the mid-chest toward the left armpit. There was no response from the patient, except the dripping and running of dark venous blood from the skin edges down the chest wall onto the gurney.

Everyone in the room was silent and motionless as I drew the knife across the same wound again, through the thin layer of fat and then the muscle between the ribs. I rammed my right index finger through the last thin layer of tissue and felt between the ribs into the chest. I poked my other index finger in and pulled in opposite directions. Blood poured out of the chest, over the side of the gurney, and down my scrub pants. I could feel the warm liquid soaking into my socks and filling my shoes. Jim picked up the rib spreader and stuffed it in the hole I'd created. He turned the crank, exposing the cavern of the left hemithorax, which was still about half full of blood. The entire process had taken about 60 seconds.

I peered into the chest and recognized the pericardium: a thin, whitish membrane surrounding the heart. There was a half-inch gash in the inferior (lower) aspect of it, and with each feeble contraction of the heart, a bit of blood squirted out. The pericardium itself was filled with blood, limiting the ability of the heart to contract. "Metzenbaum scissors!" I yelled, "And fill him up! His heart is empty!"

He'd lost so much blood into his left chest that there was precious little remaining to pump around to the rest of the body. Jim handed me the scissors, and I slit the pericardium from the gash upward. Blood and clot poured out, revealing the heart itself, which had a small hole at its apex, or tip. The heart contractions had by now nearly ceased, and I thought the patient would very likely die, barring some lucky turn of events.

"I need some sutures: 3-O Prolene! Hurry up!" While waiting the few seconds it took Jim to get sutures on my tray, I placed the tip of my left index finger in the hole, and it fit exactly. To my surprise, the bleeding was mostly controlled. The nurses were squeezing intravenous fluids into Ronny, and after about 30 seconds, the heart began to fill up and contract more forcefully. I felt a rush of adrenaline—we might be able to save this guy! I left my finger in the dike, and in another 90 seconds, the heart was beating nicely. The bleeding around my finger was acceptable, and the ER doctors had placed a breathing tube. The EKG rhythm was fast but normal. Hot damn! Now I knew we had a real chance.

By now the suture was available. Jim loaded it on a needle driver, and I attempted to suture the hole closed. In my haste, I stuck my finger with the needle. This happened with some frequency in these extreme emergencies, and it made all the residents worry about hepatitis as well as the mystery disease I'd warned Lori about, now called HIV. No time to obsess about that now.

Since the blood pressure was much higher than before (and the heart was beating vigorously), any manipulation produced gushes of blood around my finger. Further attempts to place sutures would cause massive blood loss. I knew I would need more help and better light to complete a repair.

"What are we gonna do?" asked Jim.

"We've got to get him upstairs." I turned to the nurses. "Call the fifteenth floor, and tell 'em we're coming. Ask if they can get a cardiac surgeon in here to give us a hand." Then I looked around. Blood was everywhere, especially all over Jim and me. Where my gloves ended above the wrists, my forearms were soaked with the sticky red essence of Ronny's life.

The gurney is a rolling bed, more than six feet long, with its surface at waist height. Ronny was lying atop this gurney, still unconscious, with a yawning hole in his left chest, wound edges now bleeding more robustly since his blood pressure had been reestablished. My left forearm disappeared into this hole, my finger still in Ronny's beating heart. I knew the run up to the fifteenth floor was likely to dislodge my finger's precarious position, so I hopped up on the gurney, put one knee on each side of Ronny's waist, and yelled, "Let's go!"

For a second, everyone hesitated, but in the next instant, my team, with some emergency room staff, accelerated us out of the room and through the automatic double doors. When we burst into the hall, hospital visitors and employees turned and gaped in disbelief. On the speeding gurney was a completely naked patient with a huge, gory chest incision, a young doctor covered in blood riding along on top, and rivulets of blood streaming onto the floor. Much of the team by now was also partially covered with blood, and people were shouting for the elevator, for units of blood, and to clear the way.

We made the 200-foot dash down the hall in record time and rounded the corner into the elevator, which had been diverted for our use. As the doors closed behind us, Ronny, having received no anesthesia whatsoever, suddenly awakened. He looked up at me with terrified eyes, unable to comprehend what was happening and, I'm sure, in horrific pain. He began to thrash around, and several spouts of blood sprayed wildly around my finger, onto me, the elevator walls, Jim, and my medical student. I leaned forward and grabbed him by the neck with my free, right hand to stop his thrashing. I put my face right up to his and said, "Listen to me, goddammit! You've got a stab wound to your heart, and my finger's plugging the hole. If you don't hold still, you will definitely die!" To my amazement, he nodded, relaxed a bit, and the blood loss slowed. The elevator doors opened, and we raced down the hall to a waiting operating room.

About then, Nick Givens magically appeared. He was in his sixth year and was now the resident supervisor. It was likely that he showed up because no cardiac surgeon was available. He surveyed the scene: I was still up on the gurney with my finger in Ronny's chest.

I crawled off Ronny, who was now being anesthetized, and the team began to prep him. Jim, now in sterile gown and gloves, put his index finger in the hole as I removed mine, and a blast of blood shot halfway across the room. Nick and I scrubbed in and placed sutures in the heart tissue around the stab wound. When I tied them, Jim removed his finger from the hole in Ronny's heart. Incredibly, the hole remained closed and didn't bleed!

Feeling as though I had exited a burning building, I stepped back from the operating table, let out a big sigh, and asked the team to relax. We placed chest tubes for drainage and closed the big thoracotomy incision. Now I had an opportunity to look Ronny over more carefully.

"Hey, Jim," I said. "Check out Ronny's left earring."

On that earring it said, "Fuck off."

Over the ensuing four or five days, Ronny improved rapidly and uneventfully. The chest tubes were removed, and he came off the ventilator without incident. He didn't develop infection, despite our less-than-sterile attack on his body in the emergency room. Surprisingly, he had no recollection of anything: not the initial stabbing, the second bigger stabbing by me in the emergency room, nor the episode in the elevator. When we strolled through on rounds his last day in the hospital, he said, "Hey, Doc, thanks for stitching me up…from the bottom of my heart."

CHAPTER TWENTY-THREE

"WHERE'S DORUK?"

DORUK YILMAZ WAS A HEALTHY 31-year-old Turkish man who had been coughing up blood for several months. He came to the attention of the Pulmonary Medicine Service, and he underwent bronchoscopy for an extensive examination of his lungs.

The pulmonary doctors found a small tumor growing in Doruk's left lung. The biopsies suggested the mass was noncancerous, but everyone was convinced it would eventually bleed more aggressively. In time, Doruk would likely have a single episode of bleeding which would essentially drown him in his own blood.

At the time, I was rotating through the Chest Surgery Service as a fourth-year resident. It was my job to call Doruk to the hospital to explain the problem and advise surgery.

Doruk and I met in the clinic one afternoon. He was about 5 feet 10 inches, 160 pounds, and handsome. He had immigrated from Turkey about 10 years previously, and now worked part time in the auto repair business. His clothes were worn, but clean. He arrived by himself for this important discussion, probably because he had no understanding of the seriousness of the problem nor what I was about to recommend. His marginal English made it difficult to communicate the details of the anatomy and the risk involved. His demeanor was calm and passive.

When I began to describe the need for surgery, he asked, "Is it cancer?"

"No," I responded, "but it may act like cancer and cause you to bleed to death." He couldn't quite grasp why I wanted to cut out a piece of his lung if he didn't have cancer. I repeated the explanation several times, indicating that the bleeding would likely kill him sometime in the future. Finally, he seemed to understand and reluctantly agreed to have surgery. I didn't expect him to return.

Greg McFarland was a fellow on the Chest Surgery Service, which meant he had already completed his surgical internship and residency. He had spent two additional years performing lung surgery and major chest wall resections at one of the leading cancer centers in the nation, and was at LAC-USC to gain additional training in cardiac surgery.

Greg was about four years older than me and handled himself in a smooth, mature manner that had earned my admiration. I was his junior on the service, and he allowed me enough rope to gain the skills I needed, but was always there to help avoid a problem. Greg told me I would be the operating surgeon for Doruk Yilmaz. In other words, I would do all the significant parts of a major lung resection, with Greg as my assistant and guide. It was a wonderful opportunity, and I looked forward to it without trepidation. After all, I was already cutting people's chests open in the ER and literally saving their lives.

Doruk did indeed show up on the appointed day, again without any family members in support. I greeted him, re-assured him, and accompanied him to the operating room. Soon he was asleep on the table. I opened his chest with an incision similar to the one used on Ronny after the stab wound to his heart.

Reaching in, I gently compressed the spongy, collapsible lung tissue. This left an imprint of my thumb and fingers similar to squeezing soft bread dough, but the impressions slowly ballooned out and disappeared as the lungs received new breaths from the ventilator. By searching around in this fashion, I finally identified a small tumor in the upper lung. With further investigation, it became apparent that we couldn't resect this tumor safely without removing Doruk's entire left lung, so we proceeded to do just that.

I performed the entire operation under Greg's direction. It was done by the book. We carefully and painstakingly double sutured all the major vessels. At the end, there was no bleeding. Greg suggested we close the chest without drainage tubes, a departure from the standard procedure but something he had done in many prior surgeries. Even though we would have less warning if a vessel began to bleed, it would hasten the healing of the empty left chest cavity. And besides, he reasoned, I'd done a great job and there was no need for concern.

Postoperatively, we put Doruk in the intensive care unit. He was heavily sedated, intubated, and breathing with the help of a ventilator. I called his home and spoke to his brother, Evren. I briefly described the operation, assured Evren that everything had gone well, and said we were tucking Doruk in to the ICU. He thanked me, asked no questions, and hung up the phone. When I finished afternoon rounds and ward work, it was early evening.

Across the ICU from Doruk were two very sick patients who had recently undergone cardiac surgery. One of them needed a special catheter placed to monitor his heart function.

Doruk seemed to be stable, so I gathered all the necessary equipment for the other patient and asked the nurse to assist me. Soon I was gowned, masked, and gloved, and I started the procedure.

Doruk's nurse said, "Hey, Doruk's heart rate just increased."

I said, "Give him a bolus of fluid," thinking that his blood volume postoperatively was probably low, a very common occurrence. But my heart rate began to creep up right along with Doruk's. I continued my work and a bit later, the same nurse said, "Doruk's blood pressure is slightly low." I ordered more fluid and got more concerned, mentally reviewing the myriad problems that could be wrong. The worst would be unrecognized bleeding from a pulmonary vessel.

As I neared completion of the catheter placement, I continued to worry about Doruk. By now, I was sweating under my gown and my heart was pounding. I glanced nervously over at Doruk's monitor again and again as I finished placing a dressing.

The nurse suddenly shouted, "Doruk's heart rate is 148 and his blood pressure is 60!"

I ripped off my gown and mask and rushed to his bedside. I felt in his groin for a femoral pulse: it was barely palpable. His heart rate was now 150. He had to be bleeding! We tried to get another blood pressure. It was too low to register. Oh, God! I screamed for some scissors and a chest surgery tray as I put on some gloves. I cut all the closing sutures we had so carefully placed three hours ago, opened the chest, and was met with what I feared: a small tidal wave of blood.

By now, the nurse had obtained some instruments, and she handed me a clamp. I quickly clamped a group of vessels that seemed to be bleeding. Doruk had no blood pressure. A dark and dreadful feeling arose from deep inside my chest:

I was completely alone in my responsibility for this dying patient and the entire overwhelming catastrophe.

With nursing help and IV fluids, I succeeded in getting Doruk's blood pressure back up to a dangerously low, but slightly encouraging, level. I asked the nurses to call the fifteenth floor and inform them we had a red blanket post-op patient and were coming upstairs right now. I also asked them to call Greg in from home, stat. As we rolled out of the intensive care unit with Doruk in very tenuous condition, I said, "One more thing: please try to reach someone from Doruk's family and get them in here. Tell them…we…uh… um…have a very big problem."

When Greg arrived, I was already working in Doruk's left chest. I gave Greg the details of the past hour, and we easily controlled all the bleeding, but Doruk was too far gone at this point to recover. The massive blood loss and prolonged low pressure caused hypothermia, acid imbalance in the blood, and heart dysfunction. His pressure slipped lower and lower, along with my spirits, despite numerous drugs and interventions. Finally, Doruk died on the operating table, with me standing over him. I stood there exhausted, looking down at him, and felt a crushing sense of loss, guilt, and fear.

I stepped back from the operating table a few feet and tried to process the visual input and the swirling thoughts. I was almost dizzy. How did such a successful day degenerate so quickly into this unanticipated fatality? I had convinced this vibrant young man to leave his secure existence for an operation to presumably improve his future health. Now he lay here dead in our hospital with no future at all. With great difficulty, I turned away from Doruk and walked slowly out of the room. I wasn't sure what to do next.

Greg looked at my face and could read my feelings. As we walked down the hall, he tried to console me. "We did our best." Then, "This was just bad luck…an unfortunate accident." I said nothing. He graciously offered to speak to the family, but I refused, stating that it was my obligation.

By now it was about 10 p.m. Doruk's brother, Evren, was waiting for me on the chest surgery ward, tenth floor. As I approached, he had an anxious look on his face, but it was obvious to me that he didn't expect to hear what I was about to say.

I motioned for him to step into a side room. Greg waited in the hallway. Seeing my bloody greens, Evren, in his heavy accent, spoke first. "Where's Doruk?"

I said, "Well, Doruk's surgery went well today, and we put him in the ICU…"

Evren broke in again, more insistent this time, "Where's Doruk?!"

I responded calmly, "Then he started bleeding into his chest. We had to go back to the operating room, but we couldn't stop the bleeding, and…and…Doruk has died."

Time stood still as this news settled over Evren. He had been sitting on the edge of a desk. Now he rose slowly, almost robotically, his eyes growing wide in disbelief. He leaned forward to within about eight inches of my face, his eyes fixed on mine.

"Doruk, dead?" he asked.

I nodded my head sadly as tears welled up in my eyes. Then he yelled out, "No! Noooooooooo!"

A moment of silence passed as he processed this devastating news. He pointed at me and screamed, "Murderer! You're a murderer!" He put his face in both hands and began sobbing. After about 10 seconds, he lowered his hands, looked at me, and started saying, "No, no, no, no…" Tears streamed down his face. Tears were streaming down my face as well.

Then he cocked his right hand back and leaned toward me just a bit. I felt certain he would strike me, and I considered letting him, but his fist passed deliberately to my right and slammed into the wall. When he brought it back, several of the knuckles were bleeding and obviously broken.

I put my arm around his shoulder. "I'm sorry," I said. "I'm sorry. I couldn't stop the bleeding in time. I'm sorry." We slowly walked out to the hallway. Greg, who had heard everything, was standing there with a sickened look on his face. Evren let out another big sob and smashed his other hand against the wall, then slowly collapsed to the floor as I tried to hold him by the arms.

The elevator doors opened, and Doruk's mother appeared. She quickly surveyed the scene and, seeing Evren hunched on the floor, with me kneeling, still holding his arms, shouted a frantic question in Turkish. Without looking up, he responded with a monotone string of words I couldn't understand. She burst into tears, fixed her eyes on me, and began screaming, "Murderer!" over and over. Suddenly she collapsed to the floor with a thud. Greg rushed over to assist her, whereupon she slowly rose to her hands and knees and crawled across the floor to Evren, clutching him as she wept.

We did our best to comfort the two of them as they talked and cried, kneeling or sitting on the floor with them. Fifteen minutes later a third, then a fourth, fifth, and sixth family member arrived. With each one, the same sequence was repeated: anxious look, question, response, shriek, collapse to the floor, and embrace. I'm sure that the patients lying in their beds on the ward 30 feet away heard every word and every scream.

I wished I were anywhere else but where I was. Being dead would have been a preferable alternative. Although I realized Doruk's family felt worse than I did, I couldn't imagine my mental state being much lower; or so I thought.

We managed to get everyone off the floor and settle them down a bit. Evren asked to see Doruk. I think he didn't quite believe what I had told him, and I guess he had absolutely no reason to trust me. I warned him that Doruk wouldn't look very good, but he insisted on seeing his brother.

As a matter of routine, any traumatic, unexpected, or suspicious death must be investigated by the coroner. We are therefore instructed to leave the body as it was when death occurred, except that we are allowed to close any operative incisions. I knew Doruk would still have an endotracheal tube sticking out of his mouth, a nasogastric tube hanging out his nose, and IVs in his forearms. His hair would be wet and matted. His face and arms would be swollen. He would not have that pink, warm, vigorous look that Evren was used to seeing. He would not sit up and say, "Hi, Evren. Here I am, and I'm okay!" as he would have just a few hours ago.

Evren and I got in the elevator to go down to the pathology viewing room, otherwise known as the morgue. His hands were swollen, bleeding, and hanging limply at his sides. I wiped his tears and helped him blow his nose as he cried, since he couldn't hold a tissue. His head was bowed, his shoulders slumped, and I must have looked the same. We said nothing to each other. The elevator doors opened, and we walked slowly down the hall, side by side, my arm around his shoulders.

When we entered the viewing room, the smell of death in the morgue was oppressive; it's a rotten, putrid, permeating odor. We were standing in front of a large window covered by a curtain. An attendant inside drew the curtain back slowly, revealing a rigid, pasty-white, almost ghostly Doruk lying on a cement slab with tubes sticking out of various parts of his body. He appeared unquestionably dead, even to a non-physician; the scene was otherworldly, even to a physician.

Evren let out a guttural, choking sound and turned to his left, facing a wall made of very rough brick, the type you might find on the outside of an industrial building. He put his palms on the wall at about head level, curved his fingers into a cup-like shape, and slowly sank to the floor, crying. He dragged his fingers down the wall as though he might dig Doruk out of this building and safely take him home. I heard an awful crackling sound as he broke all eight of his fingernails over backwards. Blood dripped off the ends of his fingers, and he convulsed in a series of wet exhalations. I lifted him to his feet and nearly had to carry him to the elevator. He refused my repeated pleas to go to the emergency room to assess and treat his disfigured and bloodied hands.

When we arrived back on the tenth floor, he gathered with his shell-shocked family and exchanged a few more emotional words in low tones, the entire group looking at us with utter contempt. After a few minutes, he regained his composure and walked stiffly over to me. He cleared his throat and, staring intensely into my eyes, said, "Doctor, I know you killed my brother today. And you..." he swallowed hard, "you know I can't do anything about it, because I'm poor." With that, he and his family disappeared into the elevator. I never heard from them again.

After checking on a few of the sickest patients in the ICU, I left the hospital in the most profound state of depression I had ever experienced. I hardly slept all night.

In the morning, I met with Greg and Dr. Everett (Dr. O'Donnelly was out of town, and I wouldn't think of meeting with Dr. Rollins). I announced that I was quitting the residency program, effective as soon as they would release me. All night long, as I stared at the darkened ceiling, I heard Evren's words echoing in my mind, and I now agreed with him: I was a murderer. I had killed Doruk Yilmaz. I didn't feel worthy of continuing my training to be a surgeon. I didn't feel worthy of being alive.

"I know you went through hell last night, Dr. Harch," said Dr. Everett. "But let me ask you something. If you had to do the operation all over again to save this guy's life, what would you do differently?"

I thought about it for a minute. "Nothing, sir. I think we did everything the way we were supposed to. We were really careful. I can't figure out what went wrong, technically."

"So why should you quit? What sense does that make?"

In these situations, our chiefs and mentors are required to shepherd young surgeons through events that seem catastrophic but must, by necessity, be viewed as nothing more than tragic and difficult learning experiences. Dr. Everett informed me that he wouldn't consider my offer to quit, and that my performance the last four years, including yesterday, was excellent. Hearing him say this didn't make me feel much better.

Greg insisted that Doruk's death was in fact his responsibility since he was the senior surgeon on the case, and he had pushed me to not place chest tubes for early signs of bleeding. He said I had no justification to blame myself for this death.

By afternoon, word had gotten around the hospital about what had transpired the previous night. Some of my colleagues stopped me late in the day to share details of their own disaster cases and how they survived emotionally. Within a few days, I became so busy that I didn't have time to dwell on the Yilmaz family's misfortune.

What did I learn from this gut-wrenching experience? I realized that a major elective surgery has the potential to unravel quickly into a calamity. I now understood that others like Doruk might die in spite of my best efforts and intentions. I learned that this profession we call surgery demands much more humility than I'd ever imagined, certainly more than I possessed.

CHAPTER TWENTY-FOUR

"I LOVE WORKIN' HERE"

THERE WAS A KNOCK ON THE DOOR OF the resident's library. Dozing in a tattered recliner after a night on call, I gazed listlessly over my shoulder as a junior resident got up and opened the door. A young Hispanic cop stood in the hallway.

"I'd like to speak to Dr. Harch," said the cop.

I got up slowly and walked to the door.

"I'm Harch," I said, rubbing 20 minutes of sleep from my eyes.

"Do you mind coming out into the hallway so we can talk?" he asked.

"Sure," I said, stepping out of my sanctuary.

"Did you operate on a gunshot victim named Pablo Lopez about a month ago?"

I tilted my head, pursed my lips a little, and looked into the distance, which in fact, was the wall eight feet away. "Uh…you'll have to be more specific. I've operated on about 20 guys with gunshots in the last few weeks, and many of them were named Lopez or Martinez or Garcia."

I observed his nametag. It read, Officer Dominguez.

"This guy," said Officer Dominguez, "was about 24 years old. He was shot in the chest and abdomen, and died before he left the operating room."

"Oh, yeah," I said. "Sure, I remember the case." When someone dies while you're operating, you don't forget it. We call it "leaving them on the table," and it's almost unbearable (like Doruk's death). If you're reasonably capable as a surgeon, it should be an infrequent occurrence. This particular patient had been shot multiple times, was bleeding in his abdomen and chest, and we couldn't close all the holes before he exsanguinated (bled to death).

"What can I tell you about the case?" I asked.

"Well, I'm on the LAPD Gang Task Force, and we're trying to track down the opposing gang members who carried out this hit."

"Yeah…"

"I'm told that you removed a bullet from the patient's abdomen during the surgery. Is that correct?"

"Yeah. In fact, when the case finished, an officer asked me to scratch my initials in the bullet for later identification."

The truth is, we almost never remove a bullet during surgery. We rarely ever see them. Some bullets pass through the victims completely and embed themselves into the surroundings, but most get lodged somewhere in the body and can't be found, since there's usually so much swelling and bleeding in the tissues around the bullet. Digging around to find a bullet, even when you know roughly where it is, ends up causing more tissue damage and bleeding. Leaving it in place rarely causes any increased risk for the patient. That's why it has always annoyed the hell out of me to watch a movie where doctors labor furiously to find a bullet in a gunshot victim, then announce proudly that they have found it, implying that all sorts of troubles have been avoided by discovering it and plucking it out. The real damage, of course, happens when this high-velocity missile rips through skin, bone, muscle, organs, and blood vessels. I just happened to come across the bullet during the operation on Pablo Lopez and grabbed it.

"We're working on the forensic analysis of the case. We'd like you to come over to the county morgue, confirm that the bullet we have was removed from Mr. Lopez, and describe the entry and exit sites of the rounds that killed him."

"I can do that, but I'm limited by my call schedule. I'll come to the morgue sometime when I'm off call."

"Here's the phone number. Call them when you can come by. We really need your help on this one."

"No problem."

"Thanks, doctor."

Lori's pregnancy was coming along nicely; morning sickness had disappeared and there were no signs of trouble. But as we got into the seventh month, an ultrasound showed the baby had a transverse lie (baby oriented horizontally rather than with head or feet downward). We had to consider the possibility of a version (turning the baby before delivery) or a C-section if our daughter was to be born safely. Yes, we were going to have a girl.

Late one afternoon, Nick Givens stopped me in the hallway and asked if I could meet with him. We agreed to meet in an empty room on the tenth floor after the day's work was completed. I was nervous because I had no idea what he wanted to discuss.

"Take a seat," said Nick.

"Okay…" I said tentatively.

"Do you know that I have a sort of private practice in the community?" he asked.

"What are you talking about?"

"Well, you don't think I could support a wife and four kids on the salary they pay us to work 110 hours a week, do you?"

I had never really thought about it, having spent most of my residency single.

"I guess not, Nick."

"I've been making house calls for the last three years on sick, old people who can't leave their homes."

I was astounded, so much so that I was speechless. The rest of us were just trying to survive the training program while the best damn doctor amongst us was moonlighting to support his family. When did he sleep? Or spend a minute with his wife or kids? How the hell did his wife get pregnant?

"Now, you know I'm finishing as resident supervisor in about 10 weeks. And I've handed off all my home patients to other, office-based doctors...except for two of them. And I want to know if you'd be willing to take them on."

Now I was really shocked. And flattered beyond belief. Nick Givens was asking me to assume care of the patients he didn't want to hand over to anyone else.

"Well, of course I'll do it, Nick." In truth, I didn't want more work, but there was no other answer I could give.

"Great. Let me tell you about them. The first lady, Edna, is 85 and has hypertension and congestive heart failure. Her ejection fraction is so poor that she can't leave her home... she's on a half-dozen meds...and she's so sweet I can't hand her off to just anyone."

"I can take her, Nick."

"The other lady, Millie, is quite a different story. Have you heard of the old-fashioned iron lungs?"

"You mean the ones they used to put polio victims in before ventilators?"

"Exactly. In fact, this lady is in the iron lung because of polio."

"Wow. I didn't know there were any remaining."

"Nearly everyone has been put on small, portable ventilators, or they've died. But this lady has been in the iron lung for 30 years and is comfortable there. She has repeatedly refused to go on a vent."

"Jeez. How does she do it?"

"Well, she can breathe on her own for a couple minutes using compressed air and oxygen, so her caretakers can open the iron lung briefly to clean her and move her."

"Incredible." I was anxious to meet one of the last people living in an iron lung, and honored to think I'd be her doctor.

Officer Dominguez had called me twice in the last week to remind me about going to the morgue. I got Billy to cover me and drove to a building with a big sign that read, "Los Angeles County Coroner's Office." Once I was inside, an officer accompanied me through a thick door and into a large, cold room. There were steel autopsy tables all along the wall, with a naked body on every single one.

"This way," said the officer. The first body we passed was a young, black guy with stab and slash wounds all over his chest and arms. Right next to him was a young, white gal missing both of her arms...well, not exactly missing... they were on the table beside her. Next was a middle-aged Hispanic guy with rope burns on his neck.

We rounded a corner and entered another, larger room. There were bodies everywhere, dozens of them. The penetrating smell of slowly decomposing flesh mingled sickeningly with the chemical smell of formaldehyde. It appeared that no one in this building had enjoyed a natural death. One guy had his face blown off by a shotgun blast. I walked right past a woman who must have suffered a hatchet attack; her forehead was split open vertically and I could peer straight into her brain. This was worse than any horror movie I'd ever seen, and way worse than any day on trauma call at LA County-USC. It was a graphic stroll through the detritus of the city's daily war on itself. Finally, we stopped.

"I think this is Pablo Lopez," said the officer. "Wait here and I'll get the pathologist."

I could see my handiwork on Pablo's belly: a vertical midline incision that had been reopened by the pathologist here in the morgue. While I waited, I couldn't stop myself from looking around the room. I looked to the right. I couldn't tell the age or race of the person because the body was so badly burned. I think it was a woman. Two tables over was a guy with a knife handle sticking out of his head. His eyes were still open. On Pablo's left was a fat white guy with tire marks running from his right thigh, across his abdomen and chest, and ending on his face, which was somewhat flattened.

"Dr. Harch?" I stopped gawking and turned to see a middle-aged guy in a white coat. Under his white coat were too-short plaid pants and a plaid shirt which didn't come close to matching the pants. "I'm Dr. Percival, one of the pathologists here."

"Nice to meet you, Dr. Percival," I said.

"Oh, just call me Tom."

"This place is incredible…I've never…"

"Yeah, lots of carved-up, shot-up, broken-up, burned-up stiffs. Every sort of violence and mayhem you can imagine. Gives people the creeps when they come in here. Not me, though. I love workin' here. None of these goners give me any lip."

"Yeah, when they're alive, it's a little more complicated," I said, thinking about some of the nasty people we had to tolerate at the hospital. "But the sheer number of dead people here astonishes me."

"Crazy, huh? And lots more roll in every day. Well, let's get down to business. Your guy here…or I guess he's my guy now. Tell me about entry and exit sites, injuries, the bullet, etc."

I launched into a recap of what Pablo looked like when he arrived, where the bullets entered and exited (in my opinion), and exactly where I found the bullet.

"Can you identify this bullet as the one you removed from his belly?"

I looked at the bullet. Sure enough, it had my initials scratched on it.

"That's definitely it."

"Will you sign an affidavit confirming that?"

"Sure."

"Good. We'll finish the ballistics on the bullet. They've arrested some guys they think did the shooting, so if we can match the gun, we can nail the bastards."

"Glad to help get some of these scumballs off the street."

Nick and I were standing in a living room in front of a huge, light-green steel drum, positioned on its side and raised about four feet off the ground on steel legs. A woman's head protruded from one end. She was tilted partially on her side, so she could see us. We could hear the rhythmic cycling of the air pumps, repeatedly pulling air out and forcing it back into the iron lung. I knew I was witnessing medical history.

"Millie," said Nick, "this is Dr. Harch."

"Very nice…to meet you," she replied, limited to short phrases by her dependence on the machine.

"This is the doctor I told you about, who'll be taking over your care when I leave," added Nick.

"I hate to see you go," she said, tearing up, "but you said…I'd be in good hands."

"Dr. Harch knows all about you, and he'll take good care of you."

She looked at me and smiled. "I guess it's you and me now…and my caretakers, of course," she said, angling her eyes toward a middle-aged man sitting against the wall in a chair. He nodded but said nothing.

"Dr. Givens' shoes will be hard to fill," I said, "but I'll do my best."

"Let's open up the chamber so I can show Dr. Harch how I examine you," said Nick.

The caretaker gave Millie oxygen using a mask applied to her face, and after a few minutes, we opened the iron lung like a clam shell. As Millie took shallow breaths, we quickly examined her lungs, heart, and abdomen. Then we closed the iron lung again.

"You have two, maybe three minutes before she starts to drop her oxygen levels," said Nick.

"Got it," I said. "Millie, you are an amazing person. How long now in the lung?"

"Thirty-one years," she said proudly.

"Amazing," I repeated, shaking my head.

On the way to our next home-care patient, Nick got serious.

"John," he said, "Millie has been in reasonably good health for a long time, but she's getting older, and she's just been lying there for decades. I've been lucky that she's never gotten sick. It's only a matter of time before something happens. And then she'll be hard to manage. Just moving her would likely require intubating her."

"Yeah, I was worrying about that when we opened the iron lung. All I can say is that I'll make the best decisions I can if something happens."

"I know you will. That's all I can ask."

Before returning to the hospital, we stopped at Edna's house. She was a sweet elderly lady. Nick handed her off to me in a similar way, but he didn't need to say too much about her fragile state. We both knew she had one foot on a banana peel, perhaps more than Millie.

CHAPTER TWENTY-FIVE

QUICK BREAK
FOR A BABY

"JOHN, I'M JUST NOT COMFORTABLE with the version," said Lori.

We'd listened to the description of how they'd turn Shawna (we'd settled on her name) and what the risks were.

"I don't think they'd recommend it if it wasn't safe," I said.

"It sounds painful, and I'm worried about something going wrong with our baby."

"OK. But you know that commits you to a C-section."

"Yeah. That's acceptable to me."

It wasn't just Lori who had concerns about this pregnancy. Two rotations through pediatric surgery had scared the shit out of me. Cerebral palsy, diaphragmatic hernias, esophageal atresia, FLKs! And imperforate anus...lots and lots of time spent caring for babies without anal openings, who required numerous surgeries. I was certain our baby would have some devastating abnormality.

Our obstetrician agreed to schedule a C-section. An amniocentesis showed that Shawna's lungs were ready, and we set a date. I horse traded to get half a day off for the 7 a.m. start of Lori's surgery.

On the appointed day, we departed for the hospital at 5:30 a.m. After registering Lori, my beeper went off...it was 6:30. I wasn't supposed to be bothered until at least midday. The text told me to call Dr. Feinberg. By now, he and I had become pretty good friends.

"John," said Marc, with a strained, urgent sound to his voice, "I hate to call you, but I'm screwed and need help."

"What's the matter?"

"I've got that big esophageal case today, but when I sat on the bed this morning to put on my socks, my back went out. I've spent the last 45 minutes trying to stand up straight, but I'm in too much pain. Is there any way you could do the case for me today?"

I knew he must be in bad shape because nothing stopped him from doing surgery, especially an esophageal case, which was coveted and rare.

"Is there any way to cancel it until you're better? We've got a baby to deliver this morning."

"No. We've been getting this ready for weeks. If I cancel, it'll take forever to reschedule, and I'll be off the service. Everyone else is busy. I really need your help. I'll come in and be in the OR with you, but I just can't physically do the case."

"What time is the case scheduled?"

"Eleven a.m."

"Could we push it back to 11:30 or 12?

"Probably."

"I think I can do it. But I won't be very popular."

"Great. Talk to you in a bit. Good luck."

"Bye, Marc."

I spoke to Lori just before we went into the OR. She wasn't too happy, but she understood the urgency and agreed to let me go after she delivered. How many wives, I wondered, would tolerate this?

When the C-section got underway and the doctors sliced open Lori's uterus, our obstetrician said, "Oh, my."

"What?" I asked with alarm. I was certain my fears were going to be justified.

"This umbilical cord is wrapped around the baby's neck. I'm glad we didn't try the version. Everything's okay, though."

Soon, they lifted Shawna out of the blood and slimy amniotic fluid, and placed her on the warming table. She was suctioned, she let out a cry, and Apgars were measured. She was pink and looked healthy. The nurses wrapped her up tightly in a blanket like a little loaf of bread and handed her to me. She was beautiful. I immediately unwrapped her, lifted her legs up, and looked at her butt.

"What are you doing?" asked the nurse who'd handed her to me. She was either angry or insulted (or both).

"I'm checking for an anus…and she's got one. A very nice one."

The nurse just shook her head, then looked over at the obstetrician. He shrugged, but said nothing.

I got to spend about two hours with Lori and Shawna, said my profuse apologies, and bolted for the hospital. Feinberg was in the OR, partially bent over and in extreme pain, getting the patient ready for surgery. I did the case with a faculty surgeon helping, and Feinberg watched, wishing like hell that he could be in my shoes.

I finished the rest of my work, then met Billy, Skip, and several other buddies in the residents' library at 5:30 p.m. I announced the birth of my first child, whipped out some cigars, and we leaned back and smoked them. I received a round of congratulations. I tried to complain about being unexpectedly separated from my wife and new baby that morning, but there would be no sympathy—they were more impressed that I got a great esophageal case dropped in my lap. Ignoring their heartlessness, I was determined to savor the significance of this milestone, so I hurried back across town to spend a few more hours with my new family.

One afternoon, I was writing some orders at the nursing station on our surgical ward. Sitting across the desk from me was a clerk who was engaged in a serious phone conversation.

"Yeah, you know that guy Darron who works on 5300? He just got disability! Can you believe that?"

She listened for the response, then added, "Yeah, you know I been tryin' to get disability around here for six years...and Darron, he gets hired and gets disability in less than a year!"

I'm sure there was a similarly outraged response from the other end of the line.

"I just can't figure this place out. I'm gonna talk to Darron and find out what he did to get disability so fast. It just ain't fair."

I had to bite my tongue hard enough to need an ENT consult, but I kept my mouth shut. I also had to stop myself from slapping her. I wasn't sure I'd last here another year. Fortunately, I'd completed my orders and saw Mr. Patel walking by in the main hallway. Maybe I could cheer myself up by doing some sightseeing in his twisted mind.

"Mr. Patel," I said as I caught up with him, "what's happening?"

"Oh, well, my good Dr. Harch. Let me see, let me see." He rubbed his chin as he got a sick grin on his face. "This is truly bad. You must have heard about the 26-year-old psychotic woman who heard voices telling her to kill her babies."

"No. I haven't heard this. When did this happen?"

"Last week. Anyway, she put the babies in the tub and cut them up."

"No!"

"Yes, indeed. Then she cut her own tongue out, and slit her wrists. But, alas, she didn't die. ENT sewed up what was left of her tongue. She's in jail now for murder."

"Ooooh, that is bad…"

"Well, that's not all."

"What a surprise…continue," I said.

"Three days ago, we admitted a 13-year-old boy. He was sitting in a car between his father, who was the driver, and his drunk uncle. The father stopped and went into a store, leaving the car running. The uncle lit his lighter, held it near the boy's face, and told him to drive. The boy hesitated, so he held the lighter closer, and the boy started driving."

"I'm pretty sure this isn't going to end well."

"The uncle urged him to drive faster, holding the lighter near his clothes. As they entered a freeway on-ramp, the uncle pushed down on top of the boy's foot on the accelerator. The car sped up and crashed."

Mr. Patel stopped talking and looked at me, delighted to have snared his audience.

"Well, what happened?" I asked, impatiently.

"Luckily, the boy sustained only bumps, bruises, and abrasions."

"And the uncle?"

"I don't know."

"How the hell could you not know? You know everything around here, don't you, Mr. Patel?"

"I try to, but sometimes I don't get all the details."

My beeper went off.

"Gotta go, Mr. Patel. Find out what happened to the uncle. And save up some more good stories for next time."

One of the last trials I had to endure at the end of my fourth year was another rotation through vascular surgery. I dreaded being subjected again to the pervasive malevolence of Dr. Rollins.

The patients were handed over to me by Mike Miller (one of the six who'd made the cut from my intern class and was now a fourth-year resident, like me). By the end of the day, I'd memorized each patient's problems and the details of any surgeries done.

The next morning, I had to make rounds with Dr. Rollins and my new team. We went from bed to bed as I described each case. Several of the patients had developed post-op wound infections (generally a very serious problem in vascular surgery), and when I presented the third such misadventure to Rollins, he stopped me.

"Dr. Harch," he said very slowly and pedantically, "does every patient you operate on get a post-op wound infection?"

I stared at him. I didn't fidget or shift my feet or stammer. I just stared. He was in full bully mode, and wanted to see if I'd cower and avoid the whole false premise of his question.

It was another one of his depraved tests to see how far he could push someone.

"Dr. Rollins," I said, in a similar, slow, pedantic tone, "you and I both know that I haven't operated on any of these patients, so the purpose of your question is unclear to me." I continued to look straight into Rollins' eyes without blinking. It was a bit risky, but I'd had it with the little dickhead.

Without responding, he turned and walked to the next patient's bedside. Although he was never friendly, that was the last insulting thing he ever said to me.

CHAPTER TWENTY-SIX

SURGEON
OF THE DAY

SUNDAY, AUGUST 31, 1986, WOULD be a day of historic infamy for Southern California, but we didn't know it when we arrived to cover trauma call.

In addition to being the chief resident for the Sunday Service, I was also surgeon of the day. This designation was given, on alternate days, to the chief resident for either general surgery or orthopedics. The appointed doctor had near-dictatorial power over the emergency operating room schedule; anyone from any surgical service who wanted to schedule an urgent or emergency surgery had to call and arrange it with the surgeon of the day.

Why such an odd plan for a schedule that should be determined purely by the degree of injury or illness? The answer is that each day, both orthopedic and general surgery cases became backed up, sometimes 10 or 15 deep. Having control of the OR allowed either chief resident to spend 24 hours digging out of the hole, scheduling case after case until the backup was diminished. Consequently, there were days when our appendectomies and cholecystectomies had to wait a few additional hours while ortho stabilized fractures that had been sitting unrepaired for 12 to 24 hours. True red blanket cases continued to take precedence (gunshots, stab wounds, or motor vehicle accidents with active bleeding or low blood pressure), as did serious head injuries and open fractures.

But the surgeon of the day couldn't abuse the privilege. If another surgeon had an equal or more urgent need, negotiation ensued until a compromise was reached. It was considered poor form to "hog" the OR all day and night, and if you did, payback would come soon enough on another day. Each of us discovered that the smart, efficient way to be surgeon of the day was to just be fair.

Being surgeon of the day may sound like a great honor, or an opportunity to sashay around the hospital with an air of importance, but in fact, it was a huge pain in the ass. Beeps and calls from the other surgical specialists to argue their cases (diplomatically on a good day, irascibly on an aggravating day) sucked away critical time that could be spent getting real work done.

I set my students and interns to work on the pass-ons we'd received at 7 a.m. My junior resident and I drained a perirectal abscess in the OR, then split up to see a handful of consults. I was in the ER examining a 19-year-old man who'd been jumped, robbed, and had both ears ripped off, when my beeper went off. Simultaneously, I got an overhead page to the operator, which was unusual. The beeper text read, "Call hospital operator." It was about 10 minutes after noon.

"Dr. Harch," said the operator, "I have Dr. Rex Magnuson, director of emergency services on the line with an extremely urgent call. Please hold while I connect."

"Dr. Harch, this is Dr. Magnuson, regional director of emergency services for LA County. Are you the chief resident in charge of trauma today at LA County?"

"Yes, sir, I am."

"Well, a commercial airliner just crashed in Cerritos."

"Oh, my God. How big an airliner?"

"We don't know yet."

"How far is Cerritos? Twenty, thirty minutes?"

"Yeah, about that."

"So we don't know how many survivors?"

"That's correct. It could be in the hundreds, since they were slowing down to land. I suggest you clear your ER, your surgical admitting areas, and finish any surgeries as quickly as possible. There are obviously multiple hospitals available in the area, but you can expect to get the bulk of the badly injured."

"Okay. Thanks. Call me back immediately with any new information."

I set the phone down. Holy shit. This could make the past four years of chaos seem like a walk in the park

"Hey, guys," I yelled toward C-booth. "Have you heard?"

"Yeah," said a charge nurse, "plane down in Cerritos."

"Clear out anyone you can from these trauma bays," I said.

I phoned 9200. "There was a plane crash in Cerritos a few minutes ago. Tell the interns to transfer anyone who's reasonably stable back to Saturday Service or to our ward."

I called the OR on the fifteenth floor. "Hey, we could have dozens, or even hundreds of injured people from a plane crash. What's running?"

"Two ortho cases," said the nurse, "and the Saturday Service is finishing a take-back. We're about to go get your next appendectomy."

"Forget the appy for now. Tell everyone to finish up quickly. I'll keep you updated when I have info on numbers of injured. And call in every anesthesia person we have."

I called 9200 again and asked the clerk to call in every faculty surgeon and resident who wasn't on vacation.

We didn't know any of this at the time, but an Aeromexico DC-9 had collided with a small Piper aircraft and then crashed into a residential neighborhood. The McDonnell Douglas DC-9 was a single-aisle jet that could carry between 80 and 135 passengers, depending on the version and the seating configuration, but in my mind, I pictured a 747, with 400-600 passengers on board.

My anxiety level began to rise. What type of injuries should we expect, and how should we prepare to treat them? High-speed plane deceleration would cause internal bleeding, fractures, head injuries...and burns. With most airline crashes, there's a big explosion as the remaining fuel ignites. I called the burn unit.

"Hello, burn ICU," said a nurse.

"This is Dr. Harch, general surgery chief resident on call. Have they notified you guys about the commercial airliner that crashed in the Cerritos area a short time ago?"

"No! We haven't heard anything!"

"Well, we could potentially have many, many burn patients on our doorstep soon. You might want to call Dr. Zelinski and prepare your staff."

"I will. Thank you. This is terrible..." She hung up.

Now we waited. I beeped my junior resident and asked him to clean up any significant consults or other pending work, and delay starting anything else. I decided to remain in the ER, since updates (and patients) would likely arrive there first. Everyone got busy readying thoracotomy trays, chest tube trays, splints, and big IV lines.

Five minutes passed...then ten. The tension increased. Nervous glances were passed around as people pondered what might be transpiring out on the streets. In the recesses of my mind lurked the fear that I might not be able to handle dozens of severely injured victims. Finally, I got another overhead page and was connected to Dr. Magnuson again.

"Dr. Harch, I've spoken to our first responders on the ground in Cerritos. I'm sorry to report that there are no survivors."

I felt like I'd been punched in the gut. "None? Are you sure? None from the plane? None in the area where the plane hit the ground?"

"Unfortunately, no. There was a big explosion and fire, and everyone involved seems to have perished. They're still searching the site for injured, but right now, we have no one to send you."

"Wow," I said. "That's horrible news...let me know if something changes." I hung up the phone and looked at the ER staff. "There are no survivors," I said sadly.

"No one?" asked the doctor in charge of the ER. "How can that be?"

"He said there was a big explosion and fire, and everyone involved died."

Everyone was stunned. They slowly began putting away all the equipment that had been carefully arranged on metal stands in the trauma area. Nobody said much.

It would come out later that the small private airplane entered the DC-9's airspace without clearance, directly impacting the horizontal stabilizer of the DC-9 and completely shearing it off. The pilot of the Piper, his wife, and daughter were immediately decapitated and the plane fell into an empty school yard. The DC-9 flipped upside down and dove nose-first straight into the ground, exploding as it landed on a house. The flying debris and fire consumed several more homes. All 64 passengers and crew on the plane died, along with 15 people in the Cerritos neighborhood. An additional 8 people on the ground were lightly injured and were treated on scene or in nearby hospitals.

It was difficult to get back to work, and I kept thinking we'd get a call saying many injured were found, but no such call ever came. Everyone was, in fact, dead. I repeated my previous call sequence and asked everyone to resume caring for the patients they already had in house.

I'd been procrastinating about something that had to be done: I needed to go see Nick Givens' home care patients. It would have to be squeezed in during the few "off" hours I had on a weekend.

"Hi, Millie," I said, as I stood next to the giant, hissing iron lung. "I hope this was a good time to visit you."

"Oh, doctor…any time is a good time," she said. "You know…I'm always right here. I don't get out much." She forced a little smile.

We chatted a little, then her caretaker opened the iron lung. I examined her and checked her vital signs.

"Everything looks fine," I said, as we closed the lid. I sat and jotted a few notes. "Millie, you're impressive."

"Oh, thank you…but I don't think…I'm impressive. I'm fortunate. I have…family and friends…that come visit me. I have…wonderful caretakers…who look after me. If I were… in many other countries…I would have been dead…long ago."

"But some people might not have such a good attitude."

"Well...I can look out...those bay windows...and watch...the seasons change...such as they are...in Southern... California. I eat well...and have TV...to keep up on things. All in all...not too bad a life."

I nodded my head. "Well, to me, you're an inspiration. Keep up the good work, and I'll see you in a few months."

"You can bet...on it, Doctor."

I drove the 15 minutes to Edna's house, regretting the whining I did about my long work hours. I could be trapped in an iron lung for 31 years....

Edna's daughter greeted me at the door and guided me to a recliner in the living room, where Edna sat with her oxygen tank. She was short of breath just sitting there, but gave me a big smile.

"How are you feeling today? I asked.

"Pretty good," she gasped.

"How tough is your breathing?"

"Oh...about the same." She took a big breath. "Not too bad."

"You mean difficult, right?"

She didn't answer, but continued smiling.

"Let me listen to your lungs." I put my stethoscope against her back and listened in several places. She had rales, a crackly sound indicating she had extra fluid in her system. I moved the stethoscope over her heart and heard sounds confirming that her congestive heart failure was a little worse. "Mmmm-hmmm," I muttered as I listened, "mmmm-hmmm." I took Edna's hand. Her daughter looked at me expectantly.

"Are you eating well?" I asked.

"Yes."

"Oh, c'mon, Mom. You're not eating a thing," interjected her daughter.

"Just a little too short of breath to eat?" I asked.

"I guess so."

"Let me see your medicines." They produced six bottles, and I looked at each one. "You've got a little too much fluid in you right now, so I want to double the Lasix for a week and double the potassium. And we'll have someone come by and check your blood in a few days."

"Okay," said Edna.

"You haven't forgotten about watching your salt, right?" She and her daughter looked at each other, exchanging unspoken words.

"I'm doing...my best."

"I know. I just have to pester you a little...it's my job, you know."

"Doctor...I don't think...I'm worth...all this fussing. I'm just...a dying old lady."

"Mom!" exclaimed her daughter.

"Well, I think you're worth it," I said. "If you'll keep trying, I will too."

"We'll leave it...in God's hands," said Edna.

"Good decision. See you in a month or two."

CHAPTER TWENTY-SEVEN

A FISH OUT OF WATER

WAS IN A FOUL MOOD LONG BEFORE I GOT called to see Alonzo Guzman in the ER. I was overtired, behind in my work, and he was just another stab wound to the belly, perhaps one of five or ten we'd see that day. But Alonzo was different from many of the quiet, cooperative, young Mexican guys that rolled into the ER knowing that their survival depended on the medical professionals staffing the hospital.

"Hey, bitch," Alonzo was saying to a nurse as I walked into C-booth, "bend over a little more so I can see your ass."

"That's enough," said the ER doctor.

"Fuck you, you bald-headed dumb ass," replied Alonzo. "You can't shut me up."

"We're trying to help you here," said a nurse.

"I don't need your fuckin' white-ass help," said Alonzo.

"What do we have?" I asked the ER doctor.

"Single stab to the mid-abdomen. BP's a little marginal. No other apparent injuries, but he's not real cooperative."

"Why should I cooperate with you fuckin' losers?"

I stood at the bedside and just looked at Alonzo.

"What are you looking at, dick mouth?" asked Alonzo.

"Someone who's been stabbed," I answered calmly.

"Well, so what? Lots of people get stabbed. I've stabbed people. Some of 'em died."

"Well, that's real nice. But now you're here, and it's my job to fix whatever's wrong with you."

"Well, who put you in charge, shitface?"

"I'm not in charge. I'm just one of the surgeons here." This guy reminded me of the drunk driver I saw with Eva Brandt when I was an intern, the one who'd abused everyone in the ER until we sedated and paralyzed him. But that guy was drunk and may have had a head injury. This guy was sober (it seemed) and was just an asshole.

We bargained with the guy and eventually he allowed us to put in an IV. He answered just enough questions between insults to complete a cursory history. He finally allowed a physical exam, and when I pulled the sheet down, he had a huge, complex, full-color tattoo covering his entire abdomen, extending up onto his chest. It featured a three-masted ship, a sea serpent, naked women, and skulls. The detail and color were extraordinary; maybe one of the best tattoos I'd ever seen (and I'd seen a lot of them). In the middle of it all was a small stab wound, interrupting the perfection of the tattoo. When I pressed on his abdomen, he groaned and shouted, "That hurts, ya stupid shit!"

I wanted to slap him into the next room. But his blood pressure was dropping and I knew there was no choice but to take him upstairs.

"Alonzo, you're either bleeding or have perforated bowel or both. You need surgery now."

"Well...who made you...so smart?" His words were spoken more slowly and less angrily because of the low blood pressure. After a few seconds, he said, "Fine...do whatever you have to."

As we rolled Alonzo out of the ER, he still had enough clarity to deliver one last offensive salvo. "Hey, nurse...you with the heels...I'd like to fuck you...sometime."

When we opened Alonzo's belly, I had to cut right through the middle of the huge, beautiful tattoo. I slowly drew the scalpel along the smooth, painted skin, which lay atop a muscular abdominal wall. Once inside, we found some holes in his small intestine and multiple, bleeding vessels. Everything was easily fixed and cleaned up. But I was simmering over the entire verbal lashing we'd had to quietly endure in the ER. When we were nearly finished and had only the skin to close, my junior resident held the skin edges together with the tattoo carefully aligned, as I prepared to place the skin staples.

"Hold it, Peter," I said. "I'll align the skin and you place the staples."

"Suit yourself," said Peter, a little confused, since this was such a rudimentary part of the procedure.

Then I misaligned the tattoo by about a quarter of an inch.

"You're off," said Peter.

"I know," I said. "Just place the staples." And he did. Then we stood back and admired the final product. The ship, the masts, everything in the center of his abdomen were subtly wrong. Sort of blurred. It felt right. It felt good.

"Perfect," I said. "I need dressings." I placed a big dressing over the wound. I knew Alonzo probably wouldn't discover it until he looked in the mirror at home a week or two from now. Did I worry that Alonzo would come hunt for me? Maybe. Not really. If he came back to the hospital and shot me dead, I'd get to have a nice, long sleep.

Shawna was often down for the night when I arrived home after work, and still asleep when I left in the morning around 6 a.m. She was growing and changing rapidly, and I tried to spend as much time with her and Lori as possible, especially on the weekends.

Lori was now working at *Emmy* magazine, the official publication of the Television Academy. We got some cool perks out of it, like attending the Emmy Awards and the post-award party, where we got to rub elbows with television celebrities. But Lori's life was now as hectic as mine, despite having found a kind, older family friend to assume child care during the work week. Meeting her publishing deadlines became increasingly difficult, particularly when Shawna would get sick and want Mommy, and only Mommy. They couldn't depend on me for anything on any day.

The stress was inescapable. Both of us began having upper abdominal pain. We both assumed we had ulcers. I had antacids in my car, my locker at the hospital, my gym bag, my briefcase, and at home…I gobbled them regularly, with relief. Lori had her stash of Mylanta as well. When the H-2 blockers became readily available, I got samples of Zantac and Tagamet for the two of us to share. And we used them.

The midpoint of my fifth year was rapidly approaching. I had to start thinking about what I'd do on July 1, when I'd be done with this insane residency. The prospect of finding a job in private practice was intimidating and exciting at the same time, and held the probability of making more than the roughly five dollars an hour I was currently getting (yes, I worked out the math; roughly five dollars an hour). But there was no standardized process for the soon-to-be graduates to search for employment. Most of the opportunities arose through personal connections with senior surgeons or from our senior faculty.

A few of my colleagues had a father or other family member with an existing surgery practice they could enter. Billy was applying for a two-year trauma fellowship. But I had no close professional medical contacts in the greater LA area (my unconnected, middle-class family was from Orange County).

Dr. O'Donnelly would occasionally post in the residents' library a typed job offer that had come to his office. There were surgeons who knew what type of training we received: early and frequent operating experience, a big variety of cases, unparalleled trauma exposure, and thick skin in the face of criticism. Some of these surgeons came looking for us. But most were in lucrative private practices and wanted a huge buy-in to join them as a junior partner, with the promise of future high earnings. I spoke to a few of these guys and didn't like the concept of signing a big IOU for the favor of being their slave journeyman. It was also common knowledge that some of them hired a new, young partner every three years, then released him/her summarily for bogus reasons, never paying them well or making them full partners. I became very wary of these offers.

In January 1987, I got a beep to call Dr. O'Donnelly's office. Since I was just down the hall, I walked over instead of calling.

"Hi, Betty," I said, as I entered. "You beeped?"

"Yes, Dr. Harch. Do you have a minute for Dr. O'Donnelly?"

"Yes, ma'am."

"You can go in."

Dr. O'Donnelly looked up at me over his reading glasses. "Ah, good afternoon, Dr. Harch," he said.

"Good afternoon, sir."

"You're actively looking for a job, I assume?"

"Yes, sir."

"Any luck so far?"

"Nothing very desirable, sir."

"Well, I got a call from an older surgeon in the San Francisco area who's about to retire. He works in a multispecialty clinic and has one junior partner, but needs to replace himself. He wants somebody who's technically capable but with the right personality. I thought you might want to give him a call."

"Absolutely, sir. Sounds like a good opportunity."

"Here's his name and number. Call him in the evening."

"Yes, sir. Thank you, sir."

"Ahh…one more thing," said Dr. O'Donnelly.

"Yes, sir."

"Keep this conversation between you and me, okay?"

"Yes, sir. I'll do that. And thank you again."

"Now get back to work," he said, with a grin.

I nodded, turned, and walked out, self-conscious about adding another "sir" or "thank you."

I ran to an empty room, found a phone, and dialed Lori. "Lori, Dr. O'Donnelly just gave me a possible job offer…I mean the phone number of a guy with a possible job offer."

"Fantastic, honey. Where's the job?"

"San Francisco area, but I don't know exactly where."

"Oh, that wouldn't be a bad place to land. A little far from Southern California and your mom, but not too far. There might be some job prospects for me too."

"Yeah, that's true. It's the best possibility we've had so far. I'll call him tonight if I get home in time."

"Great."

"I'll talk to you later."

"Bye."

That evening, I called Gordon Elman, who had started a multispecialty clinic in Redwood City 35 years previously. The clinic now employed about 40 physicians. He seemed like a very warm, fatherly guy, and the conversation was easy. He emphasized that there would be no buy-in, and the clinic could guarantee an immediate flow of patients to me. That was appealing; I wouldn't have to spend two years clawing for referrals as I slowly built a practice. We agreed that I'd fly up for an interview in the next month or so, at their expense. Lori and I were ecstatic over the possibility. And this part of the Bay Area would be a beautiful place to live.

A couple weeks later, I had a morning of elective cases scheduled (gallbladders, hernias) and was partway through the first operation when my beeper went off. The circulating nurse called the number listed, since I was scrubbed in and couldn't handle the beeper or phone. Millie Johnson, the lady in the iron lung, was having abdominal pain and vomiting. She sounded stable, so I offered to see her that evening after my hospital duties were finished.

I did get free about 6 p.m. and headed straight there. I opened the iron lung and checked her abdomen.

"Millie," I said, "I'm concerned about a bowel obstruction, but there are many other things that could be wrong. Without X-Rays and blood tests, it's hard to be certain. We have to think about moving you to the hospital."

"Oh, no, doctor," she said. "I haven't been out of this room in over 30 years. I don't want to go anywhere. Besides, how would we do it?"

"Well, I think we'd have to intubate you," I said. "You know, put in a breathing tube."

"Oh, I don't want that unless we absolutely have no choice. What else can we do?"

"I guess we can observe you for 24-48 hours and see if your symptoms improve."

"That's what I want to do."

"Alright, then that's what we'll do, and I'll call you in the morning. But if you get worse tonight, you'll have to call me."

"Okay. Thank you, doctor."

When I got home, I said, "Lori, this is a big problem. I'm on call tomorrow, and I can't leave the hospital. Taking care of Millie has just gotten a lot more complicated."

"You're gonna need help if she's still sick tomorrow," said Lori. "You can't be in two places at one time."

Millie was a little better by the next morning, so we decided to sit tight.

By noon, my team was spread all over the hospital. The Knife and Gun Club had gotten an early start. Consults were coming in like waves on a beach. When my beeper went off, I recognized Millie's number. I called and the caregiver said Millie was having much more pain, lots of vomiting, and increased difficulty breathing. The caregiver was scared.

"I'm stuck in the hospital," I said. "And even if I come out there, there's not much I can do. You need to call an ambulance and bring her to the hospital. They'll have to intubate her; tell Millie I'm sorry but there's no other choice. Make sure they bring her to LA County-USC."

About two hours later, I was notified that Millie had arrived. I met her in the ER. She was on a gurney with an endotracheal tube down her throat, and a contingent of paramedics, nurses, respiratory therapists, and doctors around her. She was wide-eyed and frantic. She seemed like a hermit crab that had been pulled out of its shell and tossed on a bare table, or a fish yanked out of the ocean and plopped on the deck of a boat.

"Millie," I said, elbowing my way through the crowd, "Dr. Harch here. Let's get you a sedative and start figuring out what's wrong." We gave her some Valium and she became calmer immediately. I ordered labs and X-Rays and moved her to the ICU.

The day got very busy and sped into evening. Millie's films were suspicious for a bowel obstruction but not diagnostic, so I decided to watch her. I looked in on her intermittently, and by late evening, her blood pressure was a little low and her urine output was dropping. I increased her fluids and ordered more labs and X-Rays for the morning.

Word had gotten around that she had spent her adult life in an iron lung, and numerous doctors and nurses stopped by just to see her.

The night was frenetic, and it was nearly impossible to keep up with the workload. Pass-ons at 7 a.m. were rather untidy, and when I sat down to review my patient list, I appreciated why. Counting the pass-ons we'd received, along with consults and admissions, we'd evaluated 54 new patients in 24 hours (a new record for me), and operated on 14 of them.

Now I had time to focus on Millie a little more closely. Her white blood cell count was up a bit, her new X-Rays were more suggestive of a bowel obstruction, and her abdomen was slightly tender.

I sat at Millie's bedside in the ICU and recommended surgery, reviewing the procedure and risks with her. She couldn't ask questions (due to being intubated) and she couldn't write any questions (due to being paralyzed). The loss of control over her environment and her modesty had a potent effect on her: she was now stoic and seemed resigned to whatever lay ahead.

After cleanup rounds, we took Millie to the OR late in the morning, found a bowel obstruction, and fixed it. She was in surgery for about two and a half hours. Post-op, her blood pressure was poor, her urine output diminished, and despite my considerable efforts, she suffered a slow, progressive deterioration. I brought Billy, Skip, and Dr. O'Donnelly to the bedside at various times for their opinions, but no one knew how to reverse her decline. She died about 48 hours later. I was shattered. I felt I'd failed her and Nick Givens because a bowel obstruction doesn't often kill someone. This remarkable woman who'd survived 30 years in an iron lung was gone, possibly because she'd had the wrong doctor at the time of her crisis, possibly because I'd been too busy to focus more intently on her problem.

I needed to call Nick and let him know of Millie's death, but I was too emotionally and physically exhausted to do it right then. Three days later, at home in the evening, I summoned up the courage to phone him. We hadn't spoken since he'd left the program. After exchanging some pleasantries, I explained how Millie had gotten sick, initially refused admission to the hospital, then worsened and required emergency admission. I told him about her workup, her surgery, and her demise.

"Well, I'm sorry to hear it," he said, "but we both knew she would have an event like this sometime, and that her reserve would be very limited."

"I know," I said, "but I have this lingering regret that I might have pulled her through by doing something differently."

"Like what?" he wanted to know. We went back and forth discussing the fine points of her case, with me unloading my guilt and him trying to reassure me. This dialogue finally waned, and he changed the subject.

"Hey, John, I've been meaning to call you for a while, but haven't gotten around to it. I'm situated about an hour outside of Seattle, and my practice has grown rapidly over the last seven months. I can't keep up with it, and I'm wondering if you would consider joining me here when you graduate from residency."

I was dumbfounded by this request. "Are you serious, Nick?"

"Yes. We could do nearly every kind of general surgery: GI, breast, cancer, vascular…you name it. There aren't too many people I'd ask to do this."

"Wow. I'm flattered…and honored, Nick. And totally surprised. I'll need to talk to Lori about it."

We discussed his exact location and details about his work setup, work hours, and caseload, then ended the call. Lori had been listening to the last part of this conversation, especially after hearing my shocked tone of voice.

"Can you believe that?" I asked her.

"Amazing," she said. "Suddenly, you have two possible job offers, and there are still five months left."

"But," I said, "this thing with Nick…it's complicated. I'm totally flattered that he'd ask me, and I'd love to work with him, but it'd mean 15-hour days. You know him; he works all day long and into the evening, then reads medical journals for several hours at night. I'm sure he works every weekend too. He'd expect me to do exactly the same. I'm not sure I want that kind of lifestyle after five years of this hell."

"Exactly what I was thinking…but I didn't want to say it first. I'm sure it would be exciting and satisfying, but you have to decide what kind of life you want. It wouldn't leave much time for me and Shawna...or playing basketball...or anything."

"You're right. This is gonna be a difficult decision, either way."

I needed to buy some time before giving Nick Givens an answer. Since I'd already agreed to fly to the Bay Area to meet with Gordon Elman, I told Nick I wanted to complete that interview before I could decide. He was fine with that timetable.

CHAPTER TWENTY-EIGHT

MORON

WE HATED THE CALLS FROM OUTSIDE hospitals to transfer post-op patients to our facility. Usually it meant some lowlife had gotten stabbed or shot and then dropped on the doorstep of a community hospital or dragged in by ambulance. If the patient wasn't bleeding to death, staff at that hospital would try to punt him to us immediately. But if the patient needed life-saving attention, they had to take him to their OR.

We self-righteously assumed that the community hospital on-call surgeons were lesser trained than we, and didn't really care about the outcome for the indigent patient. Knowing that the patient had no insurance and no money, the surgeon would try to get the patient out of his clean, orderly hospital and into our dirty, low-budget facility where he belonged. Following the transfer, the surgeon would drive home early in his Porsche to his million-dollar home while we spent the next 10 days cleaning up the complications. That was the worst aspect of this arrangement: someone else got to do the fun part (the surgery), and we did the difficult post-op care.

In some cases, the patient would arrive in pretty good shape. We'd read the operative note and credit the surgeon with a job well done. But in other cases, injuries were missed, bleeding was poorly controlled, or decisions were made in the operating room that required an immediate trip to our OR to correct. Often the patients were so unstable that they had to go straight into our ICU for evaluation and treatment.

The maddening thing was the lying that went on in the doctor-to-doctor phone calls about transfer. The community hospital surgeons would tell us anything to unload their no-payers. They'd conveniently forget to tell us about major injuries; tell us the vital signs were stable when they weren't; tell us the patient had been transferred to a ward bed when they were, in fact, still in the ICU. This last lie was especially galling, because part of the decision to accept these people was contingent upon whether we had an appropriate bed in which to place them.

Therefore, if you were the on-call trauma surgeon at LAC-USC, you learned to grill the surgeon calling in, and you tried like hell to extract the truth. If a bed was available, the transfer rules dictated that you must accept the patient, no matter how overwhelmed you were in your other work.

We felt that these patients were being "dumped" on us, and it just made our underwear burn.

When I was notified of an incoming call from an outside surgeon on my admission day, my antennae were up. The call was routed through the Medical Alert Center (MAC), which handled all potential transfers to our facility. These conversations were recorded for reasons of liability, accuracy, and record keeping.

"Dr. Harch, I have Dr. Hanjar on the line, from Inglewood Memorial," said the operator.

"Hello," I said, in an unfriendly tone, "this is Dr. Harch."

"Hello," said Dr. Hanjar glibly, with a Middle Eastern accent. "Are you the on-call general surgeon?"

"Yes, I am."

"Well, I have this guy who was stabbed in the chest and abdomen yesterday, and we took him to the OR and repaired some intestinal injuries, stopped some bleeding, and put in a chest tube. I'd like to transfer him to your care."

"Okay," I said. Then I began a polite but careful questioning about the injuries, what was done surgically, and how stable his patient was at this moment. I was told the patient had stable vital signs, and the bleeding from the chest tube had slowed to nearly nothing.

"Where is the patient now?" I asked.

"He's in our ICU," said Dr. Hanjar.

Bingo, I thought. Caught in my trap.

"Well, Dr. Hanjar," I said, "if your ICU patient was stable enough to transfer here, I'd take him, but I have no

ICU beds. You'll have to call back tomorrow, and we'll be happy to take him if he's out of the ICU or we have an ICU bed open." This was the absolute truth. Every single bed in our ICUs was occupied, and the day was yet young.

"We can transfer him to the ward and then to you a little while later," he said, desperately.

"I'm sorry," I said, "but if he's currently requiring ICU care at your facility, I can't take the risk of accepting him to a floor bed. It's not safe. I have to refuse the patient." And this was also true; these patients were often sent over from ICUs as "stable" when they shouldn't have been loaded into an ambulance at all.

Poor Dr. Hanjar made a few more attempts to persuade me to take his patient, but I stood my ground and ended the call. I went back to work.

About an hour later, another call came from the MAC about a transfer—a transfer from Inglewood Memorial. The patient was en route to our ER, and the MAC wanted me to find him a bed on my service.

"Is this the same stab wound they tried to send me about an hour ago?" I asked, incredulously.

"It's from a Dr. Hanjar," said the operator. "I can patch him through."

"I refused that patient!" I yelled at the operator.

"I'll patch Dr. Hanjar through to you," said the operator.

"Hello, this is Dr. Hanjar. I'm sending the patient over."

"I already told you I don't have an ICU bed for him! Who approved this transfer?" I was incensed.

"I spoke to Dr. Columbero. He approved the transfer," said Dr. Hanjar.

"Who the hell is Dr. Columbero? Is he gonna find an ICU bed and take care of the patient?"

"Dr. Columbero is one of the ER faculty physicians, and he's the MAC supervisor today," said the operator.

"Is that so? Well, Dr. Columbero is a moron who just sits at home and accepts everything while we're here actually taking care of the patients!" I screamed into the phone. On the other end, there was dead silence, except for the clicking of the recording device, which had just secured my words in perpetuity. I surmised immediately that my outburst was likely to land me in trouble, but I was too mad to care. And it was too late to take it back.

"So, at this point," I said, "There's nothing I can do to stop the transfer, correct?"

"The patient has left their hospital and will arrive here in a few minutes," said the operator.

"Well, shit, that's just great," I said, and slammed down the phone. I reached into my pocket, pulled out two Mylanta tablets, and tossed them in my mouth.

I took the elevator down to the ER to evaluate the transfer patient. His heart rate was high, he had a low-grade fever, and he just didn't look good. I wrote ICU admission orders and returned to the ninth floor to review every other patient in the ICU. It was now my responsibility to push a borderline stable case out of the ICU to make room for Dr. Hanjar's discard. This process had to be replayed for every critical patient we'd receive that night: a sort of high-stakes musical chairs game, except that we were adding contestants instead of removing chairs. It increased everyone's stress levels to know that sick, ICU-level patients were being sent to wards where the nurses didn't have enough time to watch them closely. It meant that my team had to check them more frequently, if we weren't too distracted by other problems.

The following day, I expected a call from Dr. O'Donnelly's office to explain my unprofessional behavior. I felt fully justified in refusing the transfer, but I'd have trouble defending my description of a senior faculty physician as a "moron," as well as my closing comment, "Well, shit..." When the day ended without a call, I decided to just stop worrying about it. Maybe I got away with it....

That weekend, Lori and I left Shawna with my mom and flew to San Francisco. I'd had to trade my soul to get coverage for the two days. We met Dr. Elman, many of the staff and doctors at the multispecialty clinic, and looked around the Redwood City/Menlo Park area. Even though there was no formal job offer, they seemed very interested, and we discussed specifics of employment, partnership, and pay. The real attraction was a ready flow of actual surgical cases from the other partners, and a guaranteed income.

On returning to Los Angeles, we now had a dilemma. We had to truly focus on whether joining Nick Givens in practice would be a good, long-term decision. Nick was the best surgeon I knew. He was my mentor. In a way, he was my professional idol.

After several late-night conversations, Lori and I concluded that working with Nick would be rewarding, but the demands would eventually become unbearable. I envisioned stepping out of residency and right into 20 years of…residency, with the only difference being that I'd get paid a lot more. It was not a future either of us desired.

I got the chance to sit down with Billy as well. He had landed a trauma fellowship position in Maryland and would be near his family, so he was set. Billy clearly understood my conflicted feelings about Nick, who was Billy's mentor and role model too. Billy agreed, however, that I would probably work day and night if I were Nick's partner.

Within a few days, Dr. Elman called and formally offered a position at the clinic, and I accepted it. I now had the onerous task of calling Nick and declining his offer. After all, finding a private practice opportunity with someone you knew and trusted, with no buy-in, was exceptional.

The conversation with Nick was tough. I didn't have the guts to tell him I didn't want to match his work ethic, because I worried he might perceive it as a judgement on his lifestyle choices. Instead, I told him we had too many family, friends, and connections in California, and that we wanted to stay here long term. And I thanked him profusely for his confidence in me.

About a week later, I got a summons to Dr. O'Donnelly's office. I sat down in front of his desk.

"Dr. Harch, do you know why I asked you to meet with me today?" he asked.

"I can make a pretty good guess, sir."

He handed me a letter, which I have kept to this day. The important sections are excerpted below.

Feb. 3, 1987
Patrick J. O'Donnelly
Professor and Chairman
Director of Surgery
Los Angeles County/USC Medical Center

Dear Dr. O'Donnelly:

I am writing to you in regard to an incident that occurred recently regarding one of your surgical residents and one of our attending physicians. Dr. Alan Columbero was on duty as the Medical Alert Center (MAC) supervisor. As you know, in that role, he has been given the responsibility by Dr. Goldstein for making a final determination on all requests for in-patient transfers. Your resident, Dr. Harch, had apparently refused a patient for transfer but Dr. Columbero, working from guidelines that were recently distributed by the Department of Health Services, felt it appropriate to overrule that refusal and to accept the patient.

Dr. Harch subsequently had a telephone conversation with the referring physician in the community hospital and during that conversation referred to Dr. Columbero as "a moron who sits at home and accepts everything." These comments were made with the MAC operators on the line and the conversation was tape recorded. I have a copy of that tape if you wish to hear it.

What is most disturbing, is the extremely unprofessional, demeaning and downright rude manner in which your resident conducted himself. During our meeting with Dr. Everett, we played this tape for him but he was apparently unimpressed and seemed to dismiss Dr. Harch's comments as simply juvenile. It has been my experience in dealing with you in the past that you set and expect not only high clinical standards from your residents but high professional standards as well. Dr. Harch's comments, particularly to a physician outside of our Medical Center, reflect very poorly on our Institution and I believe, on your Department. We all function under very difficult circumstances and personally attacking each other certainly does nothing to improve the situation.

I bring this to your attention because I feel that you would want to be aware and would reciprocate if any of my staff or myself had acted in an unprofessional manner.

Thank you for your consideration in this manner.

Donald P. Mellin, M.D.
Associate Director
Department of Emergency Medicine
cc: Alan Columbero, M.D.

I looked up from the letter. Dr. O'Donnelly was looking at me over his reading glasses, eyebrows raised.

"Dr. O'Donnelly," I said, "do you know the particulars of the case?"

"Yes, I do," he said.

"Sir, I had no ICU beds that day, and I felt it would be poor judgement to accept another ICU patient."

"I understand," he said.

"And when the guy arrived, he wasn't floor ready, so I had to bump another ICU patient out. And we had to do that all night, sir."

"I get it," he said, sympathetically. "And I think you made the right decision...but you handled it poorly. Now it's thrown in my lap, and it makes our department look bad."

"Yes, sir. I'm sorry about that. I was just pissed off that the final decision was made by someone with no clinical responsibility for the patient...and I lost my temper."

"Well, I can't really blame you, but you have to be more prudent with your words."

"I will, in the future. Would you like me to write an apology letter? Or meet with Dr. Columbero and apologize to his face?"

He stroked his chin and thought about it. Then, to my surprise, he said, "No. I'll write the apology letter and you can sign it. Is that okay with you?" With this question, he seemed to have a slightly different look on his face...maybe. I couldn't be sure.

"That would be fine, sir. Anything else?"

"No. You can go now."

"Thank you."

Several days later, I was back in the office, and he handed me another letter. It is reproduced in its entirety below.

Feb. 6, 1987
Alan Columbero, M.D.
Department of Emergency Medicine
1018 General Hospital

Dear Dr. Columbero:

I apologize if my comments made during my recent conversation with a referring physician from an outside hospital were offensive to you.

Sincerely,
John Harch, M.D.
PPG-5, Surgery
cc: Dr. Mellin

I looked up from the letter to see Dr. O'Donnelly with his lips pursed, again looking over his reading glasses. Was he suppressing a smile? This wasn't an apology at all, and it would be obvious to Dr. Columbero and Dr. Mellin that by sending this letter, I was essentially saying, "I did nothing wrong. Here is a weak, qualified apology, and my boss agrees with me. Fuck you." I loved it, but I tried not to be too smug or happy about it.

"Sir, are you sure this is what you want me to send out?" I asked, with just a flicker of delight in my eyes.

"Yes, I'm quite sure. It will go from this office via intra-hospital mail to Dr. Columbero."

I signed the letter, stood up, and said, "Thank you very much, sir...for your support." And I walked out. It was clear to me that Dr. Everett had had my back the day he heard the tape, and that Dr. O'Donnelly wanted to send the message that Dr. Columbero was in the wrong to unnecessarily overload our already strained system. For the first time, I felt I was part of the fraternity here.

CHAPTER TWENTY-NINE

DR. JEKYLL
AND DR. HYDE

MORE THAN THREE MONTHS REMAINED in my residency. It was satisfying to feel accepted as an insider now, but the carousel of crazy was wearing me down. The shootings and stabbings were relentless. This Dude and Some Dude were brutalizing innocent (and some not so innocent) Jane and John Does. Every day was a marathon sprint to get the work done while hoping to avoid a major screw-up. And the hospital staff…they were in a conspiracy to stop us.

I wanted the hospital to issue a Colt .45 to the surgeon of the day at the start of each 24-hour call shift. That resident would have the authority to shoot one uncooperative hospital employee each day. He wouldn't have to shoot one each day, but the mere threat would make the place magically efficient. And as time went by, fewer shootings would be necessary. Skip loved the idea, but we couldn't get it adopted.

So, how to survive these last few months…just screaming "moron" into the phone wouldn't do it. If I couldn't change the system, maybe I could fully embrace the absurdity. Maybe I could even turn it up a notch.

I devised a new strategy. Typically, I would manage the trauma service about once a week and would also be surgeon of the day, on average, every other week. I decided that when I was SOD, with a huge backlog of work, I would increase the tempo—and my demands—to overdrive.

Late one evening, we had six cases sitting on 9200 waiting for surgery. One ortho case was running, and my junior resident was upstairs doing an appendectomy. If we didn't get rolling soon, we'd be handing a plate of shit to the oncoming team at 7 a.m. I phoned the anesthesia chief resident on call.

"Hello," said a sleep-thickened voice.

"Who's this?" I asked.

"Will Thomas," he said.

"Will, this is John Harch, general surgery. We have a half-dozen cases down here waiting to go. I want to run two more rooms…now."

"I already got two guys working. We're trying to spell each other and get some sleep."

"That's great, but no one down here is sleeping. I want you to get up and get two more cases going."

"We'll get to your cases. Just be patient." He hung up the phone.

I looked at my intern, who'd been listening to the conversation. "Come with me," I said. "I know where their sleep rooms are." We took the stairs two at a time, ran down the hall, and stopped at the entrance to the anesthesia sleep rooms. There were four doors. I started banging on the first two doors.

"You bang on those two," I said to my intern. "Will, get up!" I yelled. There was no response, so we kept banging. "Will, get up! We're not going away!"

One of the doors opened, and I knew it wasn't Will, because it was a female in scrubs.

"Who are you?" I asked.

"Dr. Renowski," she said.

"Great. I need you to start a case. Come down to 9200." Then we continued to bang on the other doors. Soon, one of them opened.

"What the hell are you doing?" asked a guy who I presumed was Will.

"I'm trying to get my work done. I want you to get your ass out of bed and come do my cases, or I'll leave my intern here to bang on your door all night long. You will not sleep a fucking wink; I guarantee it. I'll also call your staff at home to come in and do your work."

He looked at me while he considered his options, which were really limited to one.

"Fine," he said. "But you're an asshole."

"Thank you," I said. "The first case is a gunshot named Watson, and the second is a stab named Martinez.

I turned to my intern. "Let's go."

Later that night, when an X-Ray technician refused to schedule a study, I ripped into him in front of my team. Gradually, the interns, junior residents, and even the med students learned that "no" or "later" weren't acceptable answers. My group got aggressive all over the hospital, and we got an enormous amount of work done in 36 hours.

The following week, to keep my blood pressure down and my adrenaline levels low (and to give myself and everyone else a break), I'd meekly request whatever I needed. Often, the carryover from the prior week's hostility would produce compliance. If not, then I'd say, "Okay, thanks. Let us know when you can do it." My team was baffled. When each call day began, they didn't know which chief resident they would have for the day, until the first confrontation occurred. Would I be Dr. Jekyll, or would I be Dr. Hyde? Playing the unpredictable role was devilishly entertaining. It also distracted me from the despair that pressed in from every direction.

I found another way to inject fun into our daily activities. Often, when we received a consult for, say, belly pain on a patient in the hospital (maybe on the medical service), the real reason for the consult was that the patient was crazy. The requesting physician hoped the consulting doctor was stupid enough to transfer the difficult, time-consuming patient off her service. Most of us would avoid these cases if at all possible, unless there was a clear surgical problem. But if the patient was interestingly crazy, then I'd consider bringing him onto my service just for the hell of it, even if there was a low probability of operating. The interns absolutely hated it, but it made rounds far more amusing.

One such guy was Jerry, a 46-year-old admitted to a medical ward for bloody stools. The consult was called, and I got a sample of Jerry's thinking early in my history taking.

"Have you been in the hospital before?" I asked.

"Yeah, about two months ago," said Jerry. "I put a highlighter up my butt."

I nodded my head.

"Then I pushed it up further with a broomstick…that gets it up out of your reach, you know."

"Well, how…"

"Usually the shit brings it out. But the plastic wouldn't stick."

"Did the doctors take it out?"

"I don't remember."

"Have you had any surgeries?"

"Yes. They put a module on the back of my head."

"A module?"

"Yeah, the kind that sends messages into your brain."
Jerry was dead serious, wanting me to understand his story.

"Who put this module on you?"

"The visitors...I call them controllers. They're from another place...another planet."

"Alright."

"They took it off..." he said, showing me the back of his head, where there was, indeed, a two-inch scar, "after they got all the information they needed."

"What's this scar on your belly?"

"Oh, the doctors took out a can opener that went up my penis."

"Did you put it up there?"

"No. Someone else did."

"Why'd they do that?"

"I don't know...I wasn't there."

At that moment, I was certain: I just had to have Jerry on my service.

One night, I was the backup resident for the on-call team. The evening had been steady, but not out of control. One of the consults I'd seen was a young, straightforward appendicitis case I'd consented for surgery, and we were just waiting for an operating room. As the wee hours of the morning crept toward pass-ons, I thought it was likely I'd have to give the patient over to the next team for surgery.

At 5:50 a.m., however, I got a beep to come to the fifteenth floor for the appendectomy. When I emerged from the elevator, I turned left and headed down the hall to the rooms where we did all our emergency cases.

"Dr. Harch," yelled a nurse from behind me. "Your appy is down here in room one."

"Room one," I repeated. "Where is room one?" Suddenly it dawned on me that every time we brought up a red blanket or arrived to do any emergency case, it was always room two, or three, up to eight. But never had I gone into a room one.

I walked slowly down the hall toward a door that was, in fact, a right turn from the elevators and at the very end of the hallway.

"Right in here," said the nurse, holding the door open. I walked through a short, low-ceilinged tunnel, then stepped out into an expansive room. Straight in front of me was my patient, on an operating table, with the anesthesiologist standing over him. Behind them was a magnificent bay of windows, perhaps 20 feet wide and 30 feet high, looking west over Los Angeles toward the Pacific Ocean. The sun was just rising in the east, casting shadows to the west and spreading soft rays of orange light over the wakening city.

I turned and looked behind me. There were stairs leading up to six, steep, curved rows of seats, arranged one above the other, occupying the entire east wall. It was an old-fashioned surgery observation theatre. My mouth was hanging open.

"Say good night," said the anesthesiologist, as he put the patient to sleep.

"Good night," I said to the patient. "See you in about 45 minutes."

When the patient was unconscious, I asked, "What is this place? And how did I spend five years here and never know this room was here?"

"I think this auditorium was put in when they originally built the hospital," explained the nurse, "you know, when they actually had groups of doctors observing surgery."

"It's absolutely amazing," I said, examining the details of this antiquated room.

"They used it to film some of the scenes in the TV series *Dr. Kildare* in the early sixties," said the anesthesiologist. "And they shot other scenes in and around the rest of this building."

"You gotta be kiddin' me," I said. "How did I not know about this?"

"This room is usually locked," said the nurse. "But a couple of the rooms are getting repairs done, and others are getting cleaned this morning, so they told us to put your case in here."

I scrubbed, gowned, and gloved. We prepped the patient and placed the drapes. I gazed out over the sprawling city of Los Angeles as the light slowly changed from orange to yellow to white, and the long shadows of the buildings retreated toward their bases. In the distance, the dark of the ocean began to turn blue. I looked up at the empty seats and imagined them full of spectators, all less experienced than I.

"Knife," I said. And I set it gently on the patient's abdomen and drew it decisively across the skin....

CHAPTER THIRTY

REVENGE, PIZZA, AND PARMESAN CHEESE

"GOOD LUCK," I WHISPERED TO BILLY and Skip as we filed into a room to take our final (we hoped) in-service exam, on which a passing grade was an absolute requirement to finish the program. We'd taken this exam, which changed each year, four times previously, but we still worried. None of us had been able to study very much, given our work schedule.

"I'll need it," said Skip, "since my previous scores on this penis-twister have been one notch above flunko. If you smell stool during the exam, you'll know whose underwear to check."

"I won't be checking your underwear," I said, "for fear of encountering a toxic PCB."

Skip thought for a second. "No...no toxic PCB today. More like a toxic ITS."

"What's a toxic ITS?" I asked.

"A toxic in-test-shrinker."

"You'll do fine," said Billy. "You may be nuts, but you're smart enough to pass."

"Easy for you to say," said Skip. "Your admission to this program wasn't a clerical error."

We took our seats and ground through the three-hour test. Having seen much of the material before, I felt pretty good about the outcome. Still...

Around this time, the fourth-year residents began preparing for the residents' skit. It was their job to roast the outgoing senior residents, and despite the near impossibility of getting five or six surgery residents together for meetings to create this nonsense, it somehow happened every year.

Most anything that had transpired over the prior five years was fair game: errors in diagnosis, technical mistakes in the OR, illicit sexual encounters in the hospital, stupid comments made on rounds, and lazy behavior. Nothing was sacrosanct, except that each year's writers had to consider the entire audience that would be present. Husbands, wives, girlfriends, boyfriends, and our faculty were invited. If it got too raunchy—and it often did—people could get offended. Consider what might happen if a liaison (or a rumor about a liaison) with a nurse was referenced with a spouse in attendance.

It was also the only opportunity for the residents to take shots at the faculty. It was strictly forbidden to challenge or mock the faculty in the hospital, but all bets were off at the residents' skit. I had been intimately involved in the writing of the skits for the past two years, but now it was my turn to sit and hear tell about my failings.

On the appointed evening, we gathered at someone's house and the insults flew. Embarrassing moments were dug up and broadcast for everyone's consumption. Since special arrangements had been made to prevent any of us from being called to the hospital, many at the party drank too much and embarrassed themselves even more.

The residents took scrupulous care to lambaste Dr. Rollins. He was universally despised by the residents, and this was their only chance to get even with him. They used the opportunity to attack both his short stature (and thus his need for a step stool, or lift, to reach the level of the other surgeons in the OR) as well as his habit of looking through the window of the OR door but failing to enter the room and assist on a difficult case. Later, he'd attack the decisions made when the case came up for review in M and M Conference.

Using the melody from "On the Street Where You Live" (*My Fair Lady*), they enacted a spoof in which the resident playing Rollins slowly ascended a ladder in the OR, singing:

I have often looked
Through the OR door
But I never had to scrub
Into a case before
All at once am I
Several stories high
Standing here, all alone
On my lift.

We laughed uproariously, but Rollins sat in stony silence, forcing a small pseudo-smile. I should have had more compassion for him, because he really was all alone at that moment, but all the empathetic blood in my body had long since been drained by five years of malicious interactions with him.

They dug up some slightly humiliating things about me, but I was "played" by my favorite junior resident. He repeatedly cleared his throat loudly (which was an unconscious habit of mine, one that was immediately confirmed by my amused wife). He had an NG tube hanging out of his nose for the whole scene, reminiscent of my response to the nurse's dare back in my internship. Overall, however, he went easy on me. A senior resident was pretty safe in the skit if he spent his time in the hospital working hard alongside his juniors, but if he regularly dumped his work on them, he could bank on a crucifixion during the skit.

When my roasting was done, I looked around and noticed that Dr. Rollins had departed the festivities early.

One morning, I had scheduled an elective inguinal hernia repair, an operation I'd done many times. In fact, it was such a common and presumably simple case that chief residents usually gave the case to the junior resident to do. This was exactly what I'd done, except that we were scheduled to have Dr. Anton, a senior community surgeon, come in to help on our cases that day. My plan was to retract and help while the senior surgeon guided the junior resident through the case. I assumed I'd be bored.

Before we got started, Dr. Anton began instructing my junior, Mike Chan, on exactly where the incision should be placed and why. He continued to direct him very specifically on how to open and retract each layer of muscle, and he pointed out the structures in a way that I'd never seen done. I kept quiet and watched, learning about as much as Mike did. A simple hernia repair had become an elegant lesson in technique and anatomy.

After the case, Dr. Anton went downstairs to chat with Dr. O'Donnelly, and I had a chance to speak with Mike in private.

"Damn," said Mike. "That was a great case. It seemed so easy."

"Yeah," I said. "It was easy because you had a very experienced guy guiding you through each step. I could have gotten you through that case, but not that efficiently."

"Well, you know what they say," said Mike. "See one, do one, teach one."

"No, Mike," I said. "After today, I'm changing the saying. Around here, the saying should be, 'Do one, teach one, see one done the right way.'"

Fortunately, Dr. Anton stayed around to help us with two more elective cases that day, both more complicated. He led me through them in the same graceful way that he did for Mike. We finished quicker than expected, and both cases went very well.

Fifth-year residents at LA County thought they were pretty hot shit after operating on everything from appys to cancer to gunshots to car accident victims. We finished many nights covered in blood. But today I recognized just how much remained to be learned about surgery, especially elective surgery. It was humbling, even a little scary.

I was making my way through one of the last days I'd be on call for trauma. Most of the pass-ons were already sorted out. The workload had been manageable. I had a consult in hand to see a 500-pound woman on the medicine ward who had a bellyache.

As I stepped out of the elevator, I ran into none other than Mr. Patel.

"Hi, Mr. Patel," I said, jovially.

"Oh, hello, my good Dr. Harch," he replied, in an equally cheery way. I can't deny it: I enjoyed it when he addressed me that way. And I loved his East Indian accent. And the stories; I lived for them at this point. I clasped my hands together.

"What do you have for me today?" I asked, in a very serious tone.

"Well, this one is quite good....I think you'll like it."

"Don't make me wait any longer."

"Yesterday, they released a 35-year-old man from the psychiatric jail ward. He went straight to his mother's house. A short time later, the neighbors hear screaming, and the police come and break down the door..."

"Yeah..." I said, fascinated.

"When the police enter, the man is sitting on his mother, who has been stabbed to death. He is sprinkling Parmesan cheese on her face, and biting off chunks of it..."

"No!"

"Yes, Dr. Harch. And when he sees the police, he pulls the knife out of his mother's chest, and attacks them. After a fight, they are able to subdue him and bring him to our jail ward. His poor mother gets sent to the morgue."

"You know, Mr. Patel, you've told me some pretty wild stories around here over the last five years, but this one... Parmesan cheese? Are you sure that really happened? I mean, maybe someone made up those details."

"Oh, Dr. Harch, at first I didn't believe it myself. So I went over to the morgue, and had the mother's body pulled."

"You didn't!" I was aghast.

"Yes, I absolutely did!" he said, smiling broadly. "And there it was, Parmesan cheese sprinkled all over her face, and big hunks of her face missing!"

"You are such a detective!" I exclaimed. He beamed.

"Thank you, Dr. Harch."

"I will never forget that story, Mr. Patel. Thank you for telling me. But right now, I have to see a 500-pound woman with a bellyache."

"Oh, yes, I heard about her..." he said, as I walked away. I was going to miss Mr. Patel.

Lila occupied the whole bed, at least side-to-side. She was in the hospital because her diabetes was out of control, but now she'd developed belly pain. I took her history, then started her exam. When I got to her belly, I pulled the sheet down and marveled at the massive expanse of her abdomen. A huge pannus (fold of fat) hung down nearly to her knees.

After determining that she had very little abdominal tenderness (although knowing what was going on deep down in her belly was, admittedly, difficult), I had to grapple with whether I'd look under her pannus. Doctors avoid doing this for several reasons: it's embarrassing to the patient; it's difficult to do if it weighs 80-100 pounds; it doesn't smell very good under there; and it's time consuming.

Anyway, I decided to be compulsive and do a full exam; you never know when you'll find something that impacts your diagnosis or treatment. After putting on some gloves, I lifted the left side of the pannus. It was kind of cheesy under there, and foul smelling, but no infection or tenderness. Then I lifted the right side, which was heavier and larger, because the patient was leaning right. I brought the pannus up farther... and there it was...a piece of pizza. A whole piece. It was perhaps a week old, I estimated. I wasn't quite sure whether to tell the patient or not. I put the pannus back down. When I was done with the interview and exam, I went to the nurses' station to dictate a note and order some X-Rays.

"Are you Lila's nurse?" I asked.

"Yes, I am."

"Well," I whispered, "there's a piece of pizza under the right side of her pannus. She might be a little less embarrassed if you remove it rather than me doing it."

CHAPTER THIRTY-ONE

PASSING IT ON

WHEN I WAS A KID, MY SIBLINGS and I had a lot of problems with asthma. All four of us were seen by the local allergists, who performed extensive skin testing and then instituted allergy desensitization. The treatment required frequent office visits and injections—sometimes four or five times a month. My dad died around this time, and my mom knew she couldn't afford to continue the therapy. The two physicians who owned the practice decided they'd treat us for free, and this arrangement persisted for years until all of us gradually improved. Their practice lost a lot of money on us.

In my third year of medical school, I returned to Santa Ana, California (where we grew up), to thank the allergists and to inform them I was pursuing a career in medicine. One of them had died, but the other, Dr. Kosanic, was still in practice. He interrupted his office hours to receive me. After chatting for a few minutes, I thanked him for providing gratis care to my family for so long.

He leaned back in his chair, tilted his head back a bit, and said, "It was our pleasure to do it. Now it's your turn… just pass it on."

As the fifth year of my surgical residency ended, I understood that my time to pass it on had arrived. LA County had given me the tools to treat diseases and trauma of many kinds. My family background, especially my mother's influence, gave me the mindset not to care whether people were gay or straight, outcasts or victims, criminals or cops. I'd entered people's lives in the most intimate ways: shared their stories, fears, grief and joy. I had lived the excitement of the unexpected, the exhilaration of life and death situations. I knew my professional calling would be to see anyone who walked through my doors, no matter where I practiced.

On the last day, when I walked out of that monolithic, concrete hospital leaving behind so many remarkable memories, I recalled a conversation I had as a medical student with a fifth-year surgical resident from UCLA.

"You gotta love this job," he said. "I mean, what other profession lets you come to work each day, get dressed in pajamas, and cut people up? And they pay you to do it. It's gotta be the best job in the world."

EPILOGUE

<hr/>

LORI AND I SURVIVED THE FIVE-YEAR surgical residency, unlike many couples, and had a second daughter, Lia, in 1989. We spent a year in the Bay Area, then five years in Southern California, finally moving to a small mountain town in Northern California called Mt. Shasta.

Life in Mt. Shasta wasn't boring. One day I treated a mountain climber who had impaled himself with a 30-inch ice axe while descending from the summit, and the case ended up being dramatized on the television show *101 Things Removed From the Human Body*. This video can still be found in a variety of places, and the case is number 100 (second to the last).

Small town medical practice had other quirky surprises for us. Lori and I drove to the grocery store one afternoon to pick up a few things, and we split up to find the items more quickly. As I entered the meat section, I discovered

Lori talking with two of my breast surgery patients. They both had pulled their blouses forward and insisted that Lori inspect their incisions to see the final results, with which they were pleased (fortunately). This demonstrates another axiom: no one forgets what you do in a small town.

At the 10-year reunion of LA-County/USC surgery graduates, Dr. O'Donnelly introduced all six of us, describing what each had done over the past decade. Most were in high-profile private practices in big cities, and Billy was well into an academic career of trauma research, teaching, and operating. I felt slightly embarrassed by my humble practice.

When Dr. O'Donnelly finally got to me, he said, "And then there's Dr. Harch, who seems to have made the smartest decision of all. He works in a small community hospital in the mountains far from here, and gets to perform the full gamut of general and vascular surgery that we trained all of you to do."

I'm still in touch with Skip, who's just as sarcastic and raunchy as he was when we trained. I text or speak to Billy regularly. He's nearing the end of an illustrious career, and is the chief of surgery at a major medical school.

I don't know where the hell Mr. Patel is.

ABOUT THE AUTHOR

FOLLOWING HIS SURGICAL RESIDENCY, John Harch received board certification in general surgery and surgical critical care. He spent 25 years in private practice, retiring in 2012. He is a guest lecturer for the College of the Siskiyous vocational nursing program. John has served on the ethics committee at his local hospital in Mt. Shasta, California, and chaired that committee for 12 years. He also gives anti-tobacco speeches for county behavioral health conferences and is a member of Project Prepare, which provides free counseling for end-of-life decision making.

John joined the Mt. Shasta Trail Association some years ago; being on their trail crew gives him an excuse to continue wielding sharp objects. If you visit Mt. Shasta, you might find him chainsawing in the forest or careening down single track on his mountain bike.

Made in the USA
Las Vegas, NV
17 October 2021

32537140R10236